THOSE WERE THE DAYS

A History Of Wolverhampton Wanderers
1964-1977

THOSE WERE THE DAYS

by
Clive Corbett

Geoffrey Publications

First published in Great Britain in November, 2007
by Geoffrey Publications, Kingswinford, West Midlands

ISBN 978 0 9557220 0 4

Printed and bound by Cromwell Press, Trowbridge

Contents

Foreword

Ronnie Allen was appointed manager of Wolverhampton Wanderers in September 1965, initially as a so called caretaker. He at once began rebuilding a club which had in the past dominated the footballing headlines for well over a decade in the forties and fifties. With the support of chairman John Ireland, Ronnie assembled a side of young talent that he hoped would emulate the success of their glorious predecessors. This book seeks to capture this colourful period in the club's history.

In 1974 I had the privilege of leading the Wolves team up the steps to Wembley's Royal Box at the end of the League Cup Final against Manchester City. I felt enormous pride in holding the trophy above my head to the Wolves end of the ground. In all I spent eleven years at Wolves and the club is therefore very dear to my heart. My children Andrew and Victoria were born at Cosford. We lived in Brewood, and Barbara and I still have many good friends who live in and around Wolverhampton and who we will still see today. The Old Gold blood still runs freely through our veins and if it does through yours you are sure to enjoy this book.

Mike Bailey

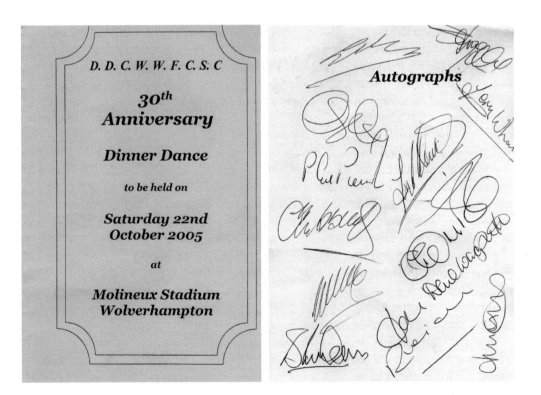

D. D. C. W. W. F. C. S. C

30th Anniversary

Dinner Dance

to be held on

Saturday 22nd October 2005

at

Molineux Stadium Wolverhampton

Autographs

Acknowledgements

It is interesting to consider the origins of any book and I must confess that 'Those Were The Days' has been largely written in my head for many years. Its completion was dependent on more detailed research to support my failing memory but rested on my ability to contact and meet as many ex-players as possible. A wonderful evening at Molineux in October, 2005 set me on my way. Organised by its chairman Chris Cox, it was the 30th anniversary dinner of The Daventry Dun Cow Wolverhampton Wanderers Football Club Supporters Club (DDCWWFCSC), and virtually everybody who was anybody in the story of Wolves in the late 1960s and early 1970s was there. With my wife Heather and friends Lin and Richard Chell, we were fortunate enough to be on the same table as Dave Wagstaffe and his better half. A great night was enjoyed by all and it encouraged me to make the approaches needed to set about this book. Interestingly, in the midst of Glenn Hoddle's reign, there was no sign of the manager or any players, although Richard Skirrow and Stuart Cain represented the club.

In the 18 months that followed, I was lucky enough to meet a host of former players, beginning with John McAlle. The warmth of his hospitality and his generous time commitment was typical of what was to come in meetings with John Richards, Derek Dougan, Dave Wagstaffe, Derek Parkin, Phil Parkes, Mike Bailey, Frank Munro, John Holsgrove, Geoff Palmer, Ken Hibbitt, Steve Daley, Willie Carr, Barry Powell, Steve Kindon and Terry Wharton. Of course I would love to have spoken with others who are sadly no longer with us, like Ronnie Allen, Bill McGarry and John Ireland, but I quickly became aware of the enduring bond that ties these men together, the love they still share for the Wolves and the respect and genuine affection they will always have for each other. I hope great interest for the reader lies partly in the fact I am addressing a relatively neglected period in Wolves history but primarily in the remarkable insight afforded by the memories and views of the key players in the story.

From the outset, I was generously supported and advised by David Instone, who was always there when I needed him and ever-indulgent of my pesterings. I would also like to thank his wife Liz for her technical help and Tricia Mills for her design skills with the cover. Similarly, I acknowledge Coxy and John Lalley for putting up with phone calls, e-mails and the odd bit of proof reading. I am also grateful to the Express & Star and Wolves for allowing the use of press cuttings and old match photographs - some of which have been scanned direct from my faded scrapbooks.

Thanks to mom and dad for introducing me to Wolves and for finding the cash to get me in during the early years, and to uncles Barry and Cliff for transporting me some of the time. I am especially grateful to my ever patient family, especially my wife Heather and children Emily and Tom, who have tolerated my infatuation with the book and the fact it has occupied much of my spare time over the last three years.

Finally, this book is dedicated to Reg Corbett, 1933 to 2006, who ensured that gold and black blood will always flow through my veins. Thanks dad. Although I'm sorry that you can't be here to read it, I think you will know every word.

Clive Corbett (November, 2007)

We are the G-R-E-A-T-E-S-T

THOSE WERE THE DAYS

Once upon a time there was a tavern
Where we used to raise a glass or two
And as we used to while away the hours
Thinking of the things we used to do

Those were the days my friend
We thought they'd never end
We'd sing and dance forever and a day
We'd live the life we choose
We'd fight and never lose
For we are Wolves, oh yes we are the Wolves!

With apologies to Gene Raskin and Mary Hopkin

1964-65: Paradise Lost

There was never any doubt I would become a fan of Wolverhampton Wanderers. My paternal grandfather attended the 1949 FA Cup final and one of my most treasured possessions remains my dad's scrapbook of that glorious campaign. Its yellowing press cuttings chart the route to Wembley through matches against Chesterfield, Sheffield United, Liverpool, West Bromwich Albion and two epic semi-final encounters with Manchester United.

It seemed propitious that it was on dad's 16th birthday that Wolves beat Leicester City and family synchronicity was secured when my son Tom and I proceeded to witness the 1974 League Cup and 2003 play-off triumphs in our respective 16th years. There had been a dangerous time early in his teens when my dad had been taken by his Uncle George to the Albion, presumably to punish some serious misdemeanour on his part. Grandad's sister Evelyn was married to George Froggatt and they ran The Happy Return public house that still sits where Wordsley's Brierley Hill Road splits one way towards the town and the other to the small village of Brockmoor in which my parents were raised and married. Thankfully, my dad was singularly unimpressed with his experience at the Hawthorns and pleaded with his father to take him to Molineux the very next week. This he did on the fateful day of April 21, 1945, when Wolves overcame Cardiff 3-0 in the first leg of a round-three Wartime League Cup North tie. Billy Wright scored twice and guest Johnny Kirkham the other. The die was cast!

Mom and dad spent much of their courting time in the 1950s either on the train between Brockmoor and Low Level stations or on the South Bank. Together, they witnessed a first League Championship, the floodlit matches against the likes of Honved and Spartak, crowds of tens of thousands turning out simply to see the Wolves kit drying on the clothes line and the time when the only issue in home games was by how many the Wolves would triumph. One hot August afternoon at West Bromwich, mom fainted and was passed over the heads of some of the 45,306 that packed The Hawthorns for that first match of the season. This was clearly a tactic to get pitch-side and closer to the action that she had picked up from her brother-in-law Fred. Constricted by a tie, he had done likewise at a scorching Molineux in the title decider against Liverpool on May 31, 1947. The season had overrun due to dreadful weather - even the snow was more memorable in those days!

Liverpool ultimately triumphed on the day Stan Cullis played his last game for Wolves. Unsurprisingly, the manner of my own coming into this world on Saturday, August 31, 1957 was closely linked to the fortunes of the Wolves. It was entirely my fault for choosing to leave the comfort of the womb on a match-day, giving my dad no option but to leave my mum and me to it in Wordsley Hospital. I completely understand his motives as, had he waited for me to arrive, he would have missed a fine 5-0 victory over Sunderland (Murray 2, Booth, Deeley and Mullen) and the crowd would have been reduced to a mere 38,644.

Not only was I blissfully unaware of this result but also the two League titles, one second place and FA Cup win that were added to the club's honours boards in my first three years on this planet. Terry Wharton recalls his first impressions; "Tommy Lawton was doing some scouting for Wolves and sent me down here. When I joined, they had just won the League, Central League, Birmingham League, Worcester Combination and FA Youth Cup, and both amateur sides had won their divisions of the Wolverhampton League. B internationals played in the reserves, youth internationals in the third team. I came down from Bolton, gaberdine mac and a little briefcase with my boots in, and thought, 'What am I doing down here?' I walked into the dressing room and looked at the team sheets, Mullen, Deeley, Lill, Horne, Hinton, Mannion, and wondered how I would ever get through that lot?"

It was unfortunate that as I became increasingly aware of football, the fortunes of Wolverhampton Wanderers began to take a distinct turn for the worse. The first FA Cup final I can remember on television was in 1964, when West Ham overcame a plucky Preston North End 3-2, but the Division One season that followed was hardly one to lure my parents to part with the hard-earned cash required to introduce me to the live Molineux experience. Wolves began 1964-65 with just one draw from the first seven League games, a situation exacerbated by the unwelcome absence of Stan Cullis.

The day before a 3-2 defeat at Leeds, Cullis had become unwell at work and was ordered by his doctor to take a few weeks' rest. Just over a fortnight later, on Monday, September 14, he was back preparing for the visit of West Ham United, as reported by Phil Morgan in the Express and Star; "After a week at the seaside, Wolves boss Stan Cullis returned to his Molineux office today to step straight from recuperation into crisis." Although Fred Davies and Ray Crawford were back in action, Ron Flowers was out injured and a decision was made to rest Jimmy Melia in favour of Peter Broadbent. Cullis, who had not seen his team in action since a 3-2 setback at Leicester on August 26, was upbeat on the subject of his health; "At least the tests I have had for the suspected virus infection and the subsequent examinations, followed by the rest, have shown me to be in good health." Morgan was blissfully unaware that the Wolves boss had been greeted on his return by John Ireland, who had taken over as chairman on July 29. Ireland initially sought Cullis' resignation on health grounds but a predictable refusal left him with no alternative but to sack the club's most successful manager ever. Keeping the discussion private, the returning boss led Wolves to a pulsating 4-3 win over a West Ham team containing the eventual World Cup winning threesome of Bobby Moore, Martin Peters and Geoff Hurst. The FA Cup holders had handed Wolves a 5-0 thrashing at Upton Park just a week earlier and, in any other circumstances, the stirring match in which Wanderers exacted some revenge would have lingered long in the memory for the right reasons.

Wolves stormed into a two-goal lead in 34 minutes. Ray Crawford headed in a Terry Wharton corner, then Peter Knowles drove home to allow himself an exuberant in-the-net celebration. However, when Peter Brabrook reduced the arrears six minutes before the break, it seemed the miserable early-season pattern might continue, a fear confirmed when full-back Gerry Harris first turned a Brabrook effort into his own net and then conceded a penalty that Johnny Byrne converted around the hour mark. But the committed club man was determined to go down fighting and, with 13 minutes left, drove in a hard cross from the left that rebounded off the chest of Jim Standen for Crawford to fire the equaliser. Roared on by a relatively meagre crowd of 19,405, Harris then picked up the ball a few yards inside the Hammers half on the Molineux Street side and slammed in a shot that somehow eluded the cricketing goalkeeper to secure Wolves' first win of the season. Phil Morgan described it thus; "There has not been a more popular goal on the ground since Bill Shorthouse beat Sam Bartram, or a more vital one since Roy Swinbourne's decider against Honved."

Unfortunately, victory did not change the decision made earlier that day and the dismissal that ended 30 years of unsurpassed service was made public on the Tuesday afternoon. The official statement read; "The Wolves board of directors have informed Stanley Cullis they wish to be released from their contractual arrangements with him. This he has consented to." Phil Morgan reported the shocking news of the loss of a man who as recently as the club's AGM in August had

Phil Morgan reflects on Wolves' options.

pledged; "I will never leave the Wolves unless I am sacked." Morgan called him 'one of the greatest' and speculated on the possibility of a two-manager arrangement.

In saying it looked 'as though a rot had set in,' Morgan asserted that big money spent on the likes of Melia, Crawford and Woodruff had not really paid off while the flow of good youngsters was beginning to dry up as other clubs were increasingly prepared to do 'under-the-counter' deals; "Wolves abided by the rules and Cullis felt they were now paying the penalty." Terry Wharton agrees; "The better players were probably kept for too long, no disrespect to Peter Broadbent and Ron Flowers but the greats were getting older. I was at Blackpool with Alan Hinton and opened the papers to find that Stan had been sacked. It was a shock but the directors were very old-fashioned and had never thought Wolves would go into a slump. They started signing hopeful players, for example replacing Alan Hinton with Dick Le Flem. Stan never sat us down with the old blackboard and told us how we were to play. When I came, it was deep in dust in one of the rooms. He just told us to go out and play, telling me to get the ball, go past people and cross it."

The feeling the sacking still engenders is summed up in the title 'Betrayal' that Jim Holden chose for the relevant chapter in his book, 'The Iron Manager.' Whether it was Ireland's own decision or he was simply acting on behalf of the board remains an issue of contention. Derek Dougan maintained that Jim Marshall, believing the manager's time was up, persuaded Ireland to become chairman, at first for an interim period. Dougan, who once lived near Ireland in Wrottesley Road, commented; "I admire John Ireland so much. He was a wonderful director who wrongly took the flak and didn't realise it." John Holsgrove concurs; "John Ireland was a wonderful chairman but they were bound to react this way to the man who sacked Stan Cullis. Bobby Thomson used to tell me all about Cullis, how hard he was. This man was God and he was sacked but somebody had to draw the sword. It was someone else's time. I liked John Ireland. He always came back with us from away trips and fell asleep on the coach. In 1965, he could have walked out on the club and they could have gone all the way down to the Fourth Division as they did in the 1980s."

Although John Richards understands the views of players who worked under Cullis, he argues it was unjust to later rename the Molineux Street Stand after Steve Bull and take away John Ireland's honour. Steve Daley makes the same

Happier times....Cullis and his players at Niagara Falls on their USA Tour in 1963.

point; "John Ireland had done a great job for the club and to take it off him was unacceptable. They could have found another way to honour Bully, make him life president or something. Do you rename the Billy Wright, melt the statute down and flog it off?" Frank Munro agrees; "John Ireland was a fantastic chairman. The board insisted Cullis would have to go and it was Ireland who had to do it. The fans think it was John Ireland who sacked him and that's why they didn't like him. I was so disappointed when they changed the name of the stand. I like Steve Bull a lot but if it had been for one of the guys I played with, I would still have been against it."

Ken Hibbitt's opinions are typical of his contemporaries; "John Ireland was a magnificent person, he never interfered. Of course I don't know what went on behind the scenes. It wasn't for the players to understand that. But you wanted to be successful for him because he was chairman and paying our wages and you knew he worked hard for the club. Every time we played in Europe, he went. He was very talkative and friendly with us but had no favourites. I remember he smoked a little pipe. In Norway or Sweden, we were getting on a boat to go to an island and he fell down the ladder. We picked him up and he was laughing his head off, saying; 'What a stupid thing to do!' He was brilliant. All I remember about him is good."

Phil Parkes agrees; "You won't find any player with a bad word against him. He was a great man and that's a word sometimes used too easily. He always came on tour with us and was always first to buy the players a drink. 'Want a drink, Mr Chairman?' you would ask. 'It isn't nine o'clock,' he'd reply, 'you know I don't drink until after nine.' 'It's OK, it's nine in England.' 'Oh, go on then.' He took a lot of stick for sacking Stan Cullis but people must realise, and this is no disrespect to Stan, who was a legend, that it was the right thing to do." Wharton remembers an act of great kindness by Mr Ireland during the 1967 USA tour; "My wife had our first child when we were in LA and John Ireland rang his wife to get a bunch of flowers sent over."

Whatever the rights and wrongs, the split made little difference on the field, seven straight League defeats following up to late October. The first in a sorry sequence, that included a 5-1 humiliation Albion, saw an angry crowd jeer at the directors before the 2-1 home loss to Blackpool. With the management of seven League clubs behind him, former Scotland full-back Andy Beattie arrived as caretaker before September was out. The 'Flying Doctor,' as he was known, enjoyed only occasional successes, notably three wins out of four in November at the expense of Stoke, Tottenham and Sheffield Wednesday. Sadly, even this proved to be a false dawn with a further five straight defeats suffered around the turn of the year. Nonetheless, some invaluable additions to the squad were made in this dark period, including striker Hughie McIlmoyle from Carlisle for £30,000 in October. He replaced Ray Crawford, who moved to West Bromwich after contributing a very healthy 39 goals in 57 games.

On Boxing Day, Dave Wagstaffe arrived for the same fee from Manchester City, having first come to John Ireland's attention with a good performance against Bobby

Thomson in a 3-3 draw at Maine Road in December, 1962. This was the same season in which relegation-bound City had been thrashed 8-1 at Molineux in the opening match, when Ted Farmer scored four. Ireland went into the dressing room after the game in Manchester and congratulated Waggy on making life difficult for a defender who was highly thought of at Wolves.

Ireland set his mind on signing him and, just before Christmas, 1964, Dave was called in by City manager, George Poyser, a man who had been instrumental in bringing Peter Broadbent to Wolves. Wagstaffe remembers arriving to sign at 11.50am on the 26th, joining his new team-mates for lunch in the Molineux Hotel and playing in the 1-0 defeat against Aston Villa. His debut was Broadbent's farewell. The glory days were an increasingly distant memory and Waggy's background left him unaware of Wolves in the 1950s; "Living in the North West, the papers were full of City, United, Liverpool, Preston and Blackburn, not teams like Wolves. I'd heard of Stan Cullis and knew they'd been on telly a few times but we didn't have one!" As City had been relegated in 1963, Dave didn't play against his old club until 1965-66 when Wolves lost twice to a City team who won promotion, scoring one of Wolves' goals in a 4-2 defeat at Molineux at the end of August.

In the winger's opinion, things were looking bleak as, although Wolves had a big squad, there was much uncertainty and coming and going; "Everything needed re-organising. Joe Gardiner, Jack Dowen and Bill Shorthouse were in charge of training but were not coaches in the real sense. They were smashing, really nice people, and I was friends with them all my life, but they were of the old school. It had been the same at City. The warm-up was four laps around the track. Just as at Wolves, long pre-season runs on Cannock Chase and you never saw a ball, until Ronnie Allen came." John Holsgrove, who arrived almost a year later, remembers the negative mood; "It was a club on the down. Tremendous players; Ron Flowers as captain, Gerry Harris, Bobby Thomson, Dave Woodfield, Fred Davies, Terry Wharton. But the feeling in the club was almost like shell-shock. In two or three years, this great club had gone from being champions and FA Cup winners to Second Division also-rans."

However, to a tall, 16-year-old keeper from West Bromwich, Wolves had not lost all their sparkle. When first introduced to the club in 1962, Phil Parkes was hugely impressed by the coaching; "They had 30 kids with five or six coaches; Bill Shorthouse, Joe Gardiner, Jack Dowen, Alf and Billy Crook, Wolves legends. I told my dad who the coaches were and they were the reason I went there. It was so much better organised than at Albion." Parkes signed as a pro in September, 1964, a year before a starry-eyed Huyton youngster arrived as an apprentice. John McAlle describes John Ireland and others at the club as 'lovely people,' reflecting; "What an honour it was to be at a club where great players like Wright, Slater and Flowers had played."

As my first visit to Molineux was not until the March after, I never saw a Stan Cullis-managed Wolves team play. From below the old clock, now relocated in the

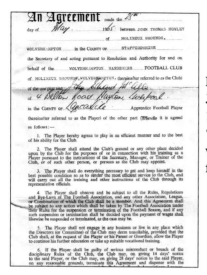

Left: A proud day for John McAlle in May, 1965. Right: The 'Flying Doctor,' who was palpably unable to fill Stan Cullis' shoes.

Cullis stand, I saw Beattie guide Wolves to a 3-1 victory over Stoke. This was the last in a three-game run that also included wins over Birmingham and Albion, although the crowd of below 21,000 was symptomatic of the slide. My strongest memory remains the smell of pipe tobacco and cheap cigars, quite different to the pungent odour of Woodbines - the popular drug on my eventual regular haunt, the South Bank.

A hammer blow fell on Cullis' hapless successor a week later with a 7-4 defeat at Tottenham that came the day before the birth of a certain Stephen George Bull. Apart from an enjoyable FA Cup run, the season held few highlights. Most positively stored away for me is grainy black and white BBC Sportsnight film of a 3-0 round-five second replay win over Aston Villa at Albion. But the joy was swiftly extinguished as Manchester United visited Molineux on a Wednesday night and progressed to the last four. Nearly 53,600 saw McIlmoyle strike twice in the first 15 minutes and, although Peter Knowles also netted, United won 5-3, with Best and Law among their scorers.

With George Showell and Peter Broadbent moving to Shrewsbury and Bristol City respectively, only an ageing Ron Flowers remained from the glory years. In spite of his best efforts, the inevitable could not be halted as Wolves were relegated for the first time since 1923, condemning them to a first spell outside the top flight in over 30 years. The final match was played out before only 13,839 hardy souls on April 26, when FA Cup finalists Liverpool fielded a virtual reserve side yet still triumphed 3-1. Wolves finished 21st, either side of Fulham and Birmingham, and demotion was fully deserved by a team who lost 25 of their 42 matches, conceding 89 goals. Andy Beattie had simply led the team with, "an earnest wish that the players should enjoy their football." Quite simply, he did little more than fiddle while Wolves burned, using a staggering 28 players in a season in which three goals were conceded on seven occasions, and four or more no fewer than eight times.

1965-1967: On The Up Again

Interest in Wolves' first Division Two season for 34 years remained somewhat peripheral as the team struggled to manage anything better than a top-six finish, this in an era when the play-offs were not even a twinkle in the eye of a football administrator. As Wolves strode out at Highfield Road on August 21, 1965, Bobby Thomson, David Woodfield, Peter Knowles, Terry Wharton and Dave Wagstaffe provided the nucleus of what would ultimately be the promotion-winning team of 1967 but much had to be done before this would become a reality. As John Holsgrove remembers, it was also a time of adjustment for coach driver Sid Kipping; "Sid was always immaculate and the loveliest man you would ever wish to meet. He had driven the great teams of the fifties and sixties for Don Everalls. That was what the club was like then, now it's all corporate and saving money. When Wolves got relegated, Sid had to go to a lot of new grounds, like Carlisle. When he had a day off, he used to drive there so he knew exactly where to go. That's what the game was all about then, people and characters."

It was somewhat ironic that Wolves' first opponents were Coventry City, who would accompany them on their promotion 21 months later. In his programme notes, their manager Jimmy Hill referred to Wolves somewhat condescendingly; "for so long virile pace-makers at the head of everyone, but who now have fallen out of the front-runners." On the day Charlton's Keith Peacock became the first substitute to appear in a Football League game, Hugh McIlmoyle put Wolves ahead on 58 minutes. However, a double from the gritty George Hudson secured a 2-1 home victory that was to be the first of four straight wins for the Sky Blues in second-flight encounters with the Molineux men. This setback was one of four defeats for Wolves in their opening six league games, with Manchester City (twice) and Rotherham sending them away pointless. In the home match with City, David Woodfield became the first Wolves player to be sent off at Molineux for almost 30 years.

During this uncertain start, Peter Knowles netted hat-tricks in the 3-0 and 4-0 home wins over Carlisle and Derby - part of an spree that spanned six games. He was to end the season as top scorer on 21, followed by McIlmoyle (15) and Hunt and Wharton (12 each). Waggy remembers his old next-door neighbour Hughie as an underrated striker who; "like Hughie Curran had the knack of seemingly hanging in the air." Terry Wharton was an admirer, too; "Did you know there's a statue of him in Carlisle? He's really loved up there." Scoring was not a problem in 1965-66, with Wolves smashing 97 in 45 games. The problem was that 65 were haemorrhaged at the other end, typified by a 9 - 3 hammering at the Dell on September 18.

At 11am the previous day, another new acquisition was made, this time from Swindon Town for £40,000. John Holsgrove recalls; "I'm in digs with Joe Gardiner's mum. Joe was a lovely man, one of the nicest people I ever met in football. One day, Ronnie Allen said to me; 'Got another signing coming, he's sharing digs with you.' What hit me but Ernie Hunt! With no central heating, it was so cold at night there was ice on the inside of the windows. Ernie had a harmonica, I played my guitar and we sang and had a laugh." When Ken Hibbitt knew I had interviewed John, he asked; "Did Holsy still have his guitar?" Holsgrove continues; "Ernie was exactly the same as now, a great character. If ever a man's gone through life living the way he wants, it's him. I'm not sure it's the right thing for his health but he was always going to live his life and when the light goes out, the light goes out! A great man." The intention was for Ernie to start at the Dell but he was not match-fit and watched from the stands as four goals from a young Southampton striker named Martin Chivers set up a thrashing.

As Holsgrove says, Wolves' biggest league defeat in living memory accounted for Beattie; "Andy Beattie, think Gordon Brown! No disrespect but he was a dour Scot. His reputation was as a fire-fighter but I'm not sure he put out many! For 30 years at Wolves, there had been hardly any change and all of a sudden the rot sets in. Beattie was the wrong man. I've always wondered why Billy Wright did not go back as manager. I'm only speculating but John Ireland must have offered it him. I never spoke to Billy about it but I don't think he wanted it." Wharton agrees that the Flying Doctor was not right for the job; "I can't really remember what he did, Billy Shorthouse picked the team and was on the training field with us. There were no tactics and Andy never came out on the field."

Beattie's departure saw Ronnie Allen take over as caretaker and his first act was to put six of the under-achieving side on Central League duty for a visit to Anfield. Allen's approach is viewed in retrospect as modern, as John McAlle maintains; "Great coach with great ideas. One of his first steps was to replace the old 'casers' used in training with modern lightweight balls." Dave Wagstaffe agrees; "Ronnie had a lot to do. His methods were very inventive, so you enjoyed training. He organised everything well. I remember he'd say after training, 'Waggy, do you fancy doing a few crosses? Phil, fancy half an hour in goal?' It finished up with me on the wing, Ronnie outside the box and Lofty in goal. All I had to do was clip balls over for him to volley in. He was brilliant and rarely missed the target but it was good practice for me and for Phil."

Parkes agrees; "As a kid, I was an Albion supporter and Ronnie was a real favourite. He was still a great striker of the ball and a great coach. He had a really good way about him and was ahead of his time. He was the only one who could get Waggy back in the afternoon because he got him a new ball to train with!" Derek Parkin comments; "Ronnie could still do it. He was still a good player and I hate to think what he was like when he actually played. He loved to be out there with the players. It was all ball-work and wherever possible we were on the pitch pinging balls about." Wharton also appreciated Allen's approach; "Ronnie was a different kettle of fish. We trained with the ball and had lots of five and six-a-sides. With Stan, it had been all about power, 16 laps at Aldersley to warm up, then 440 and 220 sprints." John Holsgrove chips in; "He was a tremendous personality. He was naturally two-footed and knew that the difference at the top level was hitting the perfect pace of pass."

Players also remember the 15-minute team building the boss led before matches, involving a small cricket set with a kid's bat and rubber ball. Holsgrove explains; "Joking in the dressing room, he was not everyone's cup of tea, especially Ron Flowers and others who had played under Cullis. We used to play cricket in the dressing room before games as a way of relaxing. Ronnie introduced it because he was good at it himself. He used to get the ball and spin it like Shane Warne." Waggy also remembers Allen's party piece on the golf course of putting a ball down on the tee in its wrapper and smacking it down the fairway, releasing the cellophane en route. Little wonder his various skills earned him the affectionate nickname of 'Hot Shot' among the players.

Although Allen occupied nothing more than an acting role until the following July, he was responsible for the highly significant acquisitions of Holsgrove and Mike Bailey. Holsgrove moved for £18,000 from Crystal Palace in the summer but did not make his debut until lining up at no 5 for the home game with Bury on September 25. It was a dream come true; "I was a Wolves supporter as a boy. My hero was Bert Williams and I have a picture somewhere of me in a green jersey like Bert. I followed the great players and particularly loved to watch Ron Flowers and Peter Broadbent. Nothing any of us could do would ever match what they did."

It was due in part to another Wolves great that Arsenal junior Holsgrove had ended up at Palace; "In 1962, George Swindin got the sack and Billy Wright became manager. He saw me in training, wasn't impressed and decided not to take me on." Holsgrove then spent about 18 months at Tottenham before the great Arthur Rowe persuaded him to sign professional terms at Selhurst Park in 1964; "Newly promoted to Division Two and who was club captain? Ronnie Allen. He became my mentor. I had a good attitude and always wanted to learn. He seemed to pick up on this and I got into the Palace team that got to the Cup quarter final, losing only to finalists Leeds. Ronnie came up to me just before the end of 1964-65 and said, 'If I leave this club, I'm coming back for you.' Next thing I hear, he's gone to Wolves as coach and, lo and behold, the manager rings me up in the summer and says, 'Wolves want to buy you'."

Holsgrove turned up for pre-season training and, although in the first-team squad of 20, soon discovered that Andy Beattie didn't know him; "I've come to Wolves to try to get in the team and find that the manager doesn't know me! The squad goes off to Kaiserlautern in Germany in pre-season and I'm left behind! I'm thinking, 'What have I done?' Willie Miller was preferred but the Southampton defeat changed everything; "I was so ambitious and knew I could play at that level but was in the reserves. Then they went to Southampton, got slaughtered and next game I'm in."

Holsgrove greatly admires the man who was his first defensive partner, loyal club servant Dave Woodfield; "He was the best trainer I'd ever seen, some even thought he over-trained. Most of us had cars then and we'd drive to training but Duggie used to walk there and back. On a Friday morning, he trained and then he'd lie on either the bed or a settee all afternoon. He was so dedicated he didn't want to waste energy. He always played to his potential and was part of the furniture when I turned up. He could also put centre-forwards into the third row of the Molineux Street stand!" The pairing of Duggie and the lanky Londoner gave the team an immediate defensive stability that set them on the road to a ten-match unbeaten run that lasted until a visit to Bolton on December 4. The last of six wins in this spell was a magnificent 8-2 demolition of Portsmouth in which Wolves were six up at half-time and in which Holsgrove, McIlmoyle and Bobby Woodruff all netted twice. But if this raised fans' hopes of an immediate return to Division One, Holsgrove and his colleagues knew this would be a case of too much, too soon; "The team needed to be stabilised. We weren't going to get promoted that season but we had to be sure we didn't go down again."

Sure enough, the old inconsistencies returned in December when a 4-1 home win over Ipswich was followed by a 3-1 loss at Middlesbrough. Shortly before, Tom Phillipson, one of Wolves' greatest strikers and a key figure in the promotion-winning season of 1932-33, passed away. The period from late December to the end of January did see another undefeated run, this time in six games before the old enemy, Coventry, came to town and sneaked a 1-0 win. During this successful spell, table-topping Huddersfield Town visited Molineux and returned home pointless courtesy of Hunt and Woodruff goals. The Terriers subsequently faded badly and were edged out of the top two by Manchester City and Southampton. Looking forward to the World Cup tournament that would of course dominate the English summer, Ivan Sharpe's programme notes make particularly interesting reading. Reflecting on England's Goodison Park draw with Poland, he wrote in very positive terms; "The 4-3-3 format has brought England new hope. No doubt about it." Prophetic words indeed from the Sporting Star columnist but the fulfilment of his soothsaying would have to wait a few months...

The FA Cup again brought most interest to a season that ultimately petered out into a respectable sixth place. Cheshire League outfit Altrincham were dispatched in the third round courtesy of a two goals from Hunt, one each from McIlmoyle and

Woodruff and a Dewar own goal. Three weeks later, 32,456 saw Sheffield United eliminated as a result of another strike from the big Scottish no 9 and a Peter Knowles double. A potentially glorious run was again ended by the star-studded Red Devils but, on this occasion, a round earlier. Amid wild excitement, Terry Wharton put Wolves two up in ten minutes (one a penalty) but Law (2), Best and Herd brought the Molineux masses back to their senses. As the Wanderer wrote in the next programme; "It was a fine effort while it lasted, but, alas, our FA Cup hopes ended at the same obstacle as last year, the redoubtable Manchester United."

Just seven days later, Southampton came to Wolverhampton with the teams six and five points respectively off the top. Mike Bailey, signed for £40,000 from Charlton Athletic on March 4, made his debut in a 1-1 draw that did little for either team but the Saints would kick on to secure promotion alongside Manchester City. At Charlton, Mike had won two full England caps, making his debut at no 4 on May 27, 1964 in New York City when Ramsey's men won 10-0. His second start came in a Home International match at Wembley against Wales. England won 2-1 and future team-mate Frank Wignall scored twice. In both matches, Bailey played alongside then Wolves skipper Ron Flowers but a broken leg suffered in an Cup replay against Middlesbrough in February, 1965 put his English ambitions on hold.

Bailey reflects on what attracted him to Wolves; "My first experience of playing at Molineux came in November, 1965 when I was in the Charlton team for a 2-2 draw. I already knew Ernie Hunt from sharing a room with him on an England under-23 trip. What really impressed me was the crowd. They made a tremendous noise every time Waggy or Terry Wharton fired in a cross for Hughie McIlmoyle. They really got behind the team. The atmosphere was friendly but electric and I knew I wanted to play in games like this every week."

Affectionately, Mike reflects on the circumstances surrounding his move; "The Charlton boss, Bob Stokoe, called me into his office, told me of Wolves' interest and asked if I would like to go to Molineux and talk to them. Having had a look around and spoken to John Ireland and Ronnie Allen, I was impressed but wanted time to discuss things with my wife Barbara. She was working in London, had never been to the Midlands, so it was a big decision for her as well. I had already made up my mind but told Mr Ireland I needed some time. However, the chairman, who I admired very much and was loved by the players, was very shrewd and insisted things had to be sorted quickly. He got me to phone Barbara, so I did and we agreed I would sign. Later, cheeky Ernie Hunt asked me what I'd got as a signing-on fee. When I told him, he said he'd got more! I respected John Ireland a great deal but he certainly pulled the wool over my inexperienced eyes! Bob Stokoe was surprised to find I had signed so quickly. When I later heard that Spurs had enquired, I realised Mr Ireland had known exactly what he was doing. It was the best for the club. Given what I achieved at the Wolves and the great life we had there, I have no regrets."

The long-term significance of securing the services of players like Bailey and Hunt is not lost on John Holsgrove; "Ernie, then Mike, great signings. The atmosphere changed. The club got what it needed, fresh blood. The players Andy Beattie brought in were to stave off relegation. That was his reputation. Ronnie wasn't seeking stopgaps. He was building a side to get us back up." Holsgrove is particularly fulsome in his praise of Bailey; "I always tell people Mike had everything. He was a better player than Alan Mullery, who could pass the ball and was a great striker of the ball but who couldn't tackle like Mike. The whistle went and the first tackle, like the side of a house, straight in there, bang, got the ball. He set the tone for the team, a fabulous player."

As the season ebbed to its close, five wins, two draws and three defeats was a reasonable return for Wolves from the last ten games but encouraging triumphs over the likes of Preston, Palace and Birmingham were undermined by setbacks in the style of a last-day 5-2 reverse at Ipswich. A leaky defence once again proved the Achilles heel in a term when eight fewer points were gained and one fewer goal scored than in the 1966-67 promotion season. Dave Wagstaffe remembers an incident on the night before the match at Ipswich, when the team were staying in Bury St Edmunds and Peter Knowles threw a bucket of water out of a hotel window. Waggy got the blame, was replaced by Paddy Buckley and sent home in disgrace on the Saturday morning train to Wolverhampton. He reached Molineux at half time in the Central League game and was called before the directors as the true story emerged!

Until the glorious summer of 1966, my interest in football was somewhat half-hearted but this would never be the case after the World Cup left a ten-year-old star-struck. It all came right at Wembley on July 30. Ron Flowers made Alf Ramsey's final 22 but did not add to his tally of 49 full caps. England carried off the Jules Rimet Trophy to prove Ivan Sharpe's optimism to be well-founded but, like hundreds of thousands of boys of my generation, I will never be able to truly forgive Wolfgang Weber. Logic and hindsight combine to remind me that his injury-time equaliser in normal time only delayed England's celebrations by 30 minutes but when West Germany's second goal was slid

Above: Alf Ramsey works with Wolves youngsters, including Phil Parkes, Alun Evans and John Farrington. Top right: Farrington, John McAlle, Peter Knowles and (at front) Paul Walker. Bottom right: McAlle, Les Wilson and Lutton.

past the despairing dive of Gordon Banks, a bolt shot to my heart and sent me charging down the back yard of 143 Brettell Lane, Amblecote. My petulant sprint was a hopeless attempt to escape the reality that the Germans had forced extra-time. Although a tear-stained return to the BBC TV coverage was rewarded by the unforgettable denouement, this was my first taste of the extremes of emotion that were to accompany my footballing experiences from that day. My son Tom was to undergo a similar, more bitter outcome in viewing (from behind the settee) the shoot-out against a reunified Germany in the semi-final of Euro 96.

The new English season was eagerly anticipated, with increased attendances and extensive TV coverage of what for Wolves would truly be, in the title of John Lalley's 'We are Wolves' article, 'A Season to Savour'. However, early matches gave little indication of the success that lay ahead. As in the previous August, they started with two defeats, this time at home to Birmingham and at Ipswich. However, they would not lose again until mid-October and only seven more times in total. Wolves were still languishing in the bottom third of the table for the visit of Crystal Palace in early September, a match that marked Dave Burnside's first outing in a Wolves shirt. The programme for this match is a curiosity piece in itself, showing Burnside at no 8 for his previous club Palace. In the end, he was replaced by Steve Kember, took Knowles' no 10 shirt and went on to score Wolves' goal!

As Lalley recalls, the transfer led to Knowles no longer being an automatic choice. Having won their first-ever League Cup tie (against Mansfield on September 13), Wolves won eight league wins out of ten up to early November. John Holsgrove sensed things were beginning to move; "If you're putting in the effort and the manager has the tactical nous then, suddenly, results start going your way. Ronnie was tactically very good and people tended to play for him. Off we went, it suddenly snowballed. Failure sometimes breeds failure and success breeds success. Two years before and they couldn't buy a win, now all of a sudden the results are going well."

The only setbacks were a 3-1 reverse at Hull and a 5-0 League Cup thrashing at First Division Fulham. The pick of the victories was the 7-1 demolition of Cardiff on September 21, a match that fired my personal interest and undoubtedly that of many more. A Terry Wharton hat-trick helped Wanderers overcome a side who had John Toshack on the bench and, by early October, Wolves were established in the top six. Molineux, meanwhile, hosted an under-23 international for the first time and Bobby Thomson played left-back for England in an 8-0 drubbing of Wales. Wharton knew things were on the up; "We had a good side. Waggy and me were flying on the wings and we had Ernie Hunt, Mick Bailey, Holsy, Duggie Woodfield and Bobby. If you win, you get on a roll and you feel you are going to beat sides. That was how things were."

A Bonfire night match against Millwall saw a blanket collection in aid of the Aberfan disaster and a win that consolidated the club's top-two slot. The programme is of particular interest for a Football League Review that featured Wolves in its Club Call section. Harry Brown interviewed secretary Jack Howley, who had already completed 43 years with the club and was to serve just two more before his retirement in 1968. Jack began by complimenting Molineux's North Bank choir or "soccer's pop singers" for its support. "Their loyalty is amazing"; Howley purred, while reporting that as many as 500 fans had followed the team to Carlisle and Plymouth. Jack admitted there had been occasions when the 'choir' had been near the knuckle but offered a simple solution; "We did have a little trouble, so we had the leaders in the office. We have taken steps to root them out." On a more positive tack, he proudly revealed details of the new Indoor Training Centre and Social Club being built next to Molineux Alley. He said; "We shall have everything there; bars, clubs, dances, bingo, everything our fans could wish for a place to go and enjoy themselves."

In the same article, Ronnie Allen outlined his plans, speaking of his intention to blend the old and new at a Molineux where all fondly remembered the good old days. Although admitting that the weight of historical expectation was resting heavily on the shoulders of players and management, he was prepared to trust the Wharton-Wagstaffe partnership and turn his back on Ramsey's 'wingless wonders' policy. Brown wrote; "In days when wingers are at a premium, Mr. Allen has two fast touchline flyers who can and do all the things orthodox wingers used to do." Holsgrove appreciates the importance of the duo; "Waggy could be described as physically flimsy but had great skill and flair, and could hit a ball on to a sixpence. He was swift, not lightning quick. Terry Wharton was a tremendous player, two-footed and took all the penalties. They gave us great balance. Ten years before, it had been Johnny Hancocks and Jimmy Mullen, now it was Terry on the right and Waggy on the left."

Terry Wharton greatly admires his ex-partner; "He was quick, he had little ankles and it was a wonder they weren't broken in two sometimes. He had that trick of pretending to cross and checking back. He was good at that and was a great crosser with his left peg." Wagstaffe also remembers the freedom Allen allowed both; "In all my career, I was never coached. An outside-left played on the wing. Ronnie put me on the wing and told me to play there." The back page of this same review had the interesting headline; 'Finding Out: About Toilet Rolls'. Alongside a photo of Derek Dougan, then with Leicester City, was a brief discussion of the pros and cons of what the Football League felt to be, 'a stupid and senseless practice'. While today's fans might be regular visitors to the club shop, the roaring trade in local stores of the day was in toilet tissue and not replica shirts.

Above: Derek Dougan was to generate more than his fair share of toilet-roll-related celebrations during his eight-year Indian summer at Molineux. Right: Club spotlighted.

On November 19, Phil Parkes made his debut against Preston at Molineux. Although this was a memorable experience, at this stage he was to be just a temporary replacement for Fred Davies; "At the start of the season, I was fourth choice behind Fred, Dave McLaren and Jim Barron. Two left and I finished up in the reserves behind Fred. Fred got injured and Ronnie said, 'You're playing.' It's one you look back on when you play your first game for a club like Wolves. We won 3-2 and Terry Wharton scored a penalty in the last minute." At the start of a December in which Walt Disney died, Wolves briefly topped the table but there were also a few worrying wobbles as expectation began to rise. First, I stood in the paddock with John Froggatt in a 44,000 crowd that saw Coventry comfortably overcome Wolves in the first of a 3-1 'double.' A fortnight later, my first away game resulted in a 3-2 defeat at St Andrew's. Managed by Stan Cullis, Birmingham secured a two-goal half-time lead that Wolves were unable to peg back. Recovering well, they celebrated Christmas Eve and Boxing Day with home (5-3) and away (3-0) wins over Derby. McIlmoyle, Wharton and Hatton hit the target both times, with Terry and Bob doubling up at Molineux at a time when questions were beginning to surface over McIlmoyle's long-term future.

The new year began gloomily with a single-goal defeat at Bristol City and two uninspiring draws, and the drab goalless affair at Ewood Park saw Dave Wagstaffe dismissed against his eventual employers, Blackburn. By the end of the month, the Sky Blues had unsurprisingly supplanted Wanderers at the top, and the Molineux men seemed consigned to a dogfight with the likes of Millwall and Carlisle for second spot in a league where at that stage only five points separated second place from 12th.

Another brief FA Cup adventure started with a draw at Oldham - and a 4-1 replay success was rewarded by a fourth-round home tie against holders Everton. In the Wolverhampton Chronicle and Midland Counties Express, Tony Butler predicted a three-goal victory for the Toffeemen but still argued; "It is not just another tie but a golden opportunity for Ronnie Allen and his team to prove to their loyal followers that Wolves are on the way back to the big time." Terry Wharton put Wolves ahead, only for Alan Ball to net a late penalty to earn a replay that was a personal nightmare for Fred Davies. It was lost 3-1 despite a Wharton goal but one man's misfortune was Phil Parkes' gain, as he recalls; "We absolutely murdered Everton at home and Gordon West had a fantastic game and saved everything. In the replay, Fred had one of those games keepers have and Ronnie left him out on the Saturday and put me in. It was Portsmouth away and I played the last 13 games of the season."

The promotion charge began in earnest with a 5-2 home win against Bolton on February 4, courtesy of two from Hunt and future Trotter Hatton, and one from Wagstaffe. It was the first of eight successive victories and was the game when, according to Waggy, Peter Knowles' antics possibly cost Wolves the services of Francis Lee; "Peter sat on the ball and Frannie was so incensed that he took a wild swing at him. We were all set to buy him but John Ireland said that he would not have a person at the club who tried to kick people like that."

Key wins followed at Charlton and Portsmouth, the latter bringing the return to action of Phil Parkes. Wolves came back from two down to win, the recovery starting with about 20 minutes to go when a long clearance by Parkes found Ernie Hunt in the Pompey half. He fed Wagstaffe, who spotted Bailey's strong forward run. The captain took it on his chest and fired in right-footed. Soon after, Hunt won a drop ball and fed Wharton on the right. His pass was intercepted but ran loose to Bailey, who crossed for Knowles to head in from six yards. He marked his equaliser by kicking the ball out of the ground as Dave Burnside closed in to congratulate him. The conduct drew harsh comment from Percy Young; "At his best, gracefully gifted and incisive. At his worst, exhibiting personality problems through erratic spasms of tiresome showmanship".

On 82 minutes, the win was secured from a left-wing corner by Wagstaffe. Burnside collided with the keeper and both were grounded when Hunt nodded home as the ball was flighted back in. BBC doyen Kenneth Wolstenhome commented; "This is real promotion form. Wolves haven't hit the heights but they picked themselves up when everything seemed lost." Parkes has affectionate memories of his second Wolves

game; "I shared a room with Peter. It was my first trip and my mam had put an apple and orange in for me. Peter got the orange and, instead of peeling it, bit into it. He had two false teeth at the front and the orange pulled one of them off the plate. He said he wasn't going to play because the match was on Match of the Day! Ronnie and Jack Dowen stuck the tooth back on the plate with glue and chewing gum. When Peter kicked the ball out of the ground, they made him pay for it. It cost him a fiver, I think."

With 11 games to go, Ronnie Allen pulled off what Dave Wagstaffe calls 'an absolute master-stroke' by signing Derek Dougan from Leicester City for a mere £50,000. John Holsgrove chips in; "The signing of Dougan, the old man of the sea as I called him, really was the icing on the cake. You must give credit to Ronnie. He came in, stabilised the team and then made a classic move that guaranteed us promotion. He knew that, although we weren't losing, we needed something more. The rumour came that Dougan was coming. His reputation preceded him but I've always treated everybody as I find them and I took to him straightaway and we became great friends. I found him outspoken and some of the time I didn't agree with him but what he did was amazing. The Doog, Bobby Thomson, Les Wilson and I became good friends and were called the 'tea set' as we had tea every day after training."

The move was in March, 1967, almost a year to the day since the equally influential Mike Bailey had been lured north. Waggy continues; "People had written Derek off, not so much as a footballer but as a trouble-maker. Really, he was frowned upon. He was on the other side from the managers but Ronnie took a chance on him." Bailey agrees; "The Doog joining us was perfect timing by Ronnie. With the season three quarters over, we were top and he gave us the final push to win promotion. It was an excellent team and the future looked good, especially with the young talents of Peter Knowles, Phil Parkes and John McAlle emerging. Most of these players stayed together for ten years and gave wonderful service and success to the Wolves."

The Doog recalled being summoned back to Filbert Street one Tuesday from Brighton, where Leicester were staying after a match at Chelsea. Without preamble, he was told by Matt Gillies; "We've agreed to sell you to Wolves." The manager refused to reveal the fee when Dougan pressed him. When the Doog returned later in the day to collect his kit, he saw a number of colleagues returning from Brighton, including inside-forward Davey Gibson, whose response to the news was to throw his suitcase to the ground and kick it while issuing a torrent of expletives.

Two days later, the Irishman still hadn't spoken to Ronnie Allen and, after training, Gillies sent for him again. Never one to stand on ceremony, he knocked and walked straight into the manager's office to be told; "They've agreed £50,000 and want to discuss things with you. You've got to get over to Sandwell Golf Club." Dougan made it clear he was "getting over nowhere" and met Allen instead in a motel car park on the A5 near Hinckley. He maintained that the transfer was finalised in Allen's blue Ford Capri, with Bob Hatton discussing a move to Bolton the next day.

Dougan's link with Wolves went back some 12 years to when a scout had been sent to Belfast to look at the possibility of signing the 16-year-old then centre- half. The scout baulked at the £5,000 asking price; "He wouldn't get in the third team." Ironically, the Doog went on to score his first League goal for Portsmouth in a 1-1 home draw with Wolves on November 9 1957, equalising an Eddie Clamp opener.

The signing gave Wolves just the boost needed to mount the final push, while, in other respects, Allen's starting line-up had the makings of a familiar look. Phil Parkes was now preferred to Fred Davies, and Gerry Taylor was drafted in at full-back alongside Thomson. Bailey, Woodfield and Holsgrove were settled at 4, 5 and 6, with future manager Graham Hawkins providing cover. With Wharton and Wagstaffe on the wings, Hunt, Dougan and Knowles or Burnside made up the usual starting 11. At 28, Dougan was one of the oldest on the playing staff but saw great potential in the squad and reflected affectionately; "Wolves! The very name was a kind of magic spell. It was like starting again. When I looked around the side, there were two Londoners; a Scotsman; a big kid of a goalkeeper from West Bromwich; Bobby Thomson, probably the most noteworthy one there because Bailey's career hadn't taken off then; Waggy was an enigma; Terry Wharton, probably a relic of the old days; and Peter Knowles." Dougan did no more than a morning's training before travelling to Plymouth, where he first donned a gold shirt. Many fans travelled to South Devon to see his debut, among them Stuart Earl, who had founded London Wolves the previous July, and they saw Peter Knowles score the only goal of the game.

A week later, Knowles scored again as the Doog marked his home debut in typically theatrical fashion with a hat-trick in the 4-0 win over Cliff Britton's Hull City. Midway through the first half, the tall forward laid the ball to Dave Wagstaffe lurking on the left in front of the Molineux Street stand. Waggy cut inside, chipped the ball to Bobby Thomson on the right hand edge of the box. The classy full back controlled before angling a right-foot drive goalwards. The Tigers keeper could only parry into the path of Dougan who lashed in. On the hour, Wharton picked the ball up in midfield and sprinted purposefully through the opposition defence. Leaving two men in his wake, he set Dougan in on the right edge of the box to loft gently over the advancing McKechnie. The celebrations at the Cowshed End were memorable, with Peter

Notes by "Wanderer"

WELCOME FOR ONE — AND ALL!

THE stage seems set at Molineux today to make this a really big occasion. We have attractive visitors in Hull City, we welcome our own team back again after five successive victories and, of course, we have a personal welcome to Molineux for new signing Derek Dougan.

The tall Irish International is no stranger to Molineux and it is a special pleasure to be able to have him with us as we embark on the last stages of the promotion fight.

We feel he can be a big help with his wide experience and his well known flair for the centre-forward role. We are sure our followers will be only too happy to give him a big hand, as with the rest of the team, he takes a bow after the extremely useful victory at Plymouth last week-end.

Knowles swinging on the crossbar and the Doog managing an athletic pirouette. Wolves' new signing left the best until last. On this occasion, Waggy crossed from the right for Wharton to head back across the six-yard box. Just as it seemed the ball would drop behind the Doog, he extended a leg backwards to lob the ball over his own head to set up a left-footed volley he gleefully rifled into the roof of the net.

Dougan remembered; "It really was meant and I'd done it many times in training. The first guy I'd ever seen do it was Jimmy Scoular, who played for Newcastle." Derek clearly relished sharing Lawrie McMenemey's opinion on the goal; "Quite frankly, had it been an English player now in the Premier League, they'd still be showing it 40 years later!" Holsgrove jokes; "I obviously remember Derek's first game at Molineux. We were on a roll, played some good football and a couple of mis-hits from the Doog bobbled in!" A hero was well and truly born, and I saw it all courtesy of a home-made wooden box that raised me up above the crowds behind one of the huge stone exits on the South Bank. These matches late in the sixties were real family affairs before the onset of serious hooliganism began to drive some away. Mom, Dad, sister and a number of mates were in tow for the fortnightly routine of parking in Oaks Crescent and frequenting a little café in Chapel Ash before the match. The Doog shared fond memories of this time; "Wolves renewed my career and raised my sights."

After his first few games, Dougan approached Gordon Banks, who was a year or two older; "Gordon, would you come to Wolves? I see a lot of potential here. There are all these young guys, the oldest is probably not 25 yet." Encouraged by a positive response from England's no 1, he approached Ronnie Allen; "I've spoken to Gordon Banks and he'll come if you look after him." The manager's answer, "he's too old," now appears something of an error of judgement given the fact Bansky was still three years away from that save from Pele in the Mexico World Cup. John Holsgrove remembers; "When Derek came in 1967, he said to Ronnie Allen; 'You can buy Leicester's goalkeeper for 45 grand. This is not being unfair to Lofty but we all know who Leicester's keeper was. But, for once, Ronnie didn't follow it up. Because Peter Shilton was coming through, we could have had Gordon, who was still the greatest keeper in the world. Doog said to Ronnie, 'Buy him, buy him' and Ronnie later admitted his mistake."

Banks moved instead to Stoke City and Allen, over six years later when coming to watch son Russell in league cup action at Molineux, admitted to Dougan that he should have listened. Dougan said he offered no more advice on signings or tactics; "I've been accused of trying to pick the team, run the team and tell the manager who to sign. That is sheer fiction. Half of the situations have been made up by people who don't know me or haven't even met me. Quite simply, I've always wanted to play with the best players, but unfortunately I've been described as the rebel, which is nonsense. I had 30 managers in my career and when the man who is the manager of the football club has got less intelligence than you, it's sometimes very difficult to take."

Derek Dougan and dark-shirted Derek Parkin watch Terry Wharton net Wolves' winner in the Easter game with Huddersfield at Leeds Road.

The Hull game was the first in a ten-match run-in of seven wins and a draw that were to sweep Wolves back to the promised land. A tense Bank Holiday weekend saw home and away wins over Huddersfield. I followed the Easter Monday Leeds Road game on the car radio on a family trip to a freezing Whipsnade Zoo, where, fittingly enough, only the arctic wolves made much of an appearance. It was in this double-header that Derek Parkin first really came to the club's notice; "I got in the Huddersfield team when I was 18 and played that weekend against Waggy because I played right-back at that time . I think that was the reason they bought me." Although Parkin saw this as the end of Huddersfield's promotion challenge, Terriers fan and Prime Minister Harold Wilson remained defiant and stoically predicted that the Yorkshiremen would still gain promotion if they secured enough points!

A hard-earned draw at Millwall on April Fool's Day was an eye-opener for the young Phil Parkes; "Cold Blow Lane was frightening, just its reputation. The pegs in the dressing room were so high that even I had to stand on a bench to hang my things up. The first thing you think is; 'F...in hell, they've got some big lads playing here!'" Mike Bailey was presented with a bunch of flowers, an unwelcome gesture and a misleading one given what was to follow. Millwall took the lead and Parkes took a fearful battering from a big centre-forward nearing the end of his career; "Len Julians knocked seven shades of s..t out of me. Every time we went for the ball, he hit me. It was Spring and there was no grass on the pitch. It was a dust bowl and when I went down, it took the skin off my nose."

Julians gave Millwall the lead and, in the second half, the home team netted again but this time the referee was brave enough to disallow it. This was the sign for bottles, bricks and coins to rain down onto the pitch, as Parkes remembers; "The big old pennies. They used to sharpen one end and throw them at you. All the back of my neck was cut." With ten minutes left, there was more drama, sparked off by a Dougan equaliser, an assault on Wolves' recent signing and a last-gasp penalty opportunity. Holsgrove chips in; "Typical bloody Den! A supporter ran on to the pitch and started to go for him. Derek was accosted and we all laughed and said, 'The Doog's got his

Phil Parkes shows his command over Len Julians in the 1-1 draw at The Den. But Derek Dougan, tangling with Bryan Snowdon, was worried about balls of a different kind.

handbag out!' " Lofty adds; "The Doog scored and this guy with a Wolves scarf on came past me from behind the goal. He ran with his arms out and, as he reached Derek, he kicked him in the balls! He was a Millwall fan in a Wolves scarf on. Right at the death, we got a penalty. Terry Wharton, the regular taker, wasn't playing, so Waggy took it. He must have hit it 20 feet over the bar. I still say to this day he missed it on purpose. He was petrified of what might happen if he scored!"

The draw was followed by the novelty of a Saturday evening kick-off against Rotherham due to clashes with the Grand National and FA Cup sixth-round ties. Although this was the first such experiment since October 1958, the club were rewarded with a 2-0 win and an excellent attendance of 32,338. Promotion was virtually guaranteed at Preston on April 15, the day Jim McCalliog scored at Wembley to help Scotland to a 3-2 victory over World Champions England. With only two minutes on the clock at Deepdale, a clearance found Mick Bailey, who in turn released Dave Burnside. The stylish midfielder played the ball through for Ernie Hunt to run on and draw Alan Kelly before slipping the ball past the home keeper. Just before half-time, Dave Woodfield headed on a Knowles corner to set up Hunt for a spectacular overhead finish. Bailey nearly made it three with a volley against the bar and, although Hannigan halved the lead late on, Wolves hung on for a vital victory.

Escape from Division Two, reported by Phil Morgan as 'A Division 2 bury - al', was confirmed and fulsomely celebrated a week later at Molineux as a Dougan double

Cheers – a fan-tastic feeling

GAY MOLINEUX

Bobby Noble   TONIGHT'S GAMES   VICTORY FOR WOLVES MEANT-

Celebrating being back where we belong......

led Wolves to a 4-1 victory over Bury. Wolves were two up in 18 minutes via a Wharton penalty and a Dougan strike, although nerves remained frayed when Jones reduced the arrears before the interval. Burnside and Dougan then settled things in the second period with the Doog's second providing a fitting finale. Phil Parkes fielded a cross and threw the ball out to Wagstaffe. His pass found Dougan just beyond the centre circle and allowed him to run on, drift just away from the right side of the Bury goal before firing in off the underside of the bar. Coming on for Gerry Taylor with 15 minutes left, Knowles almost made it five but it mattered not a jot. In the teeming rain, thousands poured on to the pitch amid scenes unknown since Wolves had clinched a third League title in 1959. The players gathered in the directors' box, and Allen and Bailey pledged that this was just the start.

Seven days later, Wolves went into what was effectively the championship decider. They were two points clear and Coventry needed only one to assure their own promotion. The game was played in front of 51,455 under the strangest possible circumstances, as John Holsgrove recalls; "It was phenomenal. I tell people and they don't believe me; there were spectators on top of the stands. It was effectively winner take all, whoever won was going to be champions. They were up the pylons and round the edge of the pitch. With this health and safety rubbish we have now, they'd have shut the place down, the game would never be played. It was amazing." Willie Carr, then in Coventry's second team, also saw things at first hand; "I had been playing in the reserves or youth team and it was pandemonium back at Highfield Road. We got back more or less as it was finishing. I just remember the crowds, they were sitting on the edge of the pitch." Although a Peter Knowles goal kept Wolves' noses in front until the hour mark, Jimmy Hill's men ultimately triumphed 3-1 courtesy of Machin, Gibson and Rees in what he termed the "Midlands Match of the Century."

Wolves nonetheless celebrated their promotion in style on May 6 with yet another 4-1 win, this time over Norwich. The players turned out for this last home game with bouquets of flowers that were duly presented to lady supporters. John Ireland presented the deserving Mike Bailey with the 'Evening Mail' award for Midlands Footballer of the Year, the midfielder's influence then and over the next decade is summed up by John Richards; "Mike was such a good captain and with him missing, we weren't as good. He could read a game so well and could get information to players around him. He had the ability to see how things were developing and to tell people what to do to make a difference and turn things round."

Phil Parkes wholeheartedly agrees; "Mike was a great captain and great player. He cared about the players and was always there for you if you needed anything. He led by example and was the first to win a tackle, the second to win a tackle and probably the third to win a tackle." With typical modesty, Bailey likes to refer instead to 'a wonderful team spirit.' Within 25 minutes, Derek Dougan had scored twice, courtesy of assists from Dave Burnside and Bailey, giving him nine goals in ten games. Although a thigh strain forced Bailey off to be replaced by Graham Hawkins on 40 minutes, Terry Wharton lashed home a cracking cross-shot from another Burnside lay-off. In his last match in Wolves colours, hugely popular defender Joe Wilson charged down the right eight minutes into the second half to allow Ernie Hunt to head home. After Dougan had been denied a hat trick, Tony Woolmer cut the deficit but could do nothing to mar the celebrations as thousands of fans invaded the pitch to acknowledge players once again appearing high in the Waterloo Road Stand.

In the match programme, 'The Wanderer' congratulated the team under the heading; 'Last for a long time, we hope.' Supporters were encouraged to purchase the promotion LP, 'The Hungry Wolves,' at 12s 6d, the only negative being that 'The Happy Wanderer' and the marches of John Philip Souser were replaced on the Molineux tannoy by the dire 'Up the Wolves.' Still top of the table going into the final game, Wolves were denied the title by a poor performance at Crystal Palace. As skipper Bailey clearly remembers, a side denied his influence succumbed 4-1; "I missed the match with a hamstring injury I picked up in the Norwich game." It was a first return to Selhurst Park to forget for John Holsgrove; "For totally personal reasons, I remember it. We'd had a hell of a long season, were a bit tired, but still had a chance of

With mum and friends on the South Bank for the final home game of 1966-67, against Norwich.

THE PLAYERS' PROMOTION L.P. RECORD

"THE HUNGRY WOLVES" is a Thank You Record from the Players to Supporters The Record is a medley of songs sung by the Players and interviews with each Player.

A SOUVENIR OF 1966-67 PROMOTION SEASON

Price only 12/6 (postage 1/10 extra)

On sale from Monday next, at the Office, Waterloo Road, or Development Association Office at Molineux.

Don't be the one without "The Hungry Wolves." It's a must.

becoming champions. We lost, got back to the dressing room and got in the bath. We're promoted but we hear the Palace boys singing, 'We're going to be champions.' It was as though they'd won the League!"

Three notable members of Wolves' promotion-winning squad moved on in the summer, namely Bob Hatton, Hugh McIlmoyle and Ron Flowers. Bolton, Bristol City and Northampton Town were their respective ports of call. Flowers, who had played his last Wolves game against Birmingham in January and just 14 in total that season, ended a glorious 15-year association with the club, during which he made 512 first-team appearances and secured three Championship and one FA Cup winners medals. He would eventually be awarded a testimonial in 1970-71.

Peter Knowles tangles with Crystal Palace's David Payne as Wolves' successful 1966-67 season ends in resounding disappointment at Selhurst Park.

In the close season, the team undertook a strength-sapping tour, playing as the Los Angeles Wolves in the FIFA-supported North American Soccer League or, as it was otherwise known, the United Soccer Association. Wolves were one of 12 clubs from Europe and South America to participate. It was an adventure in which Mike Bailey was not scheduled to play an early part; "As I'd been selected to play for England in the Expo 67 tournament in Montreal, I stayed behind to get fit while the lads flew to Los Angeles. I got fit, or so I thought, and flew to Canada. But, in the very first practice match, I felt my hamstring go again. As I could take no further part in the tournament, I asked Sir Alf Ramsey if I could join the lads in LA, and he agreed."

John Holsgrove remembers the allure of the States; "Ronnie had said all season that if we got promoted, we would go to America. Truth be known, we'd have gone any way with contracts having to be signed. It was a good period for me, I'm not sure if I was the only one that played all 14 games out there but I was able to cement my place in the team as Duggie and me learnt more about each other. When I heard we were going to Dallas, I thought we were going to see cowboys. When we got there, it

Ernie Hunt, Dave Wagstaffe, Terry Wharton and Mike Bailey Monkeeing around in LA.

was all very modern and nothing like that." Phil Parkes sums up the magic for a lad only just out of his teens; "I'd never been out of England before - just to Wales, that was about it. I was very lucky to go to Los Angeles, Hollywood for nine weeks. Who wouldn't want to go? We got well looked after and stayed in the best hotels."

Dave Wagstaffe met up with an old school pal from Manchester, no less than Davy Jones of the Monkees, a group as big as The Beatles in 1967. Tournament sponsor Jack Kent Cooke left much of the day-to-day work to his publicist Hank Erlich, of Paramount Pictures, who mixed with some of the biggest stars in the world, including Frank Sinatra. Holsgrove recalls; "Hank and I became very close friends and sadly he died a few years ago. Davy Jones would come to our hotel (the Beverly Hills Wilshire) in a limo with the windows blacked out. He'd rush in quickly, come and swim with us and go to games, and loved it. Waggy even got us on the set where they were filming their shows. It was great. At a time when you might go to Cleethorpes for your holiday, here we were touring America and getting paid. We all got £10 a day expenses, a lot in those days, and I put a deposit on a new house in Bantock Gardens." Terry Wharton remembers the time with similar affection; "Brilliant. Ronnie turned it down at first because they were going to send us to Cleveland, a big steel city, but Stoke ended up there. We wanted the best and weren't going otherwise, so Jack Kent Cooke sponsored it and we went to LA, just up the road from Coconut Grove. Ernie Hunt and me had two nights in Vegas before the final. The stars loved the football - the Monkees, Tommy Steele, Vic Damone. We had a cracking time and every match was live on TV."

Wolves topped the Western Division and beat Eastern champions Aberdeen (playing as Washington Whips) 6-5 in the final, with a Dave Burnside treble matching a hat-trick from future Wolf Frank Munro. Mike Bailey remembers; "It was a really fabulous experience, culminating in an amazing final. At the end, the mayor of LA said in his speech; 'Don't tell me this game isn't exciting!' When we played the opening game of the competition at the LA Coliseum we had 2,000 fans, then 17,000 watched the final. We did a good PR job for LA and eventually signed Frank!"

Bangu (Brazil) 1	Wolves 1	Houston, Texas
Wolves 2	Cerro (Uruguay) 1	Los Angeles, California
Stoke City 0	Wolves 0	Cleveland, Ohio
Hibernian 1	Wolves 2	Toronto, Ontario
Wolves 5	Sunderland 1	Los Angeles, California
Wolves 4	Glentoran 1	Los Angeles, California
Aberdeen 1	Wolves 1	Washington D.C.
Wolves 1	Shamrock Rovers 1	Los Angeles, California
ADO (Holland) 1	Wolves 0	San Francisco, California
Wolves 2	ADO (Holland) 0	Los Angeles, California
Wolves 2	Cagliari (Italy) 0	Los Angeles, California
Dundee United 2	Wolves 2	Dallas, Texas
Aberdeen 3	Wolves 0	Washington D.C.
Wolves 6	Aberdeen 5	FINAL

Munro has different memories; "We played Wolves three times but were in different sections and, in an earlier game, Burnside and I were sent off. I was as close to him as I am to you. He took a throw-in that hit me straight in the face. He ran away to the Wolves bench and I threw a punch at him, but he dived out of the way and I hit John Ireland. When I eventually came to sign, Ronnie Allen was in his office with Mr Ireland, who put his hands up to cover himself! The final was an unbelievable game that went on for two hours 25 minutes, with extra-time and sudden death!" Once the tournament was won, the players were invited to Bel Air to meet Cooke, as Holsgrove recalls; "Typical Yanks, they only wanted to know winners! Apparently, he offered a million dollars for Wolves. He thought he could just buy us and we laughed at him, saying, 'You can't buy a club like this with such a terrific history. The silly thing is that, 40 years on, he probably could!"

Bailey was fulsome in his praise of the American experiment; "I'm absolutely convinced the tour did us good. We tried out many ideas, talked a lot about the game and really blended. It was an invaluable experience." Ronnie Allen wholeheartedly agreed; "We made a tremendous impact in the States, helped promote the game and won the tourney, but what was more important was that my youngsters gained a lot from the fierce competition and really came of age." Derek Dougan added; "We came back with an amazing team spirit and camaraderie but I realised I was eventually going to have a problem with one bloke. Mick Bailey and I never got on." The Doog nevertheless added; "I absolutely admired Bailey and gave him the greatest compliment. At 25, he had the serious makings, with a good side, to emulate Danny Blanchflower as a captain." Munro says; "They respected each other for what they were but didn't get on. I liked both, in fact I got on well with all the players."

Dougan maintained it was in America that Ronnie Allen made the mistake of breaking trust with the players, an approach typified by an alleged reluctance to play younger players like Alun Evans and Les Wilson. Doog recounted an occasion when he had to restrain Wilson from seeking out the manager for a showdown. He maintained that the young Canadian was outraged at not being involved in a game that his parents had travelled over a thousand miles southto watch. John Holsgrove is more forgiving of the manager; "We've all got our faults. When you have 20 to 25 players in a squad, you can't please everybody."

Whatever the rights and wrongs of the 14-match American experiment it was an undertaking that would be unthinkable in the modern era. Whether or not it was the right preparation for the fast-approaching First Division season, fans would very soon start to discover.

1967-68: Back In The Big Time

It would be tantamount to football suicide today for a newly-promoted team to move into the top flight without significant strengthening but Wolves did exactly that in 1967-68. Waggy admits; "It was less of a jump then but we had a cracking team in 1967 and made very few changes to the squad." Phil Parkes agrees; "The divide now is massive. It was less then." John Holsgrove remembers the pressure; "Two weeks' holiday, nine weeks away in America (you don't turn that chance down) and then we're back in Division One. I'd been at the club two years and I'm thinking, 'First Division, big jump this,' but I really didn't have enough time to prepare. By the end of the season, I'd played all 42 League games and was shattered."

The last Division Two game, at Crystal Palace, had seen a side of Parkes, Taylor, Thomson, Hawkins (deputising for Bailey), Woodfield, Holsgrove, Wharton, Hunt, Dougan, Burnside, Wagstaffe. When the new season dawned on August 19, Fulham faced an identical line-up bar the return of the fit-again skipper. Of the 30 full professionals listed in the first programme, 21 had progressed through the ranks. Only Glendon Andrews, Mike Bailey, Paddy Buckley, Dave Burnside, Derek Dougan, Holsgrove, Ernie Hunt, Wagstaffe and Evan Williams had come from other clubs.

During 1967-68, there would be six major departures and four acquisitions. Those taking the out door were Paddy Buckley (to Sheffield United), Graham Hawkins (Preston), Fred Davies (Cardiff), Ron Flowers (Northampton), Hunt (Everton, £80,000) and Terry Wharton (Bolton). Wharton recalls the unsatisfactory nature of his leaving; "I played the first 12 or so games, my final one at Molineux against Arsenal on a Monday and we won 3-2. My last game in a Wolves shirt was at Sheffield and I moved to Bolton the next Thursday. The crowd were getting on my back a bit. If I shot wide, they'd boo me, but if Dougan shot wide, they'd clap him because he'd always fall on his knees and was a great character that way. I asked for a move."

Although the newcomers included the relatively transient Mike Kenning and Frank Wignall (from Norwich and Nottingham Forest respectively), the early weeks of

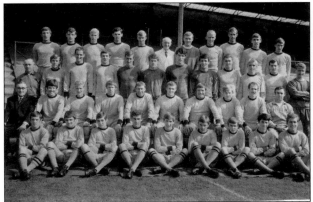

Wolves line up at their pre-season photo call - in the other shot is Mike Bailey, their no 1 driving force.

1968 saw the signing of two stalwarts who would notch up a total of 980 appearances over ten and 15 years at the club. Long-term target Frank Munro cost £55,000 from Aberdeen while Derek Parkin moved from Huddersfield for £80,000 on Valentine's Day. Percy Young marked their arrival with the uncharitable comment; "Both these players were adventurous, inclined at times to prefer imagination to industry."

How eagerly the season was anticipated is shown by the fact Molineux had its first two League crowds in excess of 50,000 (against Albion and Manchester United) since the title was won in 1958-59. There were also five home gates of over 40,000 and 14 of 30,000-plus - something never since bettered. The average home League attendance of 35,064 was also the highest since the 1959-60 'double' of FA Cup win and second in the League. Roy Ullyett's cartoon, reproduced below from an August Daily Express, sums up the bullish manner in which Wolves approached their task.

A 2-1 victory at Fulham was a welcome start, although it appeared for a while that the well-supported visitors would be foiled by the athletic Tony Macedo. Dougan eventually got on the score-sheet and a great volley from Bailey sealed full points as

Wolves played, in the words of David Miller; "like a team who had become thoroughly used to each other." Bailey remembers his winner; "Waggy sent over a great cross and it came to me on the edge of the box. I was going to bring it down but just hit it on the volley and it flew into the top corner." However, as Miller added in the Sunday Telegraph, it was never going to provide the stiffest challenge of the season; "This, you might

say, was an 'O' level paper for Wolves. The 'A' levels, the Manchester and Tottenhams, have yet to come. Wolves did enough to gain a pass if not a distinction."

On August 23, Molineux was packed to the rafters by 51,438 for the return of top-flight football to Wolverhampton. In the programme, 'Wanderer' called it; "The first steps on a hard road." The first Black Country derby since March, 1965 had the editor of Albion's programme drooling a week later; "It was a heart-stirring moment for any soccer fan. Anticipation had become reality, Wolves were back in the First Division and our rivalry, spread over so many years, was renewed with all the tension and atmosphere engendered in the Molineux Stadium. Welcome back to Division One, Wolverhampton Wanderers, and on with the game."

On just six minutes, Dave Woodfield fouled Jeff Astle but Phil Parkes dived to his right to save Tony Brown's penalty. Soon after, Hunt turned in a Dougan header to establish an interval lead. Early in the second half, the Baggies equalised when Ken Foggo received a throw-in from Astle in what in any other circumstance would have been an offside position. The little right winger, who had earlier rattled the bar, ran on without hesitation to unleash a fierce shot that went in off a combination of post and Parkes' hand. Wolves regained the lead on 65 minutes when Wagstaffe set up Bailey to leave John Osborne groping from 25 yards and, with 17 minutes left, looked to have clinched both points when Hunt set up Burnside to fire in a left-foot 'banana' shot.

However, within a minute, the visitors were back in it as John Kaye got his head to a ball hooked across goal and, despite the desperate efforts of Wolves defenders, the linesman confirmed it had crossed the line. This set up a frantic finale that the Express & Star's Phil Morgan called 'The great goal robbery' as Tony Brown clearly punched a highly dubious equaliser into the South Bank net. When Ivan Sharpe had written in the programme, "Why goalkeepers have now to watch their step," he was referring to the new 'four-step' rule. But Parkes could have done with his own warning. Having thrown a right hook at Baggies legend Astle and then grabbed Sheffield referee JE Carr, he was duly dismissed and recalls; "I think Clive Clark crossed and Tony Brown punched it in. According to the ref's report, I was sent off for foul and abusive language but I'd also given Jeff Astle a smack. The ref had to have a police escort off."

It took almost exactly 40 years for 'Bomber' Brown to admit his guilt to Steve Marshall in the Sporting Star; "Probably the Wolves derby I remember most was the first I played in. I was a young lad and the atmosphere was brilliant. We were losing 3-2 with a couple of minutes to go when I went in for a diving header but knew I couldn't get there so I punched it in. I expected the referee to give a free-kick but, to my amazement, he signalled a goal. Phil Parkes couldn't believe it and chased the ref, jumped on him and was sent off. I've only recently admitted to it because it's not something you want to be remembered for." John Holsgrove remembers a repeat the following season; "Tony Hateley did that against us at Liverpool, knocked it in with his arm from a corner and the ref gave a goal. Shocking!"

Parkes stormed off to the dressing room, tossing his green top in the direction of unlikely substitute keeper Dave Wagstaffe. Doog recalled Waggy nervously taking his place with 'a jersey practically touching the ground,' while the winger says; "Everyone was concerned at Phil being sent off, not who was going in goal. Lofty just happened to give me the shirt and I put it on. It was too big and the sleeves came right down but luckily I only touched the ball about three times." Parkes feels the winger secretly enjoyed his experience; "He fancied himself as a goalie, Waggy!" Parkes is now more appreciative of the experience; "I still lived in West Brom and you can imagine the stick I took walking through the town. My first local derby and I saved a penalty, more or less scored an own goal and got sent off. They don't come any better than that!"

Despite having a first home victory snatched from under their noses, skipper Bailey was upbeat on his team's positive start, "In taking three points from two games, we have done better than many expected. Yet, apart from the points, I feel we are playing a better brand of football. It seems the pace of the First Division suits us, although you have to think much quicker. And you are punished more ruthlessly when you make a mistake." Ronnie Allen complimented his players on the quality of their team-work, putting the emphasis on everyone backing each other up and high endeavour. As the reporter wrote; "Wolves have long decreed, 'there is no substitute for hard work.' Allen trims this to a blunt, 'be busy'." Bailey enthused about playing at the top level; "It's fabulous. It's a tremendous experience and even after two games, I feel all the waiting and hoping has been worthwhile. It's pretty plain there is no other division like it for atmosphere. The boys are really enjoying themselves."

Allen set a mid-table target for his 'resourceful' and young outfit (average age only 23), stating; "Whatever success comes, we'll accept gratefully." The pleasing start continued when a Dougan double enabled Wolves to overcome a good Leeds team the following Saturday, the same day Beatles manager Brian Epstein was found dead in his Belgravia home. Derek headed home Wagstaffe's 54th minute cross and, although carrying an injury, was put through by Ernie Hunt to score the second with a rising

DOUGAN DOUSES THE LEEDS FIRE

by ROBERT BLACKBURN

Wolves 2, Leeds Utd. 0

WOLVES had had the edge on Leeds in the first half at Molineux and a 54th minute goal by Dougan was only justice.

The Leeds defence seemed to be mesmerised 12 minutes later when Dougan added a second, giving goalkeeper Sprake no chance. Brilliant Charlton

1548
WEST BROMWICH ALBION
THE HAWTHORNS · WEST BROMWICH
HALFORDS LANE · ENTRANCE D

30 STAND D
10/- UNRESERVED CORNER STAND

OFFICIAL

ALBION NEWS
AND PROGRAMME

WEST BROMWICH ALBION FOOTBALL CLUB LIMITED

Vol. 59 No. 3 (Copyright)   30th August, 1967

ALBION v WOLVERHAMPTON WANDERERS

SIXPENCE

drive on 66 minutes. Despite a promising five points from six, John Holsgrove did not share the confidence of the former chairman's son, Harry Marshall, as the players left the dressing room; "Doog and I were walking out after the game and Mr Marshall junior said, 'We'll be in Europe next season.' We'd only played three games in the First Division but we knew what had to be done."

To get me out of mom's way on her 33rd birthday, dad took me for a first visit to The Hawthorns. Since Albion had lost 4-0 at Southampton and 1-0 at home to Chelsea, we went full of hope, but goals from Astle, Kaye, Stephens and Clark brought just a single reply from Mike Bailey. The midweek drubbing started a run of four defeats, made more worrying because they included two of David Miller's 'A' level tests (against Everton and Tottenham). On September 2, World Cup hero Alan Ball was the masterful difference between the two teams as he inspired Everton into an unassailable four-goal lead. Wolves at least showed some spirit as Terry Wharton and Les Wilson halved the arrears, the latter becoming the first Wolves substitute to score. Within four days they were pitched against a Spurs team who had lost their previous game 5-1 to Burnley. Perhaps in an attempt to deflect attention, the Spurs programme recalled that it was Wolves' first visit to White Hart Lane since the 7-4 reverse in March, 1965. A Hunt goal in his last game in a gold shirt could not save Wolves from a 2-1 loss.

Dougan was not alone in regretting Hunt's £80,000 switch to Merseyside; "At times, the life and soul of the party. He was a good player, strong, who went on to do a good job, first with Everton and later with Coventry." His old chum and business partner Mike Bailey especially missed him; "Ernie and I had gone into business together, a restaurant in Birmingham called the Savoury Duck. At the opening, we invited players from all the local clubs. The deal also included a burger van that was parked on wasteland opposite the Alexandra Theatre and I went there regularly late at night to pick up the takings. Unfortunately, Ernie was transferred to Everton shortly after and we sold both businesses for a loss." Hunt scored 35 goals in 82 games for Wolves, and Holsgrove remembers how his friendship with Bailey cost him a car.

"Mike and Ernie were close and decided they were going to have new MGBs. Mike had a blue one, Ernie a red one. When Ernie joined Everton, he drove up in his. Because it was in Liverpool colours, it got completely trashed in the Goodison car park!" Future Coventry team-mate Willie Carr recalls a great character; "Ernie was very funny and still is. When he goes to the toilet, he'll come back in a blonde wig and see if anyone recognises him, daft as a brush. But he's the best front man I ever played with. I played the ball up and knew it was going to stick there. He was great. As I was running past, he would just flick it on and I didn't even need to break stride."

Worse followed for Wolves when Leicester won 3-1 at Molineux, then they were dumped out of the League Cup by Huddersfield, although a mini-rally followed when Dougan and Knowles grabbed a brace apiece in wins over West Ham and Burnley. Alun Evans scored on his home debut in the latter, having been blooded at Upton Park, allegedly on the Doog's advice after Burnside had refused to play if he had to wear no 11.

At the end of September, I was taken to Sheffield Wednesday, my first game out of the Midlands. I am reliably informed a back-seat dispute with my sister put us in serious danger of not progressing past Chesterfield but mum and dad relented. High in the North (Leppings Lane) Stand, we saw Wolves gain a spirited 2-2 draw on the back of goals from birthday boys Evans and Knowles, who turned 18 and 22 respectively on the day. Gary Megson's dad, Don, played left back for the Owls and future Wolves midfielder Jim McCalliog turned out for them at no 10. It was great to be in a stadium that had hosted World Cup games in 1966 and BBC Match of the Day were there, with David Coleman at the microphone. Inside five minutes, Wolves took the lead as a swift Wagstaffe, Dougan, Knowles, Wagstaffe, Knowles interchange on the left found Evans with his back to goal just inside the penalty area. He laid the ball off to Knowles, who found the right-hand corner from 20 yards. Mobley and Ritchie put the Owls in control either side of half-time and, with time running out, Knowles set Bailey off on a final charge into Wednesday's half that ended in a pass apparently

Birthday boys Knowles and Evans share a joke with Wharton and the boss - but Ozzie failed (below) to similarly amuse a sixties Wolfie.

aimed for Wharton. Fortuitously, the ball found Evans near the penalty spot and the youngster notched his second goal that season with a low right-foot drive into Peter Springett's bottom corner.

Between September and Christmas, Wolves hovered precariously in the bottom half of the table, their home form keeping their heads above water. Before the visit of Manchester United on December 30, ten games at Molineux had yielded six wins, two draws and two losses. The two setbacks were hardly even 'O' level tests as Wolves lost to Leicester and Stoke. On the positive side, October saw a fine 3-2 win over Arsenal, set up by a Dougan double and an Evans strike, while a Knowles brace in November earned Wolves their first points in five encounters with Coventry.

The Stoke match was a fog-shrouded 4-3 setback that Clive Corbett, aged 11 of Pensnett, for some reason celebrated as his memory match in a programme for a match with Albion in April, 1969 (Wolves also lost that one!). Gordon Banks was kept on his

BLOOR SINKS SAD WOLVES

by GEOFFREY BEANE

Wolves 3   Stoke City 4

A BRAVE fight by Wolves, when they came back to 3-3 from 3-0, was in vain when Bloor hit the winner for Stoke at Molineux with two minutes to go.

mettle early on by John Farrington and Alun Evans but John Mahoney and Calvin Palmer soon had Evan Williams retrieving the ball from the North Bank net and, just past the half-hour, Harry Burrows crashed in a fierce cross-shot to further extend City's advantage. Ten minutes before the interval, Holsgrove's header sparked a rally that continued when Knowles calmly stroked a penalty beyond the peerless Banks. After the break, Paddy Buckley led wave after wave of attacks until meeting a long cross-field pass by Farrington to sweep home. But, just when it seemed Wolves would take a point, Stoke broke away and Alan Bloor stole a 4-3 win with a strike barely visible through the gathering gloom.

The Doog remembered off-field machinations as well as games from this period. On the day Terry Neill became chairman of the Professional Footballers Association, a thoroughly 'pissed-off' Dougan was first approached by Coventry manager Noel Cantwell, who told him he had agreed an £80,000 fee with Ronnie Allen to take him to Highfield Road, but that he couldn't at that stage make an official approach. While negotiations carried on behind the scenes, the first two games in December resulted in a win over Southampton and a double-clinching triumph over Fulham, courtesy of another Knowles double and a Woodfield header. The programme for the Saints game noted that a Wolves team had made its first appearance in the new BBC panel game, 'Quizball,' recorded at the social club. Allen, Wagstaffe, Holsgrove and Times soccer correspondent Geoffrey Green appeared in the teatime programme on December 18.

A week later, Wolves left Anfield hurt as a twice-taken penalty condemned them to a 2-1 defeat. Willie Stevenson converted after Tommy Smith had seen his kick saved by Evan Williams on the day Alun Evans first came to Bill Shankly's notice with an equaliser. Wolves were proving unusually poor travellers, with no away points garnered between the visit to Hillsborough and the draw at Burnley on February 3.

In the time-honoured fashion of being soundly kicked when down, the Wanderers had the dubious honour of meeting the reigning champions twice over the Christmas holiday. A 4-0 Boxing Day setback at Manchester United on Boxing Day was followed by a 3-2 home defeat four days later. Losses to a team who would go on to win the European Cup in the following May formed part of a run of six defeats (seven, when one takes into account a third-round FA Cup humiliation at Rotherham) that plunged Wolves deeper into the relegation mire. Indeed, January dawned with successive League losses to Everton, Leicester and West Ham before the Cup exit.

At the turn of the year, Allen snapped up an influential player first spotted on the US tour. Frank Munro remembers how things developed; "I was very surprised. I had only been married a couple of months and really liked Aberdeen. On New Year's Eve, I said to my wife, 'We'll not go out because one of four fellows will turn up'." Stuart Fraser did and we had a glass of Harvey's Bristol Cream. The next day, on the coach to Dundee, we stopped at Montrose and the manager Ernie Turnbull said; 'I'm going to leave you out today, I think you've been drinking all night'. I was staggered and it was only three or four years ago that he accepted I hadn't been." Interest from Wolves followed so quickly that Munro was taken aback; "January 5 will always be a big date in my life. I'm always glad to get to January 6 now because on the fifth in 1968 I joined Wolves. Then, on the same date many years later (1994), I had a stroke."

He made his debut the next day in a 3-1 home defeat to Everton and it wasn't love at first sight; "I was virtually at outside-right and thought, 'What am I bloody doing here?' I went back home, six inches of snow at Wolverhampton station, thinking, 'what a dump! What sort of place have I come to?' After that, though, I really enjoyed it. The midfield when I came here was Bailey, Knowles and me. Although I was bought as a midfielder, I thought I should play central defence. Even before my first game, I said that to Ronnie but he said, 'You've got too much ability for centre-half'. I disagreed, I thought that was an advantage."

The issue of a possible move for Dougan reputedly rumbled on behind the chairman's back, with the fee having risen to £90,000 the next time that Cantwell got in touch with him. The Sunday papers ran the story and Dougan knew the proverbial had hit the fan when the usually 'nocturnal' John Ireland appeared in his Molineux office smoking his pipe at 9.45am next day. The Doog recalled; "He never got out of bed until 12 or 1pm unless there was a major problem down at the Wolves. Perhaps he might if Waggy or Ernie Hunt hadn't turned up and they were still trying to find them! Ireland told me we had to sort this nonsense out." Dougan asked for a private meeting with Allen before the chairman would be brought into the conversation. Ireland agreed, disappearing into Jack Howley's office for a cup of tea.

Dougan confronted Allen, telling him he knew all about the secret dialogue with Cantwell; "I'm going to tell him (Ireland) what's been going on for the last three months. Do you want me to do it again like in America?" Allen asked to be allowed to explain things to the Chairman, and Dougan promised not to bring up what Cantwell had told him in November and on the phone the night before, but countered; "I do not make things difficult for you at this club. You make things difficult for yourself, you and your silly f...in coaches. You've gotta make up your mind." We will never know what was said between manager and chairman, but the upshot was that Dougan stayed and signed a three-year contract with an option of a further three years, although he maintained he could have moved several times; "Bill McGarry stopped me from going to Arsenal in 1969. I had Don Revie at my house twice, once at Leicester and once here in Wolverhampton. Shankly told me that there were two people he should have signed, Bansky and me."

Waggy has always accepted he was not the best trainer in the world and admits his pre-match routine was less than orthodox; "I always had a cigarette. I didn't get changed until ten to three, got the programme and went into the toilet. I hated hanging round before a game. Often I'd have a cuppa in the tearoom, everybody had a different routine. I don't understand some of the things they do today. A warm-down? I don't know what that's supposed to mean. I warmed down in the bath!" John Richards remembers; "Waggy always disappeared with a cigarette and a single match just before the kick-off bell. He was quite nervous and would go into the little toilet in the corner of the shower room. We always left it for Waggy with the window open." Ken Hibbitt adds; "Waggy was the biggest character. One match, one fag, six minutes to three and he'd walk into the toilet before the bell went. Bill McGarry would see him and knew what was happening but still shouted, 'What the f*** are you doing there?'"

John Holsgrove chips in; "Waggy was a bag of nerves. We knew when kick-off was in those days but now it's: What time does the telly want it? In the old dressing room, the smoke would pour out of the window overlooking Waterloo Road. He'd sometimes go in and pass a ticket through the window to his mate. Can you imagine that now?" Geoff Palmer, then a schoolboy player, adds; "You always knew where Waggy was. An Embassy and two matches and McGarry would say, 'Tell Waggy to put his fag out.' Some time ago, Waggy told me that, when he ran the Social Club and they were knocking the South Bank down, he was up there with the groundsman, Bill Pilbeam. You never guess what they found on a girder - an Embassy packet and some matches inside. He'd left them there during training. How's that for a coincidence?" Munro, who used to live next door to the winger, adds his own memories; "We travelled together to Molineux every day, one week his car, one week mine. He would smoke in the morning and at half-time in matches. He was always 'banging off'. My manager at Aberdeen would have sorted the nerves out with a freezing cold shower for a minute, followed by a nip of brandy, winter or summer."

Another arrival at Molineux soon after Munro was Derek Parkin; "All of a sudden, there was this interest in me. There were no agents then but supposedly the chairmen of Wolves and Huddersfield were big friends. It was done and dusted. We had no say as such. It got a lot of publicity but, being so young, it passed over my head. All I ever wanted was to play Division One football but I didn't know Waggy, the Doog or Mike Bailey. It was all new to me." Squeak's experience of Ronnie Allen was very positive; "He was ever such a nice man and made us very welcome. Norma was pregnant and we were put in a hotel and made to feel really important."

Willie Carr simply describes Parkin as 'class' while Munro remembers his new team-mate with great affection; "Derek was so right-footed but practised and practised with his left and it became better than his right. He was such a good pro and because he came at the same time as me, we stayed together at the Uplands Hotel. I remember his late wife Norma, eight months pregnant, and my wife doing handstands against the wall!" Arriving on Valentine's Day, Parkin was forced by bad weather to wait ten days for a debut that came at Newcastle, his home city; "That was unbelievable because, as a young boy, I'd supported them and St James' Park was an incredible place. I used to stand on the terraces, so, to be playing there was a dream come true." It was around this time Palmer, a Cannock-born Wolves fan and one of Parkin's future full-back partners, also came to the club's attention; "It was my ambition to play for the Wolves. When I was at secondary school, we played in a five-a-side tournament at the gym above the Social Club. Joe Gardiner came to the teacher and asked if I'd like to go training on a Wednesday night. I was 13 or 14 at the time and obviously thrilled."

Injuries to Woodfield, Wagstaffe, Bailey, Dougan and Bobby Thomson made stopping the rot difficult but mid-March yielded back-to-back 2-0 wins, at home to Sunderland and at Arsenal. Of the four late-winter signings, Frank Wignall made the most immediate impact. Having first appeared on March 9, he went on to 'do a Dougan,' notching nine vital goals in 12 games to see Wolves to safety.

The win at Highbury was nevertheless followed by three more straight defeats, at the hands of the Sheffield teams and Coventry. At the end of March, Wolves were in the bottom two and, with eight games left, were odds-on for a quick return to Division Two. Holsgrove never felt, though, the drop was on the cards; "It was great, we were playing against Jimmy Greaves, Dennis Law and Bobby Charlton. We took one game at a time and prepared well. Although it was a big step up, we never really feared relegation." In spite of his optimism the table at that point tells its own story.

17th.	Sheffield United	33	9	9	15	40	56	27
18th.	Stoke City	32	11	5	16	37	53	27
19th.	Sunderland	34	9	9	16	40	55	27
20th.	West Ham	32	10	6	16	58	59	26
21st.	**WOLVES**	**34**	**10**	**6**	**18**	**52**	**69**	**26**
22nd.	Fulham	32	8	4	20	44	73	20

The turning point came when Wignall's old Nottingham Forest team-mates visited Molineux. They were in mid-table with little to play for and Jack Ramsey certainly did not understate the importance of the match in his programme notes; "No words of mine are needed to emphasise the vital nature of today's game. Did I hear you ask, 'What on earth can we do?' If so, I'll tell you. Simply give the players every possible ounce of vocal support for the 90 minutes. Vociferously, wholeheartedly, and without cessation, other than to gulp another lungful of air to keep it going." Some rhetoric!

I don't know how it was matched by Allen's team talk but whatever he said worked wonders. Wagstaffe set Dougan up to flash home a left-foot drive after 13 minutes,

before Wignall tapped in after keeper Harby pushed out a Woodfield effort on 25. On the half-hour, he rose to head home a Waggy centre. Just before half-time, Mike Kenning hit the bar and the Doog forced the ball in to put the Wanderers four up. Although Barry Lyons reduced the deficit, a third from Wignall - known by his colleagues as 'Cheshire' - and one from Kenning saw Wolves win 6-1, their best Division One result since a 7-2 win at Burnley in April, 1963. Holsgrove admired Wignall's impact; "Spot on. He was a good player. Ron only wanted people like Frank who could improve things, he didn't just buy willy nilly."

A vital away win followed, inspired by Wignall and Knowles, and plunged Stoke into the relegation places. Nervy days still remained, with draws against Manchester City and Southampton sandwiched in between 2-0 and 1-0 reverses at Sunderland and Chelsea. John McAlle made his senior debut at Stamford Bridge, playing up front alongside Dougan, and 'Wanderer' welcomed his contribution in the next programme; "He proved a rare worker all the time he was on the pitch." Another of the 1970s regulars had staked a claim for a regular place but fans had to wait until May to see First Division status confirmed when Chelsea were dispatched by another Wignall hat-trick in a Molineux fixture watched by over 40,000. Sheffield United and Fulham took the down elevator, as Ipswich and QPR climbed in the opposite direction. As if to celebrate, the Wanderers ended with a 2-1 win against Spurs, as Wignall scored yet again and was joined on the score-sheet by Parkin. 'Squeak' would only score another five League goals in his entire Wolves career.

In-form Frank Wignall is denied in Wolves' 2-0 defeat at Sunderland on April 15, 1968 - one of the games that kept them on tenterhooks.

A week later, we had to look enviously on as Jeff Astle helped

Albion overcome Everton to bring the FA Cup back to the West Midlands. In the final analysis, however, no Wolves or Albion player was able to seize the most treasured prize of the season, that of 'Most Attractive and Personable League Footballer' as voted by readers of the Football League Review. Bewdley-born young Wolf Alun Evans made a brave last-minute charge, largely as a result of canvassing by his fan club leaders Carolyn, Judith and Louise of Bridgnorth, but was unable to make the top ten. George Ley, of Portsmouth gained 40,132 votes to pip George Best by three postcards. The 'fifth Beatle' probably never completely recovered but managed to find some solace in helping the Red Devils overcome Benfica and win the European Cup on May 29.

As for Wolves, although mere survival in the Premier League would now be a cause for great rejoicing, as it would among most teams climbing the greasy pole, it was not enough for many in 1968. The knives might not yet have been out in force for Ronnie Allen but some surreptitious sharpening had certainly begun.

1968-69: Impatient For Blast-Off

The start of August, 1968 saw a Molineux warm-up match against Scottish First Division outfit St. Mirren that was somewhat ostentatiously billed as an Inter City Challenge. However, a Wignall-inspired 2-0 success was rendered meaningless by defeats at Ipswich and Manchester City in the first two matches of the season proper. Beaten in five of their previous six League visits to Portman Road, the Wanderers found no change of luck against Bill McGarry's newly-promoted team. On 28 minutes, Duggie Woodfield thundered home a header from a Dave Wagstaffe corner, only for referee BJ Homewood to rule it out for the alleged impeding of keeper Ken Hancock by Derek Dougan and John Holsgrove. In the view of the Sunday Express reporter, it was 'an eminently forgettable match except in the amount of childishness, bickering and petty fouling.' Early in the second half, Woodfield's misfortune was compounded when he suffered a broken nose for the second time in his career as he caught the back of an Ipswich player's head. A miserable day was then completed on the hour when John O'Rourke headed home to earn his team both points. The injury did not put Wolves' defensive hard-man out of action for long as he returned to complete an unbroken spell as Wolves' no 5 that lasted until the end of November.

The following Wednesday, Wolves took on champions Manchester City and found themselves three down in 50 minutes, courtesy of Mike Summerbee (2) and Francis Lee. However, the visitors did show some tenacity as Mike Bailey urged them on to a second-half revival. Only the woodwork denied Wignall a hat-trick and Wolves a point. Ronnie Allen must have hoped the visit of Alec Stock's Queens Park Rangers would be a case of third time lucky but the third page of the new match-day magazine 'Molinews' made uncomfortable reading for him. Chairman John Ireland chose to take over what would in future be known as the 'Ronnie Allen Calling' column to lay out his expectations for improvement; "It is not so long ago that we were at the top of the footballing world and we are going back there. We came through well in the end after a hard first season back in the First Division and we saw enough, I feel, to believe we

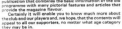

Another big stride towards the top . . .

MR. JOHN R. IRELAND
(Chairman, Wolverhampton Wanderers F.C.)

I AM DELIGHTED to be able to welcome you back to Molineux in this first issue of the clubs new match-day programme-magazine.
As you go through the 24 pages, I feel sure you will be both surprised and proud of this new-styled programme we have produced for you. It will be a regular feature of the new season, with a different edition appearing at each First Division match.
I am confident you will welcome this new official publication that combines the basic information of the old programme with many pictorial features and articles that provide the magazine flavour.
Certainly it will enable you to know much more about the club and our players and, we hope, that the contents will appeal to all our supporters, no matter what age category they may be in.

● *MR. JOHN R. IRELAND*

John Ireland cranks up the pressure on his manager.

are progressing." Hollow words perhaps since it was widely rumoured McGarry was already a firm target of the Molineux board. Rangers were unlikely to be a pushover, having risen from Third to First Division in successive seasons and collecting the League Cup on the way with a stunning win over West Bromwich Albion in 1967. Although veteran Ron Springett and the mercurial Rodney Marsh were out injured, they still included stalwarts like Frank Sibley and the Morgan twins, Ian and Ron. A crowd little over 30,000 reflected the uncertainty that surrounded Molineux.

The programme chose to allow us a peep into the holiday albums of the Wolves stars. Snapshots were published of Peter Knowles' wedding to Jean, and Phil Parkes' transatlantic romance with Robyn, whom he had met a year earlier on Wolves' 1967 adventure in Los Angeles. Parkes, we were told, would be returning at the end of the season to be wed and, carrying his American influences perhaps a little too far, 'Lofty' chose to play the first few games with a no 1 on the front of his jersey. While utility player Les Wilson had visited relatives in Canada, other photographs showed the Baileys holidaying in Djerba, Tunisia, the Dougans in Majorca and the Wignalls in Ibiza. Appropriately enough, the latter three weighed in with a goal apiece as a 3-1 win over QPR eased some of the pressure growing on Allen.

A defensive-minded Arsenal arrived four days later with five points from three games and, although the visitors' seven or eight-man barrier made for a drab scoreless draw, Wolves could take some encouragement from the fact the corner seemed to have been turned. However, the positives of the two home games were wiped out when a Wagstaffe goal at Southampton could not save Wolves from a 2-1 defeat in what Allen called a match between 'two poor teams'. What the boss readily described as 'a relatively poor start' was improved upon when two home games yielded a single-goal win over Leicester and a 1-1 draw with Stoke. Amazingly, Wolves had played seven League games before the end of an August dominated by Colin Cowdrey's cricket team's attempt to wrestle the Ashes away from Bill Lawry's Australian tourists. With the series ultimately drawn, England would have to wait another three years to bring to an end what was already a nine-year 'loan' of the famous old urn.

Wolves' tally of six points from a possible 14 was the result of too many draws as anything else. Only reasonable home form was keeping them afloat and, in more ways than one, the season was already proving every bit as tough as the previous one.

Although the first three League games in September yielded only two points, Wolves got within 22 minutes of their first away win when Frank Munro fired them ahead at Leeds. Terry Cooper equalised before Jack Charlton notched the winner with just three minutes left. Even then, there was time for a Holsgrove header to be cleared off the line by Paul Reaney. Draws were then earned at home to Sunderland and against old enemy Albion, although Wolves' bad luck with injuries was summed up when Wagstaffe was carried off with an ankle injury a minute into the goalless draw at The Hawthorns.

Morale was raised by two home League Cup wins, the first a narrow one over Southend and the second a 5-1 thrashing of Millwall, but there were growing signs of discord. Parkes was relegated to the reserves for the Sunderland and Albion games, for which former Shrewsbury Town man Alan Boswell was preferred, and Peter Knowles submitted a transfer request. As it was, Alun Evans was the man on the move - to Liverpool - although Frank Munro maintains he was not their main target; "When Alun went to Liverpool, Shankly was after Peter Knowles. He put in a £200,000 bid for both and Peter said no. He wanted Knowles more than Evans but Peter didn't want to go. I think he knew in his mind what he was going to do." Allen moved quickly to put the record straight on the issue of a move for Knowles; "Let's clear one thing up. If Knowles puts in another thousand transfer requests, he will be turned down. As far as I am concerned, his contract has five years to go and I look forward to seeing the real Peter Knowles in Wolves' colours during this time."

Little was Allen to know what lay around the corner for himself and his star man but these uncertainties were hardly the best preparation for the visit of fourth-placed Liverpool. Black Country-born Boswell, who had a worrying predilection for the punch over the catch, earned himself the tag of 'do-it-yourself keeper' and no little ridicule when it was made public that he insisted on buying his own kit and taking it home to launder. Girls were informed that he was still a bachelor, living in Wednesbury with his mother. In an ill-advised exercise in tempting fate, Boswell was quoted in the 'Around and About' section of the programme; "I must say I am enjoying life at the moment. If anything, the First Division seems just a little easier for goalkeepers, for there is more room in the six-yard area." Allen made matters worse by boasting about Boswell's first clean sheet and adding; "Let's hope he can have many, many more."

Roger Hunt, Peter Thompson and ex-Wolf Evans helped themselves to two goals each as Shankly's men handed out a 6-0 thrashing. Boswell gave a hugely convincing impression of a rabbit caught squarely in the headlights and Bailey spoke honestly in the following week's 'Sports Argus'; "To be on the receiving end of a thrashing before your own supporters is not pleasant. But now we have got over the initial shock, we are not too down-hearted as we are absorbing some useful lessons handed out by Liverpool." The match did not quite mark the end for Boswell or Allen but their wounds were to prove terminal. Imminent signing Ken Hibbitt remembers; "Alun Evans had been sold for a hundred grand and scored two on his return." And Parkes believes affairs were not helped by the fact the 19-year-old moved to Anfield a few weeks earlier after only 20 senior Wolves games; "Ronnie put Bozzy in and it didn't go very well. The week before the Liverpool game, I was going to Newcastle. Allen had done a deal with Joe Harvey for £25,000 but John Ireland said no. I was back in the week after, but they'd more or less sacked Ronnie and approached Bill McGarry, who agreed to come but couldn't get away from Ipswich straight away."

Dougan gave his boss some respite a week later as he earned Wolves a first away win of the season and their first-ever at Coventry. On the hour, he latched on to Woodfield's flick and stooped to head past Bill Glazier but the rest of October brought only one more victory, at the happy hunting ground of Hillsborough. League defeats against Leicester and Everton were followed by elimination from the League Cup at Second Division Blackpool. This heaped further pressure on Allen and, by the time the Toffeemen headed back to Merseyside with both points courtesy of a 2-1 win, Wolves were hovering precariously around the relegation zone.

The fans had certainly not given up the ghost, though, especially those in the old 'cowshed,' and the quality of this support was recognised by Allen; "It's a wonderful thing to know the crowd are behind you 100 per cent and I must confess that when the North Bank started their handclapping routine, I started to clap with them and nudged the person sitting next to me and said; "Come on, join us!" Of the eight League goals scored at home before the end of October, six were netted at this end. The North Bank choir made Wolves one of three clubs highly commended behind winners Arsenal in the John White Football Supporters Awards.

In late October, the 19th Olympic Games were staged in Mexico City, an event remembered for David Hemery winning 400m hurdles gold, the black power protests of American athletes Tommie Smith and John Carlos, Bob Beamon's incredible long jump and Dick Fosbury's famous 'flop.' Ronnie Allen was not sure altitude would have an influence on the World Cup Finals to be staged at the same venue in 1970, although, as he controversially argued, "to my mind, soccer players are fitter than athletes."

As Allen admitted in his final programme notes, Molineux performances had become the major cause for concern as Wolves had taken six points from their last five away matches, with four clean sheets. He went on; "One thing sticks out a mile. You can't possibly miss the chances we have squandered here." This was an irony for a team who had built a splendid home record until the Liverpool mauling. In the week after a 2-0 win over West Ham, secured by goals by Bailey and John Farrington, had started to address the problem, I was taken to St Andrew's to see Knowles play for England under-23s against Holland. Interestingly, then Blues boss Stan Cullis wrote in the programme about the importance of such games, stressing they prevented players being thrown in at the deep end. Criticising what he saw as short-sighted desire for success, he claimed, "People are not interested in jam tomorrow, they want jam today."

As if to prove the point, only one Dutchman (Rob Rensenbrink) and three (Peter

Under-23 games ARE important
— says Stan Cullis

The public have not always responded to Under-23 Internationals with great enthusiasm and the question has been asked: "Just what good do these matches do, apart from giving various clubs the chance to stage a representative game.

It's the difference between going in at the shallow instead of the deep end—that's the opinion of Birmingham City manager STAN CULLIS, who admits that he regrets there were no such matches when he him-

Shilton, Roy McFarland and Colin Todd) England players went on to make an impact at full international level. Of the Wolves team who handed out an eight-goal Youth Cup hammering to Shrewsbury in the same week, there was a similarly low conversion rate to first-team football. Too few of the following squad went on to grace the senior side - Rod Arnold, Jeff Wealands, Gerry Farrell, Alan Stephens, Tony Jackson, Phil Nicholls, Ken Wade, Ian McDonald, Jimmy Seal, Wayne Nicholls, Dave Molyneux, Granville Riley, Dave Jones, Jim Pepper and Roger Grice.

Such a blinkered and impatient attitude would ultimately lead to Allen's departure in the month Richard Nixon first won the US presidency. Allen had arrived at Wolves as coach in August, 1965 and taken up the reins full-time in July, 1966. In his two years two months in charge, he led the team to 60 wins and 43 defeats in 136 League games. Although most of these were played in the second tier, Allen's record still makes him the most successful Wolves boss since Cullis prior to Graham Turner. Wagstaffe is still mystified by the circumstances of his departure; "Ronnie was well liked by the players. The only other manager I've known get involved with the players like that was Jimmy Smith. It was a shock when he went, we couldn't understand the reasoning. You could approach Ronnie, you could say what you wanted as long as you were sensible."

Derek Parkin agrees; "Ronnie was a likeable man, probably too nice to be a manager. I think some people took advantage of it, I think it was naivety." John Holsgrove confirms that although the players were in the dark, Allen's departure was not a complete shock; "These are the things we didn't know about. As players, we did our bit and what happened with the directors, we didn't know. Was their expectation too high? Did they think: Ten years ago, we were the great Wolves and unless we get back to winning the League and FA Cup, it's failure? Ron had said to me, 'You'll be sorry when I've gone'. I think he knew. Liverpool was an awful game, not something you want to think about. Ron knew they'd set McGarry up." Parkin agrees that players were more in the dark then; "There's a lot of politics in football and, at that time, you never got to know the inside news."

Bailey, the man he had signed as skipper 18 months earlier, was equally shocked; "I was disappointed and upset. I thought he was a good manager who wanted us to play good football. In hindsight, things were perhaps a little too relaxed but he wanted a happy ship. There wasn't a lot of coaching. We played five-a-side daily and had a lot of ability in the team so, if there was a problem in a game, the players could usually sort it out. In that respect. Ronnie was spot on." Derek Dougan was more matter of fact, arguing that the signing of Boswell was a major factor in his leaving; "Shrewsbury had told him he could go for £10,000. I'd printed that out and put it on the board but Allen paid four to five times this. I pleaded with him not to sign that goalkeeper." The Irishman still rated Allen as a coach; "He was quite phenomenal, a brilliant coach, with great ball skills and technique." But he maintained he made the big mistake of bringing in coaching personnel, like Gerry Summers and Ron Bradley en bloc from West Bromwich Albion; "All he needed was another good coach."

Holsgrove reflects on his good relationship with Allen; "I always got on well with him. He was pretty straight with me but he bought me and, when a manager buys you, he's interested in you being successful, otherwise his reputation dips." Parkin stresses Allen's legacy; "They thought they'd get a new brush in but McGarry inherited a lot of players Ronnie brought in." Bailey agrees; "He was responsible for bringing in so many players; Munro, Parkin, Hibbitt, Hunt, Dougan and myself, joining an already talented batch of players like Thomson, Woodfield, Wharton and Wagstaffe." Munro concurs; "Ronnie signed all the players McGarry benefited from. He was a tremendous coach but too soft. On my first day's training, he said, 'Let's get on the coach, we're going to Brocton to run up and down the hills'. Mike and Waggy said, 'Hotshot, let's go up the gym and have some five-a-sides.' Ronnie said 'OK'. If that had been Eddie Turnbull at Aberdeen, he'd never have changed his mind like that."

Express & Star TOWN

ASSOCIATED WITH SHROPSHIRE STAR

W'hampton 22351; Want Ads 26641 — Wednesday, November 20, 1968 — No. 29185. — PRICE FIVEPENC

Wolves board unanimous over decision

RONNIE ALLEN IS SACKED

By JOHN DEE

Ronnie Allen today resigned as Wolves manager. Matters were ht to a head at a board meeting yesterday, when he was told was the unanimous decision of the directors that he should leave the club.

He was told he should have considered resigning immediately after his team's 6-0 home thrashing by Liverpool at the end of September.

So for the second time in four years, Wolves have sacked their manager.

The first time was, of course, that sensational day in September, 1964, when they decided to terminate the contract of the famous Stanley Cullis, now manager of struggling Birmingham City.

Cullis led Wolves to their greatest heights — the F.A.

Princess at show

The man who has turned his back on Molineux — today's picture of Ronnie Allen.

ROW BREWS

Threat of revolt on reforms

The Government's plans for reforming the House of Lords were threatened this afternoon by a growing revolt among Labour M.P.s, writes Ernest Prince.

Up to 50, including elder statesman Mr "Manny" Shinwell, Mr. William Hamilton, the party vice-chairman, and Mrs. Renee Short, may give the cold shoulder to the three line whip which has been issued by the Chief Whip Mr. Silkin for tonight's Commons vote.

The M.P. for Blyth, Northumberland, Mr. Edward Milne,

wrote to the chief whip today objecting to the time being devoted to creating a hand picked, paid, House of Lords when many of his constituents were facing unemployment this winter. He said he would not be voting with the Government tonight.

Many Labour M.P.s consider the Government is pussy-footing over Lords reform — and want the Upper Chamber scrapped altogether.

Tory M.P.s have a free vote tonight — and it is not certain how many will support the Government.

(See also Page 11).

By the time Dougan earned a point at Burnley, Wolves had ironically climbed to the respectability of 14th place, with 17 points from 19 matches. But Allen was to be given no further chances. News of his departure broke on the following Wednesday, November 20, when it was reported he had decided to go after a board meeting. The directors had unanimously decided he should leave, indeed they told him he should have considered resigning immediately after the Liverpool game. Not only had Allen taken Wolves back to Division One in his first full season in charge, his transfer deals had left the club £112,000 better off, with sales totalling £427,000 and expenditure £315,000. One significant arrival in the month of his departure was Ken Hibbitt, a 17-year-old wing forward, signed for £5,000 from Bradford Park Avenue. He didn't know much about the club he was joining; "I didn't know their history. I didn't know they'd been down and up. But I knew their colours were different and that my brother, Terry, had been approached by their chief scout. At 12, they'd given him a pair of Barbarian boots with a strap across the front and a big toe cap. And of course I knew Derek Dougan and had seen one of his classic goals, against Hull, on Match of the Day."

John Richards particularly appreciates the importance of Hibbitt's arrival and the influence he had in Wolves' midfield in three decades; "I have a lot of time and respect for Kenny as a player and a person. He and Waggy were the main sources of supply." Munro agrees; "Kenny was a good player, two great feet." Hibbitt remembers the circumstances of his arrival; "Joe Gardiner, the chief scout, saw me playing at 16 for Bradford and invited me to talk to Ronnie Allen. Joe knocked the door for me and I walked in. The first thing Ron said was, 'He's a big lad, Joe.' He offered me a contract and I signed it without looking at it, no negotiations. That was practically the only conversation I had with him but I remember the photo at Molineux with me in a grey suit, white shirt and dark blue tie. I had had seven managers in two and a half years at Bradford and it struck again in my first three days at Wolves as Ronnie was gone."

Another whose arrival seemed to curse the manager was Barry Powell; "I arrived in late 1968 when Ronnie was manager and Joe Gardiner chief scout. Joe took me up to meet Ronnie in the Molineux Hotel. We had a nice lunch and I was about to sign when he got the sack. It was a massive club. I was a schoolboy at Stoke but they hadn't registered me, so I had a look at Wolves. I was about 12 and used to travel on my own from Coventry by train. I'd walk past the market, down past the Molineux Hotel and alley, and in for training. They used to give me half a crown expenses and I got an egg and tomato roll and a cup of tea going home. I used to think I was a king. Good times, I have a lot of time for Wolverhampton Wanderers."

The day after Allen's departure (the same Thursday Allen's ex-Albion team-mate Bobby Robson was fired by Fulham after ten months in charge), Ipswich announced they had released McGarry 'with disappointment and extreme reluctance.' McGarry had managed there since October, 1964, had recently led them to the Division Two title and had signed a five-year contract just six months earlier. The irony of McGarry's arrival is not lost on Holsgrove; "Ronnie and Bill were great adversaries as players but didn't like each other. In terms of ability, there was no competition, Ronnie was streets ahead but it grated with him that McGarry replaced him and Bill liked the fact he knocked Ronnie out." His first comments on man-management were typically abrasive; "Sometimes they might want a rollicking, on another occasion they may need a little help. It is a manager's job to know which is right at the particular time."

The next home programme, for the visit of Newcastle, saw the former manager seemingly airbrushed from history. He had only one mention but Daily Express man Alan Williams reminded fans of the vagaries of football management; "There have been 685 changes at League clubs since Sir Matt Busby became Manchester United manager and, of the men currently in charge of the 92 clubs, only 22 have been in their job for five years." In the same pages, the Molineux faithful were informed a new Wolves' souvenir shop had been opened near the Pools Office at the rear of the North Bank. Manager Harvey Andrews and wife Yvonne were seen looking at some of the programmes, pennants, key rings and badges on sale. Buy of the day was a giant 24in x 18in colour team picture, available for a mere four shillings (20 pence).

On November 23, McGarry, who brought Sammy Chung with him as coach, saw his new charges almost predictably destroy Newcastle 5-0. Knowles and Wignall put them in command at the break before Dougan netted a fine header to join in the fun. Pick of the goals was a spectacular overhead kick from Knowles that left Ian McFaul clutching fresh air before the Doog also doubled up to send most of the 25,425 crowd home happy. Officially taking up his position two days later, McGarry's honeymoon was soon over as Best and Law sent Wolves home pointless from Manchester United, where Woodfield picked up an ankle injury that restricted him to just five more League outings all season and forced Wignall into action at United as emergency centre-half.

Around the same time, Hibbitt made his bow, but in the Central League; "My first game was in the reserves at United with Frank Munro. I was five grand from Bradford and played alongside a 60 grand signing from Aberdeen. It was wonderful, running on to Old Trafford and it all started from there. I'd had 16 games at Bradford and this was my first bonus, the first time I'd been on a winning or drawing side. 2-2 and I got a fiver, quite good in 1968." Steve Daley also arrived in McGarry's first week; "I come from a little village just outside Barnsley and was playing for the working men's club and had scouts coming to watch me. My brother wrote to Man United for a trial, they came and weren't that impressed. Then he wrote to Wolves and Mark Crook put me in his Wath Wanderers nursery team. I played against Chesterfield at Saltergate and soon after came for a month's trial. Ronnie Allen had gone and it was Bill's first week, Alan Sunderland came from Mexborough at exactly the same time."

Never afraid of displaying a desire to win, the new boss quickly heaped pressure on himself; "If Wolves are impatient for success and burning with ambition, it's fine by me. A manager must burn with ambition. Deep inside, I want to win every game."

EXPRESS AND STAR, THURSDAY, NOVEMBER 21

WOLVES APPOINT NEW MANAGER
And it is Bill McGarry

AND NOW THE BOOT FOR BOBBY ROBSON

After the resignation of Wolves manager, Ronnie Allen, yesterday, came the news today that Fulham have dismissed Bobby Robson.

An announcement about a caretaker-successor to Robson, former England international and Albion and Fulham star, is expected later today.

Two of Robson's appointments this summer, chief scout Harry Haslam, former manager of Tonbridge, and chief coach Roy McCrohan, former Norwich winghalf, were also dismissed.

Robson became the Fulham manager in January this year. Fulham vice - chairman, Chapple d'Amato, telephoned Robson at his Weybridge home to call him to today's board meeting.

Mr d'Amato said afterwards: "We asked for and will have to look for another manager and that we have reluctantly decided to dispense with his services.

"Our position in the table has dictated this decision."

Mr. d'Amato, accompanied by directors Tony Dean and Eric Miller, said the decision had been taken in consultation with chairman Tommy Trinder, who is touring Australia.

Mr d'Amato added Fulham have made a "generous ex-gratia payment" to Robson to cover his loss of office.

Secretary Graham Hortop drove to Kingston to tell the players, including Johnny Haynes, who has been tipped as Robson's successor of the staff changes.

Alan Humphries, youth team coach, was in charge of today's training

BOBBY ROBSON, former England and Albion star, who quickly followed his former Albion colleague, Ronnie Allen, into the soccer sideline . .

SECRET BOARD MEETING
Hagan and Allen on Villa list?

BY TOM JOHNSON

Villa Park was shrouded in secrecy today following a five hour meeting which last night kept the board of seven directors in discussion behind closed doors.

The board are believed to have discussed the question of a new manager to succeed Tommy Cummings, sacked ten days ago, and a possible candidate on their list was Ronnie Allen, dismissed from his Wolves post yesterday.

NO CHANGE

Aston Villa, without a win since September 28, today named an unchanged side for the home game with Middlesbrough on Saturday. Team:

But there is still strong support, particularly from director Joe Heath, for ex-Albion boss Jimmy Hagan.

It was felt yesterday that certain members of the board

IPSWICH LET HIM GO 'WITH RELUCTANCE'

Wolves have appointed Bill McGarry, of Ipswich Town, as their new manager.

The news, forecast by the "Express and Star," yesterday, was released by Wolves shortly after midday. They added McGarry would take over at Molineux next Monday.

Ipswich yielded to McGarry's release from his contract with "disappointment and extreme reluctance," pointing out McGarry had signed a new five-year contract only six months ago.

As he had made the request, however, they thought it in the best interests of the club to let McGarry go.

The statement by the Ipswich chairman, John Cobbold, said they felt that to bind McGarry to his contract would court difficulties and embarrassment, and added the board are grateful to McGarry for his efforts and his successes in the past and wish him well in the future.

Taking over from Jackie Milburn in October, 1964, McGarry, a native of Stoke-on-Trent, took Ipswich from almost bottom of the Second Division to fifth place by the end of the season.

Last season Ipswich collected the Second Division title and at present are three points below Wolves and three points worse off in the First Division having only won of their last eight games.

Has ambitions . . .

WINCANTON ENCORE
Loup the Loop Cervier . . .

John Sumner's Loup Cervier, who won the Remembrance Poppy Handicap Hurdle at Wincanton a year ago, today again showed his liking for the course by winning the New-quay Handicap Steeplease in a thrilling finish with Rural Gamble, the mount of Stan Mellor.

The first and second had the race to themselves in the last halfmile but it was not until the final fence that Graham Thorner sent Loup Cervier to the front to win by a neck.

Eurotus, ridden by Jimmy Utley, was gambled on from 6-1 to 3-1 favourite in the Sedgemoor Selling Hurdle, but, after showing up promin-

McGarry's reputation as a fearsome disciplinarian preceded him and he claimed to have 'discipline, effort and responsibility' as his bywords. He elaborated further; "I'm a fanatic when it comes to this game. If I see a player loafing in training, I want to go berserk. I don't want the players to like me, I want respect." Dougan remembered him entering the Molineux dressing room on his first day; "Wolves wouldn't buy the best tracksuits for training in those days, only second-hand ones or the cheapest available. As a result, McGarry was wearing a pair of bottoms that clung tightly to his legs. Around 30 players were on the 2ft-high benching that ran around the room and I had Waggy and John Holsgrove either side of me."

Dougan explained how the new boss caused unintentional hilarity by trying three times without success to put his foot on the bench before holding forth; "I've come here. I'm the manager. I'm in charge. I'm the boss. By the way, I don't want you blokes to like me. I want you to f***in hate me because you will finish up f***in hating me." The Doog forgave McGarry's approach; "That's the way it was then. Managers had no preparation to go into jobs. They didn't know any better." But he still maintained; "Mr McGarry was the most awful man God ever put on earth." Holsgrove has similar memories; "On day one, Sammy Chung came in first - a nice fellow but he knew who was boss. Sammy said, 'The manager's coming in to see you' and we were all sitting waiting. Then, bang, the door flies open, smashed back on its hinges, and McGarry just stood there. He looked around at everybody, really fearsome and didn't have Ronnie's

Left: Made in Bradford: Kenny Hibbitt is pictured in the centre of this Park Avenue quintet. Above: A souvenir shop with a view.

charm. He said, 'I figure I'm going to get the sack some day, so I tell you now I'll get the sack doing it my own way. If you don't want to play my way, come and see me and you can go. He turned round and walked out. Bang, crash, wallop! We thought, this is the man who has come to take us on to greater things!"

Geoff Palmer appreciates it could not have been easy for McGarry to deal with the mercurial Irishman; "The Doog was there, Chairman of the PFA and on all the World Cup panels. He was nearly as big as Bill, yet Bill's manager and the Doog's a player. He used to speak for us all and no way was he going to allow anyone to take the mick out of us. He was there to stand our corner." Speaking recently to the Express & Star's Martin Swain, Chung admitted Dougan needed careful handling; "He was his own man, no doubt about that. The best way to deal with him was to agree with him!"

Ken Hibbitt also puts forward the younger players' view; "Although Dougan didn't get on very well with McGarry, we were only kids and he was fair. I don't know what players like Bailey, Holsgrove and Les Wilson thought of him. Yes, Doog and he had a clash of personality but they got through it. Doog produced and did a good job for Bill and his team." Barry Powell recalls his first encounter with the boss; "Within two weeks of me arriving, Bill took over and I visited Molineux again. I was walking down the corridor with Joe Gardiner and Bill came in with his dog, Lucky. Joe said, 'Bill, this is Barry Powell, he's a good player but is a bit small.' Bill turned round and said, 'I don't give a f***in damn how big he is, so long as he's good enough.' I like to think that because he was small, he was the one who gave me my opportunity."

Derek Parkin was equally forgiving; "Bill was of the old school, a man of few words. Over the time I had with him, we didn't say very much to each other. I never had any problems with him, no shouting." Frank Munro saw likenesses between McGarry and his previous boss; "He was very similar to my manager at Aberdeen. They were both very good on the game, hard as nails but very fair. They'd played directly against each other for Scotland and England at international level, Turnbull at inside-forward and McGarry at wing-half." John McAlle also remembers McGarry's curt arrival, but, for all of this, 'Scouse' points to positive tactical changes, with each player knowing exactly what was required of him; "Bill McGarry was great for me." Palmer also accepts McGarry's approach; "He gave me my chance and I owe a big thank-you to him. He wasn't a manager who was there to be your mate. He was there to do a job, to win games and trophies. If you weren't going to do that, he would say he was a bit of a failure. He knew the game inside out."

Breaking in to the team some time later, John Richards recalls McGarry's persona but feels such an approach was necessary; "We were frightened to death of him. He was such a dictator but right for us." Willie Carr does recall a later occasion when Alan Sunderland cheekily played McGarry at his own game; "Sundy went in for a rise and McGarry said, 'Get out of here, you little t**t. I'll show you how hard it is to be a manager. You come and sit here, I'll be the player and you can be the manager and I'll come in and see you.' He goes out, knocks on the door and Sundy tells him to come in and sit down. McGarry asked for a rise and said, 'I want this and that.' So Sundy says, 'OK you can have it'. He was taking the p**s and McGarry told him to get out."

Mike Bailey is able to see McGarry in a positive light; "He was stronger on discipline, with tough training schedules, and he definitely made us harder to beat. You knew where you stood. I just did my job." Waggy was not so appreciative, though; "Ronnie had just let me play my own game but Bill McGarry came and I wasn't given the freedom. Frank Munro often says if we'd been allowed to express ourselves, we'd have been ten per cent better and up challenging for the top three."

John Holsgrove does not entirely agree; "I knew my position in the team but McGarry never said anything. He very occasionally said, 'Well done, son' but that was it. He was great to me but never let you get above your station." The manager was hot on fitness and diet, particularly, and changed Saturday eating habits. Unlimited fillet steak was replaced with steamed fish or boiled chicken and out went jam with toast and rice pudding. Players seen out on the town after Tuesdays would be in serious trouble, as Wagstaffe confirms; "What he said went, whether he was right or wrong. A while back, I'm sat talking with John Holsgrove about the first time we went away and he fell foul of McGarry for ordering prawn cocktail. The whole place went up. He was very strict and at times it was a bit over the top." Holsgrove remembers the event; "It was at Scotch Corner in April, 1969, going to Newcastle or Sunderland. What he wanted to do was impose his standards on us. I asked for a prawn cocktail. It wasn't about diet - he thought I was above my station. The bread rolls were about diet. I asked for a second one and he said to one of the staff, 'Hey buster, one roll each, no more'."

Parkin agrees McGarry was the complete opposite to Allen but benefited from his training techniques; "I had a lot of respect for him because the one thing I always really enjoyed was training and Bill was a fitness fanatic. Under him, you couldn't help but be fit and I've never been as fit as then. I never got injured and put that down to the training, I thrived on it." Phil Parkes shares this begrudging respect for the boss; "If Bill said, 'Jump', you said, 'How high, gaffer?' He was a good coach and knew the game inside out. If he lacked anything, it was man-management skills." Holsgrove is similarly appreciative of the changes made to training; "It was a lot more physical but I also used to practise free-kicks for hours in the gym over the Social Club, especially with Jim McCalliog. I would chip balls in and he'd chest and volley them. He was a tremendous striker of the ball. McGarry respected this and the fact I prepared properly and was as good as I could be. I also used to get Derek Parkin and Bernard Shaw to chip the ball up so I could practise my heading. Often on a Friday, when most of the others had gone, he'd see me knocking the ball against the wall and heading it. He never said anything but always clocked I was trying to better myself. I would have loved to sit down and chat with him but he didn't have the warmth and wanted to keep a barrier."

Steve Daley is grateful for his approach with younger players; "McGarry was hard but, with the likes of me, Alan Sunderland, Peter Eastoe, Barry Powell, Geoff Palmer and John Richards, he was brilliant. He loved us. He used to take me, Alan and Peter to the tennis centre at Tettenhall to play squash. He used to give us seven start and beat us 9-7. We were just keeping him fit. You can only judge people on how they treat you and he was great with me. When I first came here, I had no money. After three months, he called me to his office and said, 'I'm going to give you three years as an apprentice.' Within two years, I was in the team. He took some money out of his wallet, about 300 quid, and said, 'Go and buy yourself some clothes, son.' So I sent £100 back to my mam and dad, and bought clothes with the rest."

Steve Kindon advises that, in judging McGarry, we need to take out the mystique; "The manager isn't any different from the manager of a factory or a hospital. What you need is good product knowledge and man-management skills. Bill McGarry and Jimmy Adamson equally you couldn't teach them anything about football. Bill knew the game upside down and back to front but, in my opinion, his man-management left a bit to be desired. You walked down the corridor one day and said; 'Good morning, boss' and he wouldn't answer you. The next morning, you'd walk by him and he'd say; 'What's wrong with you? Don't I get a good morning?' I think sometimes he did it to keep you on your toes but, if he did it for that, he did it too much. I didn't think he was a particularly nice person but he didn't have to be. He was my boss."

For all his rhetoric, McGarry failed at first to rectify Wolves' inconsistencies. A point gained at an icy Stamford Bridge was sandwiched between home matches against Spurs and Sheffield Wednesday that resulted respectively in a 2-0 win and a 3-0 loss. Dougan and Wignall netted against Tottenham on McGarry's home debut while Kenning won a point against Chelsea with his 20th successive conversion from the spot. A last-minute penalty for the home team robbed Wolves of victory, something made all the more galling by the fact Alan Boswell had earlier saved one from Peter Osgood. The closing games of December, home to Coventry and away to Everton, were postponed, leaving Wolves with only 22 points from 23 games. In the first programme of the New Year, the manager's column was relegated to page four as John Ireland gave the McGarry-Chung partnership a ringing endorsement, telling fans; "I can assure you there is fierce determination to put Wolves back on the big-time map and to get ourselves into contention with the teams at the top. NOTHING ELSE WILL DO. Bear with him and give him time to settle in. Then I am sure we shall see a new determination and professional approach which should augur well for the future."

A tricky FA Cup tie at Hull City was negotiated in style but not before Tigers skipper Chris Chilton had headed them into a sixth minute lead. Wignall and Dougan turned it round before half-time and the Irishman made it 3-1 late on. Unfortunately, progress in the Cup was halted in the next round at Tottenham. Dave Wagstaffe put Wolves ahead, only for Neil Johnson and Jimmy Greaves to send Spurs through, although Peter Knowles was denied a replay-earning goal due to alleged hands by Dougan. By the end of February, two postponements, two draws, a loss and a single win at home to Forest left Wolves lingering in mid-table. The early part of 1969 also saw McGarry further dismantle the 1967 promotion-winning squad, as Dave Burnside joined Plymouth and, most surprisingly, Bobby Thomson moved in March to Birmingham, aged only 25, having made exactly 300 appearances for the club.

Holsgrove recalls; "Losing Bobby was a shock but what a buy to replace him! Derek Parkin, a lovely player, a great passer of the ball." Parkin is also unable to explain the departure of a man he always got on well with; "Bobby never reached the heights expected of him as he had played for England very early. He had electrifying pace but didn't really achieve what some hoped for." It was at this point McGarry converted Parkin to left-back and made him an offer he couldn't refuse; "I was a professional footballer. The club pay your wages and you play where they tell you. At the end of my career, I even played in goal at Stoke. McGarry asked me in a nice way, although I don't think I could have refused! I was naturally right-footed but he was complimentary and said that, because of my ability, I could adapt. I don't know how I got away with it really." While Parkin began to cement his place in Wolves folklore, Frank Wignall gradually fell out of favour, turning out for the last time against his old team Forest on January 11 before joining Brian Clough's Derby County in their successful fight for promotion from Division Two. Mike Kenning followed him out of the club soon after netting an equaliser against Ipswich on March 1.

Scottish striker Hugh Curran was snapped up from Norwich for £65,000 and made his debut at home to Burnley on February 1, viewed by Dougan as one of many attempts by McGarry to ease him out of Molineux. He quipped wryly; "I'm the only guy in history to replace his replacement." Hughie netted against Manchester United and Spurs on successive Saturdays and notched four in ten before the season ended. These matches marked the start of a six-game unbeaten run that included only one win, at Loftus Road, as Dougan scored to complete the double over Queens Park Rangers. Only three minutes had gone when he helped Parkes' long clearance into the Rangers net. A week later, a goalless draw at home to Southampton settled Wolves into mid-table respectability, with 31 points from 32 matches. But, amazingly, the remaining ten games were to bring just four more points. Well after the scheduled end of his month's trial, Steve Daley was convinced he had been forgotten; "It had extended itself into three months, I didn't think anyone knew I was there and I wasn't going to say anything. It came to the crunch when McGarry called me into his office and said, 'I'm going to give you three years as an apprentice.' As it was, I stayed for ten years."

Although never in serious relegation danger, Wolves' crushing losses in March at Stoke (4-1) and West Ham (3-1) sent them spiralling into a nightmare end-of-season run of seven defeats out of ten. It was a frustrating time for Munro, who made just eight League appearances and four more as substitute all season. Ironically, when Dave Woodfield was injured, it was Frank's soon-to-be defensive partner, John McAlle, who profited with a nine-game run alongside John Holsgrove to the end of the season. Holsgrove recalls; "The funny part was that McGarry finished me off and made me the player I was. He turned me from a supporting left-half to a centre-back. Towards the end of 1968-1969, Dave Woodfield got a few injuries. McGarry always felt I could contribute more and put me at centre-half. If the ball came down the middle, Duggie always challenged the centre-forward and I would tidy up. Now he moved me to the middle and John to the left."

Wolves won only once in that spell, though, 3-1 at home to Manchester City, who went on to defeat Leicester in the FA Cup final courtesy of a Neil Young strike. Knowles, Dougan and Munro scored to see off the classy Maine Road outfit. If there was any comfort to be drawn from this wretched spell, it was that in late March and early April, one draw and two losses came at the hands of the division's top three, Leeds, Liverpool and Arsenal. While this was vaguely tolerable, my first taste of a home defeat to the Albion was not, this time as a result of a Clive Clark goal. Ken Hibbitt played for the first time in the first team but only briefly as sub for John Farrington; "My introduction lasted about two minutes." The side signed off at home in a game with Coventry rearranged from Boxing Day but Knowles' goal earned only a 1-1 draw. Thirty-five points and 41 goals had come from 42 matches, condemning

The Doog leads the charge as the 1969 slide goes on at Anfield.

Wolves to a 16th-place finish. For all the comings and goings, the Dougan-Knowles partnership had still accounted for well over half of this poor League total.

Around Easter, a highly significant acquisition was made when 18-year-old John Richards was spotted playing for Lancashire at a grammar school tournament in Bognor Regis. Having previously played for England schoolboys against Wales and Scotland alongside future Wolves junior Micky Spelman, Richards caught the eye of Tony Penman, a Staffordshire teacher and Wolves fan, on whose recommendation he was invited by Joe Gardiner to play in a reserve game against Derby at Molineux. He was astonished to be playing with the professionals, Wolves winning 4-1 as a result of a Woodfield goal and Jimmy Seal hat-trick. After the game, Richards was approached in the dressing room by a stranger, who said; "Well played, son, how would you like to play for Wolverhampton Wanderers?" "Yes, I'd like that", answered our hero and, on that, the stranger left. Only on asking Seal did John discover the offer had been made by no less than John Ireland, and he put aside his plans to go on a teacher training course at Chester College. Although he realises players of the Stan Cullis era differ widely in their view of Ireland, Richards is another who had a great deal of time for the chairman; "I can't praise him highly enough. He was probably the reason many of the younger players stayed here. He was Wolves through and through, and looked after players. He was just somebody who made you feel very welcome."

The following Sunday morning, Richards was picked up by Joe Gardiner and driven to Molineux, a visit upon which he reflected in the 1977 Centenary souvenir in the Express & Star; "I remember when I first walked in, staring at the trophies and old team photographs on the wall, legends in football history; people like the Reverend Kenneth Hunt, Stan Cullis and Billy Wright. To think I was going to play on the same pitch as they had was indeed a dream come true." He continues; "I was taken to meet Mr McGarry in the manager's office just off the main entrance in the Waterloo Road. Having been kept waiting for ten to 15 minutes, I was led in to sit on one side of the huge desk." He was offered a year's contract at £25 a week but went back to Warrington to finish his 'A' levels before reporting for pre-season training.

Richards admitted he was aware of the expectation of the 1950s that rested heavily on the club at the time but felt it came more from supporters; "It was still very fresh, just a generation on, and they compared everything else to that success. Nobody was ever going to live up to that." With tea-man Jack Davies and chief scout Gardiner on the staff, the first-team trainers under both Major Buckley and Cullis were still at the club. Derek Parkin also appreciates the burden of history; "I'd heard of Wolves and knew they'd had some great teams in the 50s and 60s. They'd got some great players, really nice gentlemen they were. All the old players used to come to games and you got to know them. I was very respectful because I knew what they'd done. In the 70s, we were quite successful. We got to the UEFA Cup final, two League Cup finals and won both, and finished in the top six. The only way we could have overtaken them was to win the League, and the FA Cup a couple of times. Then we would have been on a par." Dougan summed up the magnitude of the 1950s achievements; "When I arrived, Wolverhampton Wanderers had become only the third club that century, after Huddersfield and Arsenal, to win the championship three times in a decade."

Just over a week after closing their League schedule with two defeats in the north east, Wolves were on the plane to Baltimore to play as Kansas City Wolves in the 1969 International Cup. They almost literally hit America when their Boeing 707, already short on fuel, burst a tyre on landing at Bangor, Maine. Once on terra firma, Waggy learned his suitcase was en route to Las Vegas, and Phil Parkes had £100 taken from a hotel room. Holsgrove recalls; "We stopped in Kansas City. It was a nice place but would never be as good as Los Angeles. I came down for breakfast one morning and McGarry asked me what I thought of the hotel. It was almost like a Travel Lodge and I told him I didn't rate it and he got up and stormed out. We went to Atlanta at the weekend and stopped in the same hotel as Tommy Docherty's Aston Villa. It was like the seventh wonder of the world, with lifts on the outside. We couldn't believe it. After beating Villa, we flew back to Kansas and, on the coach, McGarry stood up and said, 'By the way, lads, we're moving hotel. Go in, get your gear and we're off to the Hilton.' He never said a word to me about it, he wasn't going to admit it."

For the second time in three summers, Wolves undertook a punishing itinerary, with the following results: May 2 West Ham 2-3 (Baltimore), May 4 Dundee United 4-2 (home), May 7 West Ham 4-2 (home), May 11 Kilmarnock 3-2 (home), May 14 Villa 2-1 (Atlanta), May 16 Kilmarnock 3-0 (St. Louis), May 21 Villa 5-0 (home); May 31 Dundee United 2-3 (Dallas). The 'home' triumph over Villa secured the title and the Mayor of Kansas presented the squad with Certificates of Citizenship, and John McAlle with a watch as Player of the Tournament. McAlle was more touched, though, when Peter Knowles told him; "I didn't realise how good you were."

On tour, Dougan was reportedly approached by Nobby Clark, a character from his Peterborough days who was by now at Arsenal. Having already been told in a Kansas hotel by a bourbon-fuelled Curran that he (Hughie) had been bought to assume

McALLE WAS WOLVES STAR

John McAlle got an unusual hat-trick in Wolves 4-2 vengeance win over West Ham in Kansas City last night.

His first two goals gave Wolves a 2—0 lead but the third, when he inadvertently slipped the ball into his own net, made it 2—1, and that was the half-time score. Skipper Mike Bailey with his third goal in three games made it 3—2 and Hugh Curran got the fourth a few minutes before Trevor Brooking scored the second for the Hammers.

This victory — with six points for a win and the goal points bonus — put Wolves, with 20 points, nine points clear at the head of the table over West Ham, who beat Wolves 3—2 in the opening game last Friday.

Wolves made the most of their chances with McAlle the star.

KNOWLES' CENTRE

McAlle swept Wolves into the lead with two goals in three minutes late in the first half.

West Ham goalkeeper Bobby Ferguson punched away a free kick and McAlle quickly recovered the ball to hammer it into the net.

The second goal was a header from a high centre from Peter Knowles that went over Ferguson's head.

West Ham started to crumble as Wolves went further ahead when Mike Bailey steered home a pass from McAlle after 3½ minutes of the second half.

BRIEF RALLY

Ten minutes from time Hugh Curran swooped on to another McAlle pass and beat Ferguson for Wolves' fourth.

West Ham rallied briefly with their second goal four minutes later, when Peter Bennett drew Parkes out of the goalmouth and passed to Trevor Brooking who banged the ball into the net.

A cup match last night between Dundee United (representing Dallas) and Aston Villa (Atlanta) was postponed because of rain and will be played tonight.

John McAlle in action Stateside, in the form that earned rave reviews.

the Doog's mantle, he (The Doog) was understandably interested by Clark's suggestion that Bertie Mee was prepared to offer £90,000 to take him. It was a deal McGarry was not prepared to countenance, though, and Dougan was further frustrated when he urged his boss to bid for Kilmarnock's Tommy McLean, a skilful winger with the predatory instincts of a striker. Dougan recalled; "He scored twice against us, I think. I dreamed about Waggy on the other wing. I would create havoc, getting more chances, scoring more goals." The Doog learned McLean was available for £80,000 and that he relished the thought of playing in the English First Division. McGarry said no and, within months, McLean had started a successful 12 years at Glasgow Rangers.

Elsewhere, future legend Hibbitt came to wider attention when, at 18, he was feted in Altrip at the Europea-Festival, a junior competition for European luminaries like Inter Bratislava, Eintracht Frankfurt and Bologna. Wolves held Bologna 0-0 before slipping 1-0 to Mannheim and beating Dortmund 5-0. They ultimately secured fifth place with a 3-0 win over Fribourg and the squad, also including Eastoe and Bertie Lutton, headed to Rheinfelden for a second tournament. A particular benefit of the US tour was McGarry's discovery of Munro's defensive skills, the manager telling the Evening Mail's Neville Foulger; "Munro's performances in America were a revelation. He has often said he fancied playing in the back four. Frankly, I never pictured him in this sort of position but decided to give him a try."

It was a switch that was to serve Wolves well for the best part of a decade. In addition to the staple fare, the first programme of 1969-70 would contain skipper Mike Bailey's US diary, in which he reported on extensive sunbathing, Hughie Curran's stint as a traffic cop, fabulous drug store breakfasts for 8s 6d, and great interest on US TV of Apollo 10's Snoopy and Charlie Brown testing out space hardware in earth orbit. Two months later, worldwide attention was focused on Cape Canaveral and Mission Control, Houston, as we waited for Neil Armstrong's 'giant leap for mankind'. Back home, we eagerly awaited a take-off of a different kind.

1969-70: Changing Times

Black was the new gold in late summer, 1969, with dark shorts adopted by Wolves for the first time since their relegation in 1965. It was all change on the administrative front, too, as ex-junior player Phil Shaw replaced the long-serving Jack Howley as secretary. Bernard Shaw and Jim McCalliog signed from the steel city clubs of United and Wednesday for £25,000 and £75,000 respectively. Shaw, an England under-23 man, was introduced as the owner of a Ford Cortina and hairdressing business that was managed by his fiancée. Steve Daley says; "He was a good lad. I always told him the way he mistimed his tackles made him look hard! He liked a night out, as we all did."

Bill McGarry made it quite clear Scottish international McCalliog was seen as a vital cog in the engine-room while also expected to work with Peter Knowles and Dave Wagstaffe to take the goal-scoring weight off Derek Dougan and Hugh Curran. He had netted to help Wednesday lead Everton 2-0 in the 1966 FA Cup final before Mike Trebilcock and Derek Temple guided the Merseysiders to a famous comeback. A year later, McCalliog, 23, was feted north of the border for a goal in a 3-2 win at Wembley over world champions England. He clearly expressed his enthusiasm for the challenge; "Let me say how happy I am to join Wolves. They are a club with great tradition and have one of the most respected managers in the game. Now I hope to settle quickly and help them to honours. With the players we have, I feel sure we can get to the top."

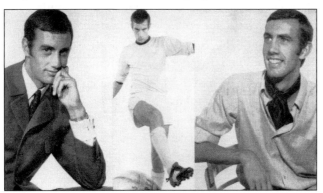

In the same article, it was revealed John Holsgrove had signed up with the Telecast Studios Model Agency in Birmingham. He remembers the 'stick' that had to be taken on this and other matters; "Football's all about banter. We used to train on Christmas Day and the worst thing you could do was wear a jumper you'd just got as a present. It was best to wear old stuff."

Close-season matters were put into perspective by the loss of Reg Hollingsworth at only 59 on July 8. He had been a regular from 1928 to 1936 in the team who helped Wolves back to the First Division. John Richards remembers that Joe Gardiner again kindly drove him down from Warrington, this time for training. Kenny Hibbitt recalls that the new boy was very quick and always prepared to graft; "When John first came, he played on the right wing and was bobbing on his toes a lot. He worked really hard because he probably lacked the skill factor then. But it didn't take him long to put his pace, bravery, eye for a goal and skill together to make him an England international. He put a lot of work in but was as brave as a lion, probably one of the bravest I've seen in the penalty box."

Steve Kindon is also a great JR admirer, on and off the pitch; "Fabulous, John was brave and strong, and from here to that door he'd beat anybody. I don't think it was his running, it was his anticipation. And he was a lucky b****rd. Centre-half knocks it down and that lucky b****rd was just where it dropped and knocked it in, anybody could have done that. I take a shot, the keeper parries it and that lucky b****rd is there and all he does is tap it in. Anybody could have done that. Then you think there must be a little more to it than being a lucky b****rd! He's my best pal in football, a hero of mine and a great guy. I know the family well, his mum as well. He and I shared hotel rooms. It was always me and John, Kenny and Willie, Squeak and Scouse."

Daley chips in; "John wasn't blessed with the greatest skill, at times it was like playing a one-two with a wardrobe door! But he was very quick, very aggressive and had that bit of selfishness. If anyone was going to score in the box, it was going to be him. He was brave and strong. He'd put his head in where the boots were flying. If the ball was to be won, he'd be there. No matter what sort of game he was having, he was 100%, he'd never hide. He knew instinctively where the goals where. You talk about comparisons between Bully and John. All I can say is that Bully would have had to be a bloody good player to be better than John." For Richards, the switch from schoolboy to professional was a huge shock; "Most of what we did for a couple of weeks was very hard cross country. I can always remember Cannock Chase because I was sick at least twice in the first week. It was two or three months before I began to feel comfortable."

At the same time, Hibbitt was eyeing progress up the pecking order; "I was only 17 when I came, so I started in the bottom (away team) dressing room, where the reserves gathered for training. Each pre-season, I hoped to be in the top dressing room. Two years went by and my number was in the home one. I'd made it!" Holsgrove also recalls the routine of the seniors assembling in one room, with younger players in the other; "Unless you were in the main squad, you were in the away dressing room and worked your way up, which was right. This dated back to Ronnie Allen, when Dave McLaren would come in at the start of pre-season saying, 'Wheat, wheat, chaff, wheat, chaff.' That's how you found out whether you were in the first team."

This was a great incentive, with the away dressing room shared in 1969 by the likes of Richards, John McAlle, Alan Sunderland, Daley and Barry Powell. Daley recalls; "We would come in at about 8.45 and the only time you got in the home team room was when you went to pick up the first-team players' boots. I cleaned Mick Bailey's. We also picked up the kit to get it washed, and cleaned the bath or shower once the first team had used it." Powell always tried to learn from older players; "You're in that environment and you watch how they prepare for games. I used to be a bugger for going into the first-team dressing room, even when I wasn't invited. I used to want to be around the senior players, and Jack Dowen, the coach/kit-man, would forever be saying, 'Get out, Powell!' A cheeky little bugger, I used to go and sit next to the likes of Bailey and Dougan and ask, 'What's it like to play in front of 50,000? What's it like to do this?' In fairness, they always told me. They were great. It helped me control my nerves when my chance came. They were a great bunch and I got a lot of help from them. I even babysat for Frank Munro."

On the eve of the big kick-off, Bill McGarry reflected on a disappointing first nine months in charge to The People's Brian Madley; "I admit it hasn't been easy. There have been problems but most problems can be overcome. I am looking forward to getting on with the job of putting Wolves where they belong, right at the top. The potential is tremendous and I want to turn that into reality." In a final Molineux friendly, Dougan scored just past the half-hour to see off a Kilmarnock side who had finished fourth in the Scottish First Division. The visitors would soon face FC Zurich in the Fairs Cup, or, as 'Molinews' termed it; "One of Scotland's big four, due to go into European orbit next month." This uneventful victory and other early warm-up games suggested that McGarry's impact was starting to be felt. Having proved his defensive worth in the USA, Munro remembers how an early-season injury to Duggie Woodfield, "a tremendous professional who I admire greatly," that gave him the first opportunity to cement his place at centre-back, initially alongside Holsgrove.

On the first Saturday of the season, most of the 32,260 crowd went home happy as Dougan (2) and Knowles set up a 3-1 win over Stoke City. Madley wrote, "Derek Dougan, that irresistible, inimitable Irishman, has done it again! These sides had over £200,000 worth of summer signings on show but you can't dismiss the Doog that easily. It took him only a few minutes to crush Stoke with a great goal and remind Wolves fans he is still the master of Molineux." The following Wednesday, Curran and Dougan joined forces to defeat Southampton 2-1 before the Wanderers headed north to Sheffield Wednesday. Appropriately enough, Jim McCalliog's first Wolves goal came in a 3-2 victory at his old stamping ground. The omens had looked bleak when Alan Warboys put the Owls ahead after three minutes but three goals in 12 minutes virtually won the match for the visitors. First McCalliog took down a right-wing cross to beat Springett from close range before Knowles and Curran chipped in to put Wolves apparently in command. A David Ford goal and a sending-off that earned Dougan a 14-

day suspended ban left us nervously listening to the radio at Geoff and Barbara Page's wedding reception at the Baggeridge Miners' Welfare Club.

A fourth win was secured, by 3-2 in the return at Southampton. The game was significant as the first known occasion that two Wolves full-backs (Parkin and Les Wilson), scored in the same game. Les had netted only three times previously for Wolves, all away. When Manchester United came to town on August 23, Wolves were joint top with Everton and Liverpool, 50,783 witnessing a hard-fought 0-0 draw. Of the 11 goals scored in the opening games, Curran and Dougan had contributed only three in total but the often shaky defence had leaked six. Another old boy, Ernie Hunt, then scored to help Coventry to a 1-0 win that put a black mark on an otherwise successful August. But for keeper Bill Glazier, though, the unbeaten run would have stayed intact.

Home crowds reflected the successful start as an average of 40,138 put Wolves seventh highest in the country, comparing favourably with a 12th-placed average of just 30,645 in 1968-69. The visit of newly-promoted Derby four days later resulted in a 1-1 draw and marked both the return of Frank Wignall and the introduction of new £20,000 floodlights. They were switched on amid concerns they might be too bright for photographers. As the Daily Express' Ron Viner said; "We did not realise they would be so powerful. Many of us over-exposed our films." The following week, Miss World, Penny Plummer, presented the award for Club of the Year in recognition of the excellence of the new Wolves Social Club on Waterloo Road - opened two years earlier at a cost of £140,000 and now with 4,500 members and a waiting list of hundreds.

Some 1,400 packed into the gymnasium over the club to see John Ireland pick up the cup in recognition of club secretary Doug Morgan's fabulous work. The 'Club Mirror' reported the success; "The Wolves Social Club possesses every amenity and a programme of entertainment that caters for all tastes. The secret of the success is in fact that it is a genuine social club. Its success, atmosphere and prosperity is generated by its members themselves, superbly guided by their genial club organiser." Two evenings

Penny Plummer hands the cup to John Ireland; and leading light Doog points the way to equality against Derby.

Just like daylight!

later, a McCalliog-inspired home League Cup win over Spurs became the first football match in Britain to be transmitted live in colour.

Unexpected storm clouds were beginning to gather, though. Fans' favourite Peter Knowles announced that the visit of Nottingham Forest on September 6 would be his last competitive game. He was a petulant teen idol, good-looking with a Beatles haircut, renowned for his brilliant skills and short temper, typified by ball-throwing dissent and a habit of celebrating goals by kicking balls out of the ground. After 64 goals in 191 Wolves games and just 24 days short of his 24th birthday, Knowles turned his back on football to devote his life to the Jehovah's Witnesses. Parkin remembers the shock of his conversion; "He was not unlike Bestie, a new generation of player and the looks to go with it. Swanky white sports car, girls, and all of a sudden he comes into the dressing room with a Bible. You can imagine it. A lad who had been so brash comes in with a Bible and starts preaching, it didn't go down very well."

Holsgrove had played with Knowles since 1965 and was surprised at his decision; "Although I never really got to know Peter, it was a big shock. He was one of the last people you'd ever think would change. I respect him as a player and he would have gone on to play for England. It's a free world, he made a decision and, 40 years later, he doesn't regret it. That says everything, good luck to him." Holsgrove points out that the departure created opportunities for others; "I often think: What if Peter Knowles hadn't given up, would John Richards have come on so quickly? He left and John got his chance." Frank Munro remembers; "When I first came here, I was very close to Peter. We used to go out for a drink in Birmingham, two halves and he'd be drunk! We used to go to the same barber for haircuts. It was about being the best looking bloke in the programme. He started reading the Bible on the coach, I think it was his wife who got him into it. We honestly thought he'd be back within six weeks."

Phil Parkes admits he was less surprised; "He told me he was going to do it. All the players have every respect for Pete, he is still doing it. It's a great shame, though, because I think he could have been ranked alongside Peter Broadbent because he had everything. He had the nasty streak in him as well that all great players have to have. It was a great shame but he's one of the most contented people I've ever met." Conversely, although Dougan considered Knowles a good player, he felt he lacked the commitment to become truly top-class. He cited an incident in a match against Coventry; "Frank Munro put a ball through but Knowles heard George Curtis coming, let the ball run slightly away from him and headed about 20 yards in the other direction behind the corner flag to get out of his way!" Munro recalls this incident but is more forgiving; "I put a cross-field ball to Waggy and sliced it a bit. Peter was through but heard the big hooves behind him, left the ball and ran off the pitch. That was Peter, he was still a fantastic player."

Mike Bailey agrees; "He had fantastic ability, bags of skill and vision, had it all." Parkin also greatly admired his natural ability; "He was one of those players that could turn a game. A good trainer and there's no escaping the tremendous talent he had. It seemed a shame he quit but he's stuck by his beliefs and I have only respect for him." Full-back partner Bobby Thomson has affectionate memories, too; "He reminded me a lot of Peter Broadbent but he had his own talent. He became a crowd favourite because of his antics." Steve Daley refers to Peter with great fondness; "Peter is a smashing bloke. He could do anything, he'd got this cockiness, an arrogance that was not big-headedness. I remember him going to the corner flag and sitting on the ball."

Munro feels Knowles was a huge loss; "If Peter had continued, we would have won more, I'm convinced. I think he was so good he would probably have gone on to become the second best Wolves player ever after Peter Broadbent. He was exactly the same, they both had tremendous feet." Richards admits it was a major regret he never had the chance to play alongside Knowles; "He was recognised as one of the best young players in the country and without doubt one of the most skilful, destined for more international honours." When first at Molineux, Powell used to clean Peter's boots and has huge admiration for him; "It was a big shock, I couldn't believe what he had done. I saw him many years later at Wolves for a Johnny Hancocks testimonial. Johnny needed a pair of boots, size five, and he had mine, the only ones that fitted him. As we're getting organised, I'm giving a bit of a tongue-lashing to some apprentices and an arm comes round my shoulder and a voice says, 'You want to listen to this guy. He did a great job with my boots and look where he is today.' It was Peter and his brother Cyril. I thought that was great. Peter was terrific and made a great impression on me. I've seen him in training waltz around the keeper, flick the ball deliberately against the bar and head it in. He's one of the greatest players I've ever seen and I played with Pele and Beckenbauer in the States."

Daley also saw Peter in action; "He had no reason to come back but played for Frank Munro at Willenhall because the club wouldn't give him a testimonial. Peter, who doesn't swear, smoke or drink, walked in with one of his 'bosses' from the Jehovah's and Phil Parkes went, 'F***in hell, look what's come through the f***in door'. Peter went, 'Hello Phil', and Phil replied, 'Knowlesy you

t**t, how are you doing?' I thought: Phil, you never fail to let me down. Peter was a bit slower but what a first touch! It used to take me three or four touches to do what he did in one. He'd got tricks as well, a great player and very fit. He looks as young today as he did then."

As a confused 12-year-old, I was one of thousands unable to accept that Knowles would never return and McGarry's programme notes for the Forest game made it clear this was a sentiment he shared; "As far as Peter Knowles is concerned, I'm still hoping there will be a happy ending. His training gear will be laid out as usual on Monday and I expect him to be here". The general feeling in the club was that he would be back and his registration was retained for years, with a contract being sent and returned unsigned for seven summers. Daley confirms; "Peter was in a club house, so Bill gave him a month to sort himself out, get another place and bring the keys back. The fourth week and he'd still not played, he brought the keys back and took them into Bill's office on the Thursday. Bill said, 'Look, we're playing Liverpool on Saturday, you can play if want to.' He said, 'No, I've finished', and that was it, off he went."

Waggy adds; "Peter was quite wayward then, always looking for something in life, but it was still a shock. We all tried to talk him out of it, one by one. He promised us he would make a bonfire on the pitch of his bibles if the world didn't end in 1972. So when it didn't, somebody phoned him up and asked him when we were having our bonfire. Peter said they'd got the dates wrong!" Daley admires his stance; "I have a lot of time for him. He's done great. Peter's a strong character and they were his genuine beliefs." Bailey regrets the loss to the game but still respects Knowles; "We all admire him for sticking to his beliefs. Good luck to him." Whatever the feelings at the time, he indeed stayed true to his word and his principles, an interview from the time offering an insight into the real Peter Knowles. The integrity of the man shines through in the stream of consciousness reproduced below. Although Peter wasn't to know it then, he had much to say on what many feel to be the woes of today's game.

"People seem to think I made a decision overnight or that the Jehovah's Witnesses have made me make the decision. But I've thought about it for three months and I'm really pleased I got out. There's nothing against football. I loved the game, I still like the game now when I see it on TV. I'm there moving about, really involved in it. I could see something was going to happen and I wanted to get out of it. I didn't want it to overcome me. And I know the personality I am, the flair I have got, that I could one day break somebody's leg. No matter how long I play football, no matter how long I am a Jehovah's Witness, or how near to perfection I come, I know the personality I am and I'm imperfect that I could break somebody's leg, and I'd hate this on my mind. It's not the thought of breaking somebody's leg, it's the thought that a person could be out of work, a cripple for the rest of his life and when you've been earning £100 a week, you come down in wages and that's a big drop, especially if you have four or five kids. And also, when you break your leg, you're hanging about the house and start being niggly with your wife and it could easily break a marriage up. I don't want this on my conscience and I know the personality I am on a football field that I could do this.

"When I started reading the Bible and trying to be a Christian, I found the nearer we got to Saturday I was dragging myself away from my wife and dragging myself away from religion. I was building myself up as I got near to Saturday. I was starting to be on my own and thinking about my game. I was thinking how I was going to play and what happened if somebody kicked me or if somebody was going to score. I was really getting involved in the game. And, from Wednesday until Saturday, I might as well not be married, I might as well have been on my own. This is wrong because the Bible expects you to be a Christian seven days a week. I think sport has gone out of football. There's that much at stake, anything can happen and it's the same with the crowds. At one time, a woman would never go to a football match but now there's all women in the crowd. There's people getting smashed over the head with bottles, getting stabbed and I can see it's going to come to a big climax in one game."

It is clear Knowles saw the game becoming dominated by business and blighted by hooliganism. Among other matters, he may have been referring to the invasion of the North Bank by Manchester United fans a few weeks earlier which had led to fights, and bottles and coins being thrown. Dougan saw the extent of the loss; "I do regret he got out and often wonder how far he could have gone. But religion turned Peter Knowles into a better bloke than I ever thought he'd turn into." Waggy agrees; "Whenever I see Peter now and say, 'How you're doing?' he says, 'Every day, I wake up is a wonderful day, I haven't got a worry in the world.' I can't argue with that, can I? How many can say that? He's perfectly happy." Munro agrees; "He's very contented and, when he sees old films of himself, he says, 'Who's that bloody hooligan running about?' When I was in hospital after my stroke, he was one of the first to visit me."

In the late 1970s, Peter looked back somewhat sadly on his time in the game; "I regret everything about football. I used to go on the field and really make sure I was centre of attraction. I think this is it with people that have got skill. It isn't just a matter of playing. They like to do things out of the ordinary. If I was playing at Wolves, I'd really make sure I did things out of the ordinary. When I look back at some of those things, it sometimes makes me ashamed." It could be argued he had things in the right perspective, appreciating the catalogue of woes that had to be tackled for the sake of the game's long-term well-being. Knowles never kicked another ball in professional anger and, although true Wolves fans will never cease regretting his loss, they have come to respect the strength of belief that fuelled his decision.

Although Wagstaffe was man of the match, the Forest game is best remembered for Knowles' farewell and final party piece. Parkes remembers; "Before the game, he said to me, 'If we're winning, I'm going to sit on the ball under the clock on the Molineux Street Stand'. Sure enough, he stopped the ball and sat on it." In an excellent first half, Curran scored two fine goals but missed three while the Doog netted one and missed two, leaving McGarry to moan; "I find it hard to recall a game in which a team made more chances with so few conversions. Perhaps it would have been better if we had not scored our third!" The lead was cancelled out in ten crazy minutes mid-way through the second half by a goal from Welsh winger Ronnie Rees and a brace by Henry Newton. Knowles squandered a chance to win it while Rees fired over in the last minute and Waggy was denied a possible penalty. My abiding memory is of a first-hand introduction to hooliganism as visiting fans kicked in the back of the South Bank and skimmed sheets of corrugated asbestos into the crowd. The club rectified it by replacing the metal with wooden boards, but my dad found it difficult ever to regain his enthusiasm for football in the 'new age.' Having begun to follow Wolves in the war years, he would never again be a regular visitor to Molineux.

The game started a September run of five draws that continued when two Curran goals in eight minutes near the end earned an unlikely point at Chelsea. Dempsey and Osgood had scored before Hughie raced onto a Dougan knockdown to drive low past Bonetti, then headed home a cross from the no 9. Three days later, McGarry's second return to Ipswich brought more frustration. Dougan put Wolves ahead and Curran looked to have made it two until the linesman ruled it out for an infringement by his strike partner. Predictably, Ipswich levelled - with a twice-taken penalty, Parkes pushing the first kick over until the same official flagged to say he had moved early.

Another chance of victory was thrown away after Jim McCalliog opened the scoring at home to Burnley but further League Cup progress was secured against a Brighton side who had previously seen off Birmingham. Ex-Wolf Geoff Sidebottom was in the Seagulls' goal and, not for the first time, David Woodfield was pressed into action as emergency centre-forward, scoring his last but one Wolves goal in a 3-2 win. Duggie then occupied the same position at Newcastle in a team stripped of Dougan and

Curran. Mike O'Grady made his debut, the 26-year-old joining for £80,000 from Leeds United. He had first made his name by scoring the goal that saw Huddersfield eliminate holders Wolves from the FA Cup in 1961. Although Newcastle went ahead courtesy of yet another spot-kick, a Jimmy Mac header made it 1-1 and Parkin almost won it with the last kick of the match against his home-town club.

On that last Saturday in September, the reserves drew 3-3 with Blackburn Rovers. In a team also comprising Alan Boswell, John Farrington, Derek Clarke, Jimmy Seal and Peter Eastoe, the nucleus

John McAlle marks John Hollins at Chelsea.

Not a bad crop of emerging and fringe players.....back row (from left): Alan Boswell, Ken Hibbitt, Bernard Shaw, Gerry Taylor, Dave Galvin, John McAlle, Wayne Nicholls. Front: John Farrington, Derek Clarke, John Richards, Jimmy Seal, Peter Eastoe.

of the 1970s team was on show in the form of Taylor, Shaw, Hibbitt, McAlle and Richards. McAlle remembers that it was under the expert guidance of coaches like Dave Maclaren that the bedrock of future success was founded, with luminaries like McAlle (30), Hibbitt (27), Richards (25) and Sunderland (4) among those racking up appearances and experience. Hibbitt adds; "We had a very good team, with five or six future internationals in there. That's how strong the squad was. I had come from a squad of 18 to 20 at Bradford but we had 40 pros at Wolves and the manager could only pick 11. So you had to be talented to get in." While others were progressing, Powell was struggling to settle; "I found it hard initially. Coming from sleepy Kenilworth, it was difficult in a big town. I'd been there almost a year and was phoning my dad constantly. He told me to stick with it, saying the first year is the hardest and once you've got over that, it will be plain sailing. He was right."

Still in the top six at the start of October, Wolves' table-topping aspirations faced the acid test with the visit of leaders Everton. The Merseysiders had won ten, drawn one and lost just once in their first 12 games. Wolves were six points behind them but had still lost only once themselves. Unfortunately, O'Grady was unable to inspire his new club against Harry Catterick's eventual champions; a team comprising England men Brian Labone and Joe Royle, not to mention the famous half-back line of Howard Kendall, Colin Harvey and Alan Ball. Royle scored a 15th minute penalty before John Morrissey doubled the lead eight minutes before the break. Curran halved the deficit on 49 minutes and it remained a lively, tightly-contested affair in front of 40,589. It was then that 43 year-old Maidstone referee Keith Walker stepped in.

Walker had been involved in controversy a week earlier when Liverpool visited The Hawthorns, the Reds equalising in the extra-time he allowed for alleged time wasting and gamesmanship. At Molineux, he controversially sent off Dougan for bad language as he argued with a linesman in front of an outraged North Bank. Ironically,

the Doog was featured as no 1 in the programme's new Action Album feature but will be best remembered on this occasion for the dismissal that provoked a mini riot that left 96 injured and a similar number arrested as the crowd surged in the old Cowshed. For this indiscretion and the reaction by the hooligan minority, Dougan was handed an eight-week ban (six weeks added to the existing two suspended from August).

Alan Williams of the Daily Express had clear views on Mr. Walker's performance; "One of the oldest adages in football decrees that the best referees are those you scarcely notice. This could hardly be the case with Walker. In my opinion, he was too fastidious about the petty indiscretions which many top referees handle with quiet words here and there. His officious 'I'm in charge' attitude only serves to antagonise the players and inflame the crowd rather than earn him respect." In what remained of the game, Harvey scored to restore Everton's two-goal lead and, although Curran converted a penalty almost right away, Wolves could not quite pull it back and Phil Morgan wrote; "It was Everton who had the poise while Wolves had the tendency to be overawed and put out of their stride."

On the following Wednesday, Wolves threw away a 2-0 lead earned by O'Grady and Dougan as they failed to kill off Sheffield Wednesday at home. Eight draws in ten matches was unmatched in the club's history, with four successive 1-1s in a run of five draws out of six in 1949-50 coming closest. This was also the only previous time they had drawn four consecutive home League matches and, in 1950, it contributed to the loss of the championship to Portsmouth on goal average. In 1969, Wolves appeared to be back on track as Curran left Mike England in his wake to power home a superb header to overcome Tottenham at White Hart Lane. By the end of the year, Hughie notched 12 goals in 23 League starts and was included in Scotland's party for the World Cup qualifier against Germany, only to withdraw 24 hours later. Parkin was called up at right-back for England Under-23s against Russia.

Brighter form was soon forgotten as Wolves were eliminated from the League Cup in the fourth round by a determined QPR team who were flying high in Division Two. Ex-Wednesday man Vic Mobley started for them at no 5 in a team of famous names including skipper Terry Venables and forward Rodney Marsh. Having contained QPR for 20 minutes, Wolves caved in as Allan and Derek Clarke's brother Frank scored twice and Barry Bridges chipped in a third. After the break, Les Wilson slotted home what proved to be nothing more than a consolation.

There were mixed fortunes in the last two League games in October, a McCalliog-inspired home win over West Ham being followed by a narrow setback at Manchester City. Following a Mike Doyle penalty soon after half time, Wilson and Bailey went close before Wagstaffe was denied a last-minute spot-kick. November dawned with O'Grady earning Wolves a 1-0 home win over the big-spending Baggies, who had new signings Colin Suggett and Danny Hegan in their line-up. The two points pushed Wolves back into the top five while condemning the Albion to the bottom six but Dougan began a ban that would last into the new decade. While Curran was to shoulder much of the burden in his absence, a future luminary was making pleasing progress.

John Richards was beginning to score for fun in the reserves and would total 16 goals in only 25 starts. On the day the Baggies visited Molineux, Richards scored all five as Wolves' second string won 5-3 at Blackburn. Just short of his 19th birthday, the fresh-faced Warrington lad admitted to favouring Spurs as a boy but reflected happily on his heroics; "I enjoyed every minute of it. It was a great feeling." Looking back now, he recognises this as the game that made everyone at Molineux sit up and take notice; "It just went right on the day, I had six shots and scored five. Nobody else scored and it made more of an impact." He was one of a number of fine young players coming through, with five or six arguably still ahead of him in the pecking order of strikers - Jimmy Seal and Derek Clarke in the reserves alone.

He was in digs in an old Victorian semi on Broad Lane, Bradmore, off Bantock Park, a Mrs Cath Eagle adhering to strict instructions at her home to build up young players with steaks and Guinness; "The club was very well organised, arranging digs for the players." In the excellent chapter 'After the Fabulous Fifties, the Sodding Sixties' from the 'We Are Wolves' book, Tony Eagle recalls March 1969 and his mum getting 'increasingly fed up with students' as lodgers, so she contacted Wolves and was called on by Joe Gardiner. A 15-year-old Barry Powell was the first house guest and was visited by mates like Peter Eastoe, Steve Daley and Alan Sunderland. "First I moved in with Mrs Screen with Kenny Hibbitt and somebody else but they were going on holiday so we needed to change and I moved in with Mrs Eagle," Powell said. "It

FIVE-GOAL FLING MAKES JOHN SMILE

JOHN RICHARDS (right), eager goalgetting reserve inside-forward, looked back on his five-goal fling against Blackburn Reserves two weeks ago and grinned : "I enjoyed every minute of it—it was a great feeling".

Yet this Johnny-on-the-spot, who celebrated his 19th birthday this week, might have now been studying in college but for his love of soccer.

was only supposed to be temporary but I ended up there for three years. She was superb, took in two of us at a time and treated us just like sons."

In September, 1969, arguably Mrs Eagle's most famous lodger arrived, as Tony describes; "Again, I walked into the kitchen to find a young man, same age as me, 18, just finished his A levels (also like me), a Lancashire accent, and sideburns. His name was John Richards." John had a happy stay of two years and life was tightly controlled with an 11pm curfew and no going out for two nights before a game. Daley and others were going through the same careful nurturing process; "At first, I was in digs in Low Hill, very nice, with Jimmy Seal who came from not far from where I lived. Then I moved in with Alan Sunderland in Dunstall, another great place!"

A few years would pass before the chance came for greater freedom and visits to the Wolves Social Club and the Lafayette. In the interim, McGarry and Chung kept the youngsters' feet firmly on the ground. The management appreciated that Richards and others were still learning and needed to gain strength and experience before earning a prolonged run in the first team. Seven or eight of them were taken to West Park on Thursday afternoons for special skills training with Chung. Different routines were arranged for strikers and defenders, and Richards appreciates the value of this hard work as the nucleus of the 1970s team came of age on the playing fields of WV1; "We were fortunate we had someone like Sammy prepared to do that with us and it paid off." Later arrival Geoff Palmer agrees; "Sammy's training was enjoyable. We loved it when he got the balls out. We used to go over West Park, the goalies trained there on Thursdays. We would cross balls in the mud for Lofty, Gary Pierce and the others while the first team had the afternoon off. The exercises were not only hard work but really enjoyable. Although the coaching and shooting was for goalkeepers, it was good because we were crossing the ball and doing what we had to do in a match."

Wolves seemed to confirm their status as title contenders when a 0-0 draw at Anfield was followed by a 2-0 home win over Arsenal. They restricted the Reds to an Emlyn Hughes shot that Parkes saved brilliantly while O'Grady had a goal disallowed for offside and Paul Walker had a shot cleared off the line by Geoff Strong. In an extraordinary incident, he was also bundled to the ground by Tommy Lawrence just outside the area. Apparently, Bill Shankly had told McGarry he rated the burly keeper as a good full-back, to which the Wolves boss ruefully replied; "But now I'm wondering which code he means!" Walker and Irishman Robert (Bertie) Lutton were making manful contributions to the cause, as the 19-year-old latter showed when he scored the first and laid on the second for Curran in the defeat of the Gunners.

Success over Arsenal was followed by a shock setback at lowly Crystal Palace. Wolves began promisingly as John Sewell deflected a Wagstaffe drive into his own net. However, despite several more first-half chances, they subsided to let Palace score twice in the second period. As 1969 drew to a close, the Selhurst Park debacle pointed to the old inconsistencies returning to haunt Molineux.

Fine wins over Sunderland and Chelsea (for the latter, Munro was an emergency centre-forward) were sandwiched between defeats at old adversaries Leeds and Nottingham Forest. A Curran goal against the Black Cats secured a fourth successive home win but McGarry was left to bemoan the cumulative effect of retirement, injuries and suspensions as he reflected upon the 3-1 loss at Elland Road; "I don't think any club in the country could have taken the punishment that has been handed out to us in recent months and got away with it." Two down at the break to Leeds, Wolves stirred through a Les Wilson header on 48 minutes, only for Allan Clarke to kill them off two minutes later. Eventual FA Cup winners Chelsea were drubbed 3-0 in mid-December, rocked five minutes before half-time by Waggy jinking inside to unleash a long-range shot into the South Bank net. Curran soon doubled the lead, scored again after 52 minutes and was denied a hat-trick by a belated offside flag.

Due to play for the reserves, Richards got his initial first-team call the following weekend for the trip to Nottingham. It was not to be, though, and JR would have to wait until the New Year for another chance. He witnessed a 4-2 thrashing at the City Ground that was only partly atoned for by an excellent 0-0 Boxing Day draw at Old Trafford. When snow wiped out the home Christmas fixture against Coventry for the second year running and further stalled Richards' potential debut, the 1960s had nearly slipped away, with Wolves languishing in seventh, a massive ten points off the pace set by Everton and Leeds. John Ireland was still upbeat in his programme notes for the Coventry non-event; "Thanks to Bill McGarry, Sammy Chung and the players, our position is much improved despite a grim list of injuries, suspensions and other events." Deprived of football at Molineux from December 13 to January 17, I stayed at home in front of a roaring fire to read the Doog's 'Attack'. It was the must-have 1969 Christmas football book, tackling the key issues of the modern game and his career in typically combative style.

Wolves found some holiday action by turning out at Bournemouth for Ray Bumstead's testimonial match. Significantly, the official Wolves Supporters Club was established in the January and many members travelled to Burnley on the third day of the new decade for a third-round FA Cup tie memorable only for Dougan's return. His suspension ended at the same time that Munro began a month's ban of his own. Martin Dobson, Frank Casper and Brian O'Neil scored without reply to leave Wolves no option but to concentrate on the League. Future acquisition Steve Kindon first came to McGarry's notice in this game but it would be more than two years before Wolves would go back for him; "I had a very good game against Wolves at Turf Moor and Bill must have noticed me and enquired. He tried to sign me straightaway but Burnley wouldn't release me. So he waited and did eventually come back for me."

Phil Parkes, who had played with a broken toe, became fall guy for the Cup exit and was replaced by John Oldfield for the League re-match a week later. Oldfield had moved from Huddersfield to re-unite with Parkin and O'Grady. The Doog set up the latter to slide home after only 90 seconds and it wasn't long before McCalliog doubled Wolves' lead. Dougan was then brought down and, although Peter Mellor pushed away McCalliog's penalty, Bailey rammed home the rebound. A late Ralph Coates' goal prove to be nothing more than a consolation. Since 1950, Wolves had been drawn in the FA Cup against a team from their own division 23 times and in only ten of them had the outcomes of Cup and League games coincided.

When Fairs Cup holders Newcastle visited Molineux on January 17, Wolves were 11 points off the top but only two off third place. A forgettable 1-1 draw in which Curran saved a point was overshadowed by the death of George Noakes at his Wednesbury home a few days earlier. Although retired for three years, George had been chief scout at Molineux for 21 years and his contribution was recognised by John Ireland; "A dedicated Wolves man, you somehow do not think of the club without George Noakes. We are all very grateful to him." Billy Wright added his own eulogy; "George must have been one of the most successful scouts football has known. I am sure that without him Wolves would not have been half the club they were."

Although Dougan and Curran scored in a home win over Ipswich, Wolves began to fall away alarmingly. The victory, on January 24, was to be their last in the League until August 25! The 16 League games played after Christmas saw two wins, six draws and eight defeats. The slide began in earnest at Everton at the end of January when Joe Royle netted a 31st minute winner for the champions-elect. Injury prevented Bailey from reappearing after the break but worse followed when the curse of Everton struck again for Dougan. A sickening clash of heads with Keith Newton just before the hour led to him being stretchered off with an appalling facial injury - and the required operation put him out of action for much of the rest of the season.

Entertaining draws with Spurs and Stoke simply delayed the inevitable descent. At home to Spurs, a brace from nemesis Martin Chivers nullified Bailey and Woodfield's

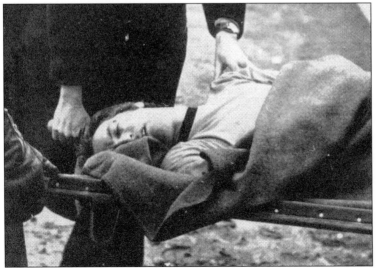

goals. Duggie's was his 15th for the club and came in the last of his 276 matches before a £30,000 move to Watford. John Farrington and Derek Clarke were also soon on their

Derek Dougan on a stretcher - and glad to see the back of Everton for another season.

way (to Leicester and Oxford), with fewer than 50 games between them. After rain and snow made preparations tough in the build-up to the trip to Stoke, McGarry discussed the idea of an 'inflatable house' on the Castlecroft training pitch; "Training can be a worry this time of the year. Our climate is ideal for coaching from the start of the season until November. But after that, you have got to keep all the players in action or they stand the risk of freezing to death."

Curran showed no aversion to the conditions as he helped a McCalliog header over Gordon Banks' line to earn a point. A week later, Wolves were probably wishing the weather had caused the postponement of the home match against League Cup finalists Manchester City. Joe Mercer's men were inspired to a 3-1 victory by Colin Bell and Mike Summerbee, and Wolves headed to The Hawthorns at the very end of February in anything other than good spirits. A 3-3 draw, enjoyed by 37,819, was earned by another long-range O'Grady effort and a penalty and header by Curran.

It was the fifth time the Molineux men had scored three in away games that season but the visit to West Bromwich is best remembered for the debut of Richards, watched by his proud parents. John remembers how he walked very slowly and proudly into Molineux in those early days hoping just to get noticed. His sole ambition was to play just one first-team game. With Dougan and Bobby Gould both out injured, McGarry only told him at 2.15pm he was playing. Considering McGarry and Chung operated on the principle of gradually introducing young players into the team, the choice for his debut was unusual but he became the latest in a growing number of strikers the management had tried in Dougan's latest absence.

Looking back, Richards appreciates his gradual grooming and the fact he was not seen as a regular until his third season, 1971-72, when he stepped into the top dressing room; "It was very good the way it worked with Bill and Sammy. They introduced you as a sub and you travelled with the team. I had the best part of two seasons, almost like serving an apprenticeship, learning how Division One was and getting used to the way the team played before I managed to break into the team. I got in when it was a very good team. A lot of excellent players were coming together like Dougan, Bailey, Wagstaffe and Hibbitt. We just seemed to gel." It was at this time that Powell also made a breakthrough; "I was only 5ft 1in and 6st when I left school. The youth coach was Gordon Ecclestone, a South African, and he was on to me all the time, working on two v one situations. We played Villa one Saturday morning and I got a two on one. Instead of passing, I tried to go by myself. Because of my frailty, I lost the ball and he said, 'Powell, I've told you so many times to pass the f***in thing?' I'd had enough and turned round and said, 'Why don't you f** off?' Afterwards, he put his arm round me and said, 'I've got inside you.' From that moment, my career kicked off."

The next two games, however, spelt out how far Wolves had sunk. A McCalliog goal could not stave off a 2-1 defeat away to a Sunderland team who had won only four games at Roker Park all season. Then, only 20,544 attended the visit of Crystal Palace on March 18. The Londoners had won only once away from home yet, in a drab encounter, Steve Kember cancelled out a Curran strike to earn a draw. It was Wolves' lowest Division One gate since Liverpool had attracted a mere 13,839 in April, 1965 on the last day of the relegation season. After the Palace clash, Hughie scored his 21st of the season but could not deny high-flying Leeds a victory secured by Clarke and Jones. McGarry bemoaned the way his team had fallen apart; "Before our game with Manchester City, it seemed we had only to jog along and we would finish in the top six. Well, the result of that game certainly shattered that illusion."

Unexpectedly, Dougan returned to replace Richards after an unproductive four-match run and joined Curran on the score sheet in a 2-2 draw at Arsenal. It was to be Wolves' last point of 1969-70. Defender Chris Lawler guided Liverpool to a win at Molineux and visits to West Ham and Derby brought three and two-goal reverses. The end of the season could hardly come soon enough and a twice-rearranged fixture saw Coventry repeat their August success courtesy of a Brian Joicey goal that earned them a European place. In an unwisely optimistic moment, Move and later ELO drummer Bev Bevan declared his faith in his beloved Wolves; "I don't think it will be long before the league title comes back to Molineux."

The Wolverhampton public had proved very patient in 1969-70, with the average attendance of 31,238 up on 1968-69. Surprisingly, it is a total never since beaten. The club made a seasonal deficit of £143,000 and lost long-serving physio George Palmer after 24 years of distinguished service. On the international front, Dougan and Lutton represented Northern Ireland, Bailey the Football League and Parkin and Munro their respective under-23 teams, Parkin facing Wales, Bulgaria, Scotland and the USSR. The star of the season had to be Curran, who scored 24 goals for Wolves and was also called up by Scotland. Parkes remembers a wicked sense of humour and other talents; "Hughie would get up and sing anywhere. On one trip, he led John Ireland to the top of the steps that should have led to an aircraft. Knowing that no plane was there, he reassured him, 'Mr Chairman another one will be along in a minute!'"

Richards rated Hughie very highly; "Excellent, one of the most underrated strikers Wolves have ever had. He was great to play alongside, worked hard, was tough and probably the best header of the ball of anyone I've ever played with or against. He was not dissimilar to Andy Gray but different to Dougan, who had more finesse." As for the Doog, he was the only other player to reach double figures that term but only if one counts his two Anglo Italian goals. Looking back, Holsgrove considers the season to have been his best at Wolves; "Now Duggie was injured for quite a bit of time, I played centre-back. Frank played alongside me at first and McGarry eventually replaced me with John McAlle at left-half. I faced people like Ron Davies and Wyn Davies and had them in my pocket. We went post-season to Yugoslavia for two or three games. I wanted to write a postcard to my wife but didn't have a pen. McGarry told me to go up to his room half an hour later for one. He gave me the pen and said, 'Big man, Jack

Charlton is going to be out of the England team soon. If you carry on the way you're going, you'll be in his place.' One thing I will say, McGarry was good to me."

After visiting Skopje, Wolves played in the inaugural Anglo-Italian competition, six English clubs being placed into the following groups with their Italian counterparts. Each team played four games and were awarded two points for a win, one for a draw, and one for each goal. **G1**: Sheff Wed, Swindon, Juventus, Napoli. **G2**: WBA, Middlesbrough, Lanerossi, Roma. **G3**: Wolves, Sunderland, Fiorentina, Lazio.

The team from each country with most points would meet in the final at the end of May, Wolves opening their account on May Day evening, offering 'Benvenuti a Molineux' to Fiorentina players and officials. Dougan and Wagstaffe scored in a 2-1 win seen by only 14,262 fans. Interest dwindled so much that over 2,500 fewer turned out the following Saturday for Lazio's visit. Bailey secured three more points but it had not been a memorable re-introduction to European football. A thoroughly unpleasant affair climaxed in the dismissal of Lazio's Georgio Canaglia, and Parkes says; "They had a full-back called Giusseppe Wilson, born in Darlington. He kept going behind Waggy, putting his finger in his back and saying, 'Roma, bang bang!' It frightened Waggy to death and he didn't want to play in the return."

On May 16, the return in Florence brought a 3-1 Wolves win, noteworthy for more goals from Dougan and Curran and also the first of many from Richards. He can not recall it but, having visited Malawi and Zambia the previous year with a youth team comprising the likes of Rod Arnold and Barry Powell, he remembers the excitement of such travel opportunities for a young man. The trips taught him how highly Wolves were regarded; "It was not until we started playing abroad that I fully appreciated the respect the name of Wolverhampton Wanderers commanded wherever we went."

Probable qualification was spurned in Rome when Lazio won 2-0 in front of a heaving 40,000-plus. Although the Italians presented their opponents with engraved 'Lazio-Wolves' leather wallets, they gave little else away. Parkes feels Wolves were most let down by referee Gordon Hill; "Lazio were the Millwall of Italy. There'd been a fight in the tunnel, they tried to kick us. Gordon was supposed to be one of the best refs in England but he sold us down the river. We needed a draw to qualify and there wasn't long to go when Derek Parkin made a great tackle and won the ball. Even Gordon said, 'Great tackle, Derek,' but

Wolves Italian squad souvenir

Back in Europe - if only after a fashion!

the crowd started booing and shouting, so he gave a free-kick and they scored their first off it. Mike Bailey called Hill everything afterwards in the lounge."

Bailey concurs; "After a fiery encounter at Molineux, which was refereed by an Italian, we felt confident with Gordon in the middle for the return. We thought we would get some protection from the cheating that the Italians were renowned for. A big mistake! Hugh Curran was poleaxed right after the kick off, completely off the ball, but neither Hill nor his lino saw it. I guess you wouldn't be looking for it so soon in the game. When you played a one-two, the Italian tactic was simply to block off the runner and they did it consistently without receiving a card for obstruction. The game changed when Derek won the ball with a great tackle just outside the box, but the Italian did five to ten roll-overs and Mr Hill gave a free-kick. Their player jumped to his feet and took the kick from which they scored. We were incensed and from then on the Italians went down at every opportunity. We lost and, in my opinion, Mr Hill was conned. I told him so after the game. It cost us the match." An enjoyable sojourn had been cut short as Wolves' tally of 13 points was overhauled by Swindon's 14.

Swindon went on to defeat Napoli 3-0 in the final but the quick demise of the competition was not greatly mourned. The violence that brought the abandonment of Albion's game at Lanerossi was an especially bad instance of the ill-feeling and disciplinary issues that dogged many of the matches.

Thoughts now turned to the World Cup, where 39-year-old Wolverhampton butcher Jack Taylor was England's refereeing representative. Dougan, having appeared with Henry Cooper and Graham Hill on BBC's Question of Sport, joined Jimmy Hill, Malcolm Allison and others on ITV's World Cup panel. Ken Jones of the Daily Mirror found England skipper Bobby Moore striking an unwisely optimistic tone; "We all feel we are good enough to keep the World Cup. If we don't, somewhere in the world is a great team we haven't heard about." This must have originated from those who felt Brazil were in tatters after sacking coach Joao Saldanha three months earlier. As it turned out, Mario Zagalo, supported by Carlos Alberto, Rivelino, Jairzinho, Pele and Co, didn't do such a bad job. I vividly remember the glorious Sunday afternoon in Pensnett on which I watched in awe as the greatest team of the modern era simply destroyed Italy in the Azteca Stadium.

It's Doog—TV personality

1970-71: First Trophy In 11 Years

The nightmare form of late 1969-70 continued deep into August of the new season. Four successive defeats soon became seven as a trip to Newcastle and visits to Molineux by Derby and Tottenham left Wolves point-less. Even the traditional home friendly had resulted in a loss, this time 2-1 against Hanover 96. New signings Danny Hegan and Bobby Gould made their debuts in this match, and the future Coventry and Wimbledon boss scored. Somewhat unpromisingly, Bill McGarry said he had stepped into the 'wilderness of reserve football' to rescue two men 'sickened by the game,' by taking Hegan from Albion for £30,000 and Gould from Arsenal for £50,000. After a successful spell with Coventry, Gould had scored only 16 times in 57 games for the Gunners and Hegan, who had played for McGarry at Ipswich, had been particularly unhappy during his season at The Hawthorns, claiming; "All I intend to do is prove some people wrong." Derek Parkin recalls a move he believes came too late; "I remember him playing for Ipswich but then he went to West Brom. He'd waited and waited because he thought Bill would buy him. I think it came too late when he did eventually buy him." Phil Parkes agrees; "Danny's problem was that Ipswich wouldn't let him come to Wolves first. Ipswich at the time was a quiet backwater and Danny went to Birmingham, the big city, and I think he lost his way a bit."

The Hanover game followed a tour of Germany and Holland that yielded three more defeats, against Groningen, Stuttgart and Hanover again. The boss blamed results on injuries and; "the wrong attitude of players. Some seem to think they are permanent fixtures and this view must be disturbed. It is very important to make a good start with a settled side." When the action began in earnest at Newcastle, Wolves slipped up badly. McGarry relegated the previous term's top scorer, Hugh Curran, to the bench to give Gould his first League start. Injuries forced him to play utility man Les Wilson beside John Holsgrove in defence. Derek Dougan and Curran scored what amounted to consolation goals in a 3-2 defeat that certainly flattered Wolves.

McGarry then played a three-man strike force against Derby on the following Wednesday, Dougan and Curran again obliging, this time in the first half. The Rams had then, unfortunately, scored four of their own and there was no further reply for a stunned home crowd. If the alarm bells were ringing, three days later they were positively clanging when Spurs won 3-0 thanks partly to two men (Alan Mullery and Martin Chivers) who were to return to haunt Wolves in the 1972 UEFA Cup Final. This time, Gould was handed the no 12 shirt but even the return of Frank Munro failed to bring the stability the team badly needed. Defeat made it 16 successive League games without a win stretching back to the Ipswich match on January 24. A crowd of below 24,000 clearly showed how confidence had begun to drain away. In the programme, it was announced Dougan, fresh from service on London Weekend TV's 'Four Jest Men' soccer panel, had replaced Cliff Lloyd as Chairman of the Professional Footballers' Association - one of few positive developments in a difficult time at Molineux.

In a major reversal of fortune, Wolves' only August win came at Coventry, venue for their only defeat in August, 1969. Curran secured the points with a left-foot strike after starting the move with a flick to Dave Wagstaffe flying down the wing. Gould chested down the cross and the Scottish forward did the rest. At the end of the week, Curran scored what McGarry called 'a hell of a goal' to put Wolves one up at the City Ground. But Holsgrove was carried off soon after and, with John Richards on the bench, the defence were left threadbare. Holsgrove recalls; "I was hurt early at Forest. It was the same as Dave Woodfield. He'd got injured and I went in. Frank came in alongside me and we made it our home for a couple of years. Then it was Munro and McAlle. But I'd lived my dream for six great six years. I'd played for the team I supported as a boy and, the first time I put the shirt on, I couldn't believe it."

This misfortune, allied to a disappointing display in goal by John Oldfield, saw Forest win 4-1 but led to Munro and McAlle being paired together. Munro had played alongside him in the reserves when recovering from injury and recommended him to

Doog is new P.F.A. chief

CONGRATULATIONS, **DEREK DOUGAN!**

Our popular centre-forward, who has won something of a new reputation as a T.V. personality on London Weekend T.V.'s "Four Jest Men" soccer panel along with Paddy Crerand, Malcolm Allison and Bob McNab, is the new Chairman of the Professional Footballers' Association.

He takes over from Terry Neill, the former Arsenal defender who is now player-manager of Second Division Hull City. And Doog, after his election in Manchester last Sunday, commented:

"I guess I have been a pretty controversial character over the years, but I have matured now and like to think I act sensibly and with dignity.

"It is a great honour to be elected Chairman of the Professional Footballers' Association. I have served on

McGarry: "I said, 'Why doesn't he get a chance'? He got in and we played together for years. It's amazing how things fall into place." Parkes was back for a trip to Ipswich that started an unbroken run of outings that would stretch to September 15, 1972. Curran scored twice and Gould broke his duck to earn Wolves a 3-2 win.

Munro and McAlle were to play at the heart of the defence a staggering 271 further times, the last of them in the promotion-clinching draw at Plymouth in April, 1977. McAlle remembers with affection how well they gelled, Munro as the skilful reader of the game and distributor, and him the ball-winner; "Wherever he went, I covered him. We played very well together." Frank agrees; "John was one of the best tacklers I've ever seen, so brave". John Richards adds; "Frank must have been dreadful for someone like John to play alongside. John was a straightforward player, defend, win the ball, lay it off. Frank had so much time, he was always looking to take players on and beat them." Dougan referred affectionately to; "the colossal Frank and John the wonderful servant." The consistency of selection in the early 1970s is clearly recalled by Munro; "We were together eight or nine years. For a season or two, our team never changed, you knew what it was going to be. I'd hate to play now, I love to watch on Sky but I couldn't bear this rotation. I'd hate to be in one week, out the next."

Parkin says; "John was great to play with because he was so consistent. He never tried to do anything fancy, just played to his strengths. He just played the ball and was probably the most left-footed player I ever played with. He couldn't kick with his right to save his life! But he had a heart like a lion and worked hard. Frank was easy to play with, a class player. He was never the quickest but read the game well and had a tremendous touch for a big man, better than John Richards! He was so skilful that he made it look easy. He and John complemented each other, that's what it's all about." Willie Carr greatly admires Frank's skills; "He was a footballing inside-forward at centre-half and used to scare the s**t out of Lofty when he went to head the ball then ducked and left it." Steve Daley remembers the same party piece and a fabulous defensive pairing; "I used to love the tricks Frank did in training. In a game, their goalie would ping the ball to the striker and Frank would shout, 'My ball!' and then duck. He would do that three or four times a game. He wasn't the most mobile of players but, like Bobby Moore, his reading of the game got him there early. As for John, stick thin but probably the hardest player I've ever seen." Waggy adds; "The talent Frank had....looking out of the corner of his eye for me, he'd ping a 50-yard ball. I first saw him in 1967 on the USA tour playing as an old-style wing-half. You should have seen him in the gym. You got him in the corner, his foot on the ball and hand on the wall. He was so big, so strong you couldn't the get the ball." Parkes is similarly effusive; "I shared a room with Frank for nearly ten years. We go back a long way and he was a great player, a real character as well."

After a shocking start, Wolves suffered just three more League defeats up to mid-February. Some tedious fare was endured before full throttle was engaged,with a 1-1 home draw with Stoke typifying the spluttering form. With Dougan at emergency centre-half, the team failed to hold on to an early lead given them by Curran but the nadir came at the Manor Ground when Division Two Oxford dumped them out of the League Cup at the first hurdle. Things seemed to be getting worse at a soggy Stamford

Hibbitt splashes in his and Wolves' first at Chelsea.

Bridge as the FA Cup holders quickly went two up. But the kick-start to the season came with a second-half fightback that earned a point. On his first start, Kenny Hibbitt fired home left-footed, then Jim McCalliog beat John Hollins to level.

The major confidence engendered by this unlikely comeback started a six-game winning League sequence reminiscent of the eight successes on the bounce that propelled them towards promotion in 1966-67. Hibbitt remembers the day distinctly; "I waited a long time for my full debut. I had a cartilage out that set me back but then I started at Chelsea. We were soaked before we got on the pitch as the rain came straight down the tunnel. they were good conditions for people like me who weren't very quick. It was nice to score and I went from there; a magnificent occasion and I wanted more of it." Kenny reveals, though, how his lengthy wait had got to him; "Many good players didn't make it or were in and out of the side and eventually drifted away. I was working my socks off and thought I was doing well but wasn't getting a break. I never even got into squads that travelled. I was getting so fed up I nearly left the club because I wasn't making any progress. Then an injury comes and, bang, McGarry throws me straight in." Fans can only thank their lucky stars......

Wolves then headed north for the first game in the new British Isles Cup. Football's new beast, sponsorship, was apparent with the Watney Mann pre-season tournament (won by Derby) and the Ford Sporting League, both in operation for the first time. The oil company, Texaco, lent its name and £100,000 to a competition involving clubs from England, Scotland, Northern Ireland and Eire who weren't current trophy holders. The English representatives were Tottenham, Albion, Stoke, Nottingham Forest, Blackpool and Wolves. Alan Smith of The People sarcastically claimed he was looking forward to; "titanic struggles between Morton and West Brom, Motherwell and Stoke, and Forfar and Airdrie". More seriously, the Sunday Telegraph's David Miller warned; "what the League has to guard against, and commendably appears to be doing so, is the danger of the tail growing until it wags the dog." John Ireland and Bill McGarry were certainly more positive when later interviewed just before the final, Ireland enthusing; "Texaco have given their whole-hearted support for the competition and we hope we can win it in its first year." McGarry wrote; "I have enjoyed the competition and it has been a great help to me."

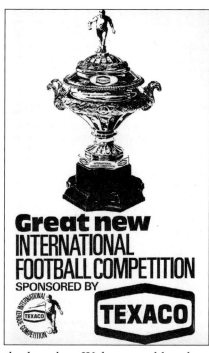

Great new
INTERNATIONAL
FOOTBALL COMPETITION
SPONSORED BY
TEXACO

In the first-round first leg in mid-September, Gould and McCalliog set Wolves on their way with a 2-1 win at Dundee.

The touch-paper was lit by a first home League win of the season, albeit one watched by below 20,000. Gould and Curran put Wolves two up before a Huddersfield team comprising Colin Dobson, Trevor Cherry and Frank Worthington cut the lead by half-time. Richards replaced Gould late on and the youngster drilled low into the corner of the South Bank goal to open his League account and secure a victory followed by a visit to Burnley, where Wolves were unbeaten in five League games. Nothing changed as McCalliog, Dougan and Gould set up a 3-2 win.

Before the next League game, a tedious 0-0 draw with Dundee did nothing to whet the appetites of the 13,042 present. It would not be the last time Wolves would make progress in the Texaco Cup as a result of superior away form. The first Saturday in October saw the visit of a Manchester United team beginning to live on the memory of their European Cup triumph over two and a half years earlier. Gould won a place in the hearts of the Molineux faithful with a hat-trick that earned a third successive three-goal League win. He had scored in all of them. On the same Saturday, one former and one future Wolves player teamed up to earn a place in folklore with the 'donkey kick' goal for Coventry against Everton. Willie Carr recalls it as a case of practice making perfect as he gripped the ball between his ankles before flicking it up for Ernie Hunt to volley home - a goal thankfully televised on Match of the Day and shown over and over again; "One of our coaches, Bill Asprey, had picked up ideas at Lilleshall. We'd tried it at Spurs the week before and Huntie nearly hit the clock behind the goal. Luckily, when Match of the Day were there, filming in colour, we scored."

In another instance of déjà vu, Wolves' fourth win in a row came at Southampton, only the second time this had happened since the return to Division One. The previous four in a row had also been completed at The Dell a year earlier. Victory had seemed distant when Mike Channon put the Saints one up after only 30 seconds but Wagstaffe equalised with a fine left-foot strike. When Dougan used his left to slide home under the advancing Eric Martin, winning suddenly felt ridiculously easy for the Molineux men. The following Monday, saw a full-strength Wolves squad turn out to honour Ron Flowers in a testimonial match. A memorable appetiser to the main event was a short nostalgic recreation of the traditional pre-season friendlies of the Cullis era. Bill Slater,

Billy Wright, Johnny Hancocks and Jimmy Mullen were among the greats turning out for the Colours, who lost 3-2 to a Whites team containing Norman Deeley, Eddie Clamp, Ted Farmer and Peter Broadbent. In what was a fabulous experience for those too young to have enjoyed such stars in their heyday, Joe Gardiner, Dennis Wilshaw and Malcolm Finlayson joined in the fun as match officials. In the main game, Flowers wore no 6 for the Wolves XI and duly scored in a hugely enjoyable 8-4 win over an England XI boasting Gordon Banks, Jimmy Armfield, Ray Wilson, Bobby Moore, Jimmy Greaves and Geoff Hurst among a smattering of local players.

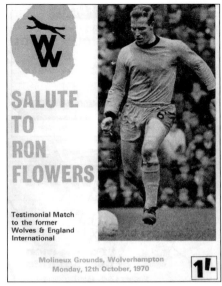

SALUTE TO RON FLOWERS

Testimonial Match to the former Wolves & England International

Molineux Grounds, Wolverhampton
Monday, 12th October, 1970

1/-

Back in the League, Wolves' first-day conquerors Newcastle were dispatched 3-2 from Molineux in what was Derek Parkin's 124th successive first-team game. Wyn Davies sidefooted the Geordies ahead but they were soon pegged back by Mike Bailey's first of the season. In a captivating second half, Wolves stormed the South Bank end and Gould slid them ahead. Despite a Holsgrove headed own goal, Wolves were not to be denied and victory was assured by another Wagstaffe strike. Wolves were now on the fringes of the top six and many of the 24,803 present were beginning to believe that sustainable progress was being made. A midweek visit to Morton pitched Wolves against Albion's round-one Texaco Cup masters but a Gould double and one from the Doog saw Wolves win in a canter. They returned home to achieve a similar margin of victory over Manchester City, Joe Mercer's men, arriving in third place and with only one defeat in 12, being dispatched by a Dougan brace and McCalliog penalty.

Wolves headed to Anfield full of hope, in sixth place but level on 18 points with two other teams, three ahead of Liverpool. As a writer said in the Anfield Review; "Wolves, renowned for their rampant attacking displays in the past, are back on the goal standard. A run of nine games without defeat, including six successive victories, has transformed what looked like being another miserable season into one so full of promise." Sadly, Wolves fell 2-0 at a habitually unlucky ground and it would be 1984 before the League win of 1950 would next be repeated. Tommy Smith converted a penalty while Wolves were denied one of their own when Ray Clemence seemed to bundle Gould over. To rub salt into the wounds, Alun Evans secured the points for Liverpool. The Wanderers still appeared to be suffering a hangover when Morton beat them 2-1 in the second leg of the Texaco Cup. Although inspired by an ageing Bobby Collins and having a young Joe Jordan, the Scots still lost 4-2 on aggregate.

The first Saturday of November saw Wolves firmly back on track when almost 40,000 packed Molineux to see Albion beaten 2-1. It seemed John McAlle had scored his first Wolves goal when he struck a screamer from the edge of the area into the South Bank net, only to be thwarted by a linesman who spotted Hibbitt in an offside position by the corner flag. Munro shared his partner's disappointment; "John never scored a League goal but, against Albion, he hit this left-foot shot from 35 yards. I said, 'John, no, no, no!' It never left the ground and went past Jim Cumbes straight into the corner, beautiful, straight as a die. What a goal and the ref gave Kenny offside on the left wing. I couldn't believe John's luck." Cumbes soon helped Waggy's corner into his own net and, although Graham Lovett equalised in the second half, the Doog swooped with the winner. The Irishman must have particularly enjoyed presenting his 'Weekend Tomorrow' programme on Radio Birmingham the following Friday.

A week later, fourth-placed and free-scoring Wolves travelled to lowly West Ham. Relying on Dickie Davies and ITV's World of Sport for news on a wet, dark afternoon, was almost unbearable as an early Jimmy Mac goal was wiped out by a strong reply that left the home side 3-1 up with ten minutes left. McCalliog and Gould somehow hauled Wolves level but, although they had taken 19 points out of 24 and scored 28 goals in the process, the side were in a mini-stutter - as shown when leaders Leeds swept into a 3-1 half- time Molineux lead. Curran's goal narrowed the gap but failed to prevent a first home defeat since August 22. A visit to Crystal Palace saw Curran earn a point against a team who had held second-placed Arsenal in their previous game, then Wolves travelled to the Brandywell Stadium in Belfast's troubled Bogside for an afternoon Texaco Cup semi-final first leg. Derry had overcome Limerick and Shamrock Rovers to reach this stage but a Gould header won a tricky tie.

In the same week, Hibbitt was selected for England under-23s against Wales at Wrexham; "I won only this one under-23 cap, which was disappointing, but, from a personal point of view, I was just happy to be playing for Wolves. That was my first concern. I was later picked for an England B tour but broke my ankle and missed out. The first Saturday in December saw Blackpool lose to a Terry Alcock own goal in a dismal Molineux clash that made many wish they had opted to go Christmas shopping. The programme for the game showed a table of spending by Division One clubs on transfers over two years. It pointed out that £4.6m had been invested at an average of £209,000 per club. Wolves were the highest spenders on £336,000, with champions-to-be Arsenal and runners-up Leeds way down on £174,000 and £180,000.

Bad weather put off the Texaco Cup second leg and, amazingly, it would not be played until March 23. However, Munro and Dougan faced each other in a Scotland v Northern Ireland game the former remembers; "I got the ball on my chest on the edge of our box and just waltzed past Dougan. He chased me for 15 yards and just hacked me down. I said, 'What are you bloody doing, we're playing at Arsenal on Saturday'. He said, 'There are no friends in this game' The Doog had the last laugh. We got beat

1-0. He had a right foot shot and I was right behind it. I could see it was going out for a throw until it hit John Grieg's heel and went into the other corner."

At Highbury, goals by John Radford and George Graham overshadowed a Dougan header and gave eventual double winners Arsenal victory. Wolves gleaned a hard-won 0-0 draw at Tottenham on the last Saturday before Christmas, when Steve Daley remembers Bill McGarry giving him a taste of the big time; "I used to love to play. Even when I was in the first-team squad and the reserves had a midweek game, I'd ask if I could play. Bill used to give you an introduction to the first team as the skip boy. It was at White Hart Lane that me and Peter Eastoe took the skips to the dressing room and helped Sammy Chung by getting all the strips and boots out."

The last action of 1970 was at Molineux in a Boxing Day fixture watched by just over 30,000 and memorable both for the quality of football and the snow on the pitch. A Doog double saw off champions Everton as my family kept warm and in favour with the constabulary on the South Bank by sharing coffee heavily laden with whisky. The goals were scored at the far end, the first theatrically slid in from a Gould pass and the second a carefully placed header past the prone Andy Rankin. Wolves entered the New Year in sixth, 12 points off the top but just a win away from third-placed Chelsea.

The day after New Year's Day was more dark and dank than cold and crisp but the fact it was FA Cup round-three day meant expectation was high if muted by the Ibrox disaster that left 66 dead and over 200 injured. Visitors Norwich were up against Hugh

Bobby Gould leads the celebrations after Derek Dougan's second goal against Everton on Boxing Day.

Curran, a man whose £60,000 transfer two years earlier was still the record fee paid to the East Anglians. Wearing white shirts in contrast to the red of the Canaries, Wolves were awarded a sixth minute penalty when Clive Payne palmed over a Dougan header. Such offences didn't bring red cards then but McCalliog duly converted the spot kick. Two minutes later, ex-Albion winger Ken Foggo established a parity that remained until just after half-time when Hibbitt dived to head in a Bailey cross. Roaring towards the North Bank in an attacking frenzy, Wolves made the tie safe. Hibbitt crashed a shot against the bar for Gould to head in, then Kevin Keelan did well to deny McCalliog but Gould was again the beneficiary via the post. The scoring ended with McCalliog deflecting in a shot by Bernard Shaw, although there was still time for Foggo to miss a penalty.

Early 1971 brought a national postal strike that rendered mom and dad almost penniless. But somehow money was found to get me to every home game despite their dependence on food parcels from other family members. Wolves' confidence was sky-high, as shown by a splendid 2-1 victory at Derby to avenge the Rams' August goal fest at Molineux. Inside two minutes, Ron Webster pushed the Doog just outside the area. Jimmy Mac ran over the ball, Hibbitt squared and Shaw's shot was deflected past Colin Boulton for his first Wolves goal. Derby levelled in the second half when Munro conceded a penalty but with little more than a minute left, Gould flashed in the winner. Elation at the result was cut short by the news Jim Marshall had died. He had been an active fan for over 60 years, a director for 20 and a former chairman. In this light, the squandering of a point in a 0-0 home draw with Coventry hardly seemed important. Holsgrove remembers Mr Marshall with great affection; "He was a really tough old man. He would shake your hand and almost crush it. His advice to me was; 'Any time Woolworth's shares are under £1, laddie, buy 'em, you'll make money.' He would keep checking, 'Have you bought them yet?'" Later that season, ex-secretary and general manager Jack Howley, at Wolves for 45 years, also passed away.

The FA Cup resumed with a quick return to the Baseball Ground - a quagmire after torrential rain. Munro remembers; "It was a dump, the mud came up over your boots." Barry Powell recalls the unusual call his room-mate received for the tie; "We shared one room at Mrs Eagle's and at 8am that Saturday, stones were hitting the window. I looked out and saw Sammy and the bus. Hugh Curran had gone ill overnight and John was needed. I had to shout him up, then drove to the game." Alan Hinton put Derby ahead and the difficulty of Wolves' cause was summed up by the award of an indirect free-kick when Dave McKay clearly felled Gould in the area. With just ten minutes left, Richards - on for Gould - seemed to have set up a Molineux replay. Boulton tipped a Dougan header on to the bar and JR pounced to force the ball in. But, two minutes into injury-time, John O'Hare put Derby through to round five.

Dougan, meanwhile, played and scored in Northern Ireland's European Nations Cup match in Greece, while Parkin went with England in the same competition to Valetta. He never got off the bench but reflects without bitterness on whether playing for a more

Jim Marshall and Jack Howley, two fine servants who died during 1970-71.

93

'fashionable' club would have brought full honours; "It's difficult to say. If you get a successful team, you'd get three or more from it. I was with Tony Brown, Albion's only player. Bill Glazier was the only Coventry player. I was the only Wolves player. Then you'd get Reaney, Cooper

Shock for these Wolves fans

"MOLINEWS" reader **JOHN WORRALL**, of Adelaide, South Australia, has sent us the cutting reproduced on the right with this note:

"Glad to see Wolves doing so well, but we had quite a shock when we read that the Chelsea result at Molineux was a 9—1 away win.

"Wolves are TV favourites over here at the moment, for in recent weeks we have seen at least 60 mins of their games against Blackpool, Everton, Norwich and the League

U.K. SOCCER

English FA Cup, fifth round — Colchester 3, Leeds 2; Everton 1, Derby 0; Hull 2, Brentford 1; Leicester 1, Oxford 1; Liverpool 1, Southampton 0; Stoke 0, Ipswich 0; Tottenham 2, Nottingham 1; Manchester City v. Arsenal postponed to Wednesday — ground waterlogged.

English first div. — Coventry 2, Blackpool 0; Huddersfield 1, Newcastle 1; Wolverhampton 1, Chelsea 9.

and Hunter from Leeds, and Ball, Royle and Harvey from Everton. The team picked itself." Elsewhere that season, Curran and Munro played for Scotland while, back in Division One, Dougan scored twice and Birchenall once in a 2-1 defeat of Crystal Palace that set Wolves on a three-match winning run. Although the Derry tie was postponed again, the following Saturday took Wolves to Bloomfield Road and their first double with a 2-0 win over seemingly doomed Blackpool. With Arsenal next due at Molineux but still in the Cup, eliminated Wolves and Chelsea rearranged a match the Wanderers won 1-0 thanks to a second-half Hibbitt goal. Aussie Wolves fans had an awful shock, though, when a newspaper reported the result as 1-9! The win sent Wolves to Leeds in good heart, occupying third place with 36 points from 28 matches, seven behind their hosts and only four behind Arsenal. Alas, three goals from Revie's men without reply put Wolves firmly in their place and allowed Chelsea to leapfrog back over them.

Wolves' all-conquering youth side met West Ham in a quarter-final replay. With extra-time running out, it seemed Daley and Eastoe had won it, only for Watson to equalise after 119 minutes. A favourable toss of the coin meant the second replay was at Molineux and Mike Collins scored after 90 seconds to see Wolves through.

Mike O'Grady returned to first-team duty to win the home game with Liverpool but, after a visit to Malta had brought a 5 - 1 romp over Marsa, the visit of Arsenal saw

ALBION VERSUS WOLVES

ALBION NEWS SPECIAL CENTENARY MATCHDAY MAGAZINE

a 3-0 defeat that put paid to any grandiose title ambitions. A badly cut forehead for O'Grady marred a useful 0-0 draw at Manchester City but another three-match run of wins was on the way. A Gould double saw off the senior Hammers but the greatest fun was reserved for the Hawthorns on March 20 in the 100th Black Country derby. The Baggies had seen off Manchester United 4-3 in their previous home match thanks to a Tony Brown hat-trick and they went in one up through a George McVitie strike. In front of 35,716, though, a shot and flying header from Curran on 52 and 58 minutes turned things around, only for Albion's 'Bomber' to level on the hour. Just two minutes later, Bailey beat John Wile to restore the lead, then Cumbes failed to

Mike Bailey fires Wolves' third goal past Baggies centre-half John Wile in the exciting derby victory at The Hawthorns.

hold a Curran shot and Gould forced the rebound home.

Three days later, the long-awaited Texaco Cup second leg saw Derry buried 4-0 under goals by Parkin, O'Grady, Curran and Gould. The fourth win and third 'four for' sent Nottingham Forest away point-less, courtesy of a Curran hat trick and a single strike by Gould. Striving to reach their first Youth Cup final since 1961-62, Wolves came back to Molineux two down after the first leg at Highbury. Watched by over 7,000, the youngsters gave everything, only to be thwarted by centre-half Brendan Batson and finished off by a Paul Davies strike on 41 minutes. The team was; Kevin Charlton; Geoff Palmer, Alan Stephens; Doug Devlin, Richard Dams, John Rutter; Eddie Gould, Alan Sunderland, Peter Eastoe, Mike Collins, Steve Daley. Substitute Barry Powell. Palmer remembers; "The team did well that year. The likes of Stevie Daley, Alan Sunderland, Barry Powell and Peter Eastoe were in and I was lucky to play in the semi-final. Then, in July, 1971, I got asked to sign as an apprentice on my 17th birthday, another big thrill."

Daley adds; "We had five teams; the first team, the reserves, the West Midlands League, the Midland Combination and Youth teams. Alan Sunderland, Dougie Devlin, Barry Powell, Peter Eastoe and me all made the step up together. We all played in the same youth team who became the Midland Combination side, that then became the West Midland League and reserve line-ups. We all progressed that way." Powell recalls how vital the youngsters were to McGarry; "He had the foresight to send us all to college. I was enrolled on two courses, went twice and decided I wasn't happy. At 15 years of age, I knocked McGarry's door, saying, 'I don't like college, I want to be a professional footballer.' He said, 'Son, I can't tell you at 15 whether you'll be a professional footballer, neither can you. If you don't want to go to college, it's your f***in look-out, not mine.' Out I went. He just said it how it was."

The season threatened to peter out for the senior side when the thrashing of Forest was followed by a single-goal loss at Stoke. However, Wolves bounced back with their first win at Goodison Park since February, 1960. Henry Newton gave Everton the lead but a minute before half-time Bailey flashed a powerful shot past Rankin, leaving Gould to drive home a left-footer to claim both points. A 1-0 reverse at Old Trafford dragged Wolves back into fourth but cup fever took over on April 14 as they visited Tynecastle for the first leg of the Texaco Cup final. Don Ford gave Hearts the lead after six minutes, but two from Curran and one from Bailey stunned most of the 26,000 crowd to give Wolves an iron grip on the trophy.

Mom and dad had scrimped and saved for a long time to send me on a school trip to Paris at Easter. It was my first time abroad but I was less grateful than I should have been as it meant me missing my first home match since 1966. In my absence, and at the time I believed because of it, Mike Channon mugged Wolves to give Southampton a win. I calculated that he scored at more or less the same time that the hovercraft sped us back into Pegwell Bay, Kent. This was the day that a clearly offside goal by Jeff Astle saw Albion virtually end Leeds' title chances and spark off a riot that saw Elland Road closed for games at the start of the following season.

The Saints setback would cost Wolves third spot but Curran and McCalliog scored at Leeds Road to beat Huddersfield and record away League win no 9. Wolves had two home games left to overhaul Spurs, the first a disappointing 0-0 draw with Ipswich that was preceded by a youth game against Grasshoppers of Zurich. Daley and Eastoe starred for Wolves and were duly called up for England youths against Spain at Luton. Daley went on to play in the UEFA World Youth Cup in Czechoslovakia and recalls; "We won that cup, beating Poland in the final. Bobby Parker, Mick McGuire, Trevor Francis and Peter Eastoe also played." The last game of the season saw Dougan return to see off doomed Burnley. He ended an hour of frustration by heading Waggy's corner past Tony Waiters. Steve Kindon was one of the brightest Burnley players on show but thankfully made a terrible hash of a good

		Home			Goals		Away			Goals		
	P	W	D	L	F	A	W	D	L	F	A	Pts
Arsenal	42	18	3	0	41	6	11	4	6	30	23	65
Leeds United	42	16	2	3	40	12	11	8	2	32	18	64
Tottenham H.......	42	11	5	5	33	19	8	9	4	21	14	52
WOLVES	**42**	**13**	**3**	**5**	**33**	**22**	**9**	**5**	**7**	**31**	**32**	**52**
Liverpool	42	11	10	0	30	10	6	7	8	12	14	51
Chelsea	42	12	6	3	34	21	6	9	6	18	21	51
Southampton	42	12	5	4	35	15	5	7	9	21	29	46
Manchester United ..	42	9	6	6	29	24	7	5	9	36	42	43
Derby County	42	9	5	7	32	26	7	5	9	24	28	42

second-half chance. As usual, Phil Morgan found the words to sum up a tentative if ultimately successful Wolves performance; "When it came to unlocking the doors leading to European football, Wolves nervously fumbled for the key after moving so confidently up the garden path."

It was only about prestige but Tottenham succeeded at the second attempt in snatching third place from Wolves on goal difference. On May 3, they lost at home to a Ray Kennedy goal that secured the double for their bitter rivals Arsenal. But, two days later, they picked up two points with a 1-0 win over Stoke. They had three fewer wins than Wolves and, had victories then carried three points, the Wanderers would have finished three points clear in third. However, 52 points was never going to be a title-winning haul as it was 13 behind the Gunners. The 64 goals scored was useful but the 54 conceded were their undoing.

Given the high finish, the most amazing statistics must be the mere 18,000 gates for the last two home games. Since the visit of Arsenal on March 2, only once had an attendance crept above 25,000. The Central League team's seventh place was their best for four seasons, with Richards scoring 17 in 20 games, a feat in itself since he had been named as first-team substitute no fewer than 19 times. He admitted to becoming increasingly frustrated at not playing and had a word with McGarry. This famously backfired when he found himself out of favour for a couple of months and wondered whether he would get another chance, feeling that; "McGarry saw it as an opportunity to teach me a lesson." In the absence of regular contributions from JR on the striking front that season, four players hit double figures; McCalliog 10, Dougan 13, Curran 20, and Gould 24, and qualification for the UEFA Cup guaranteed Wolves a first European adventure in over a decade. Those who would miss out on the experience included John Holsgrove, off to Sheffield Wednesday after 202 appearances, and Bertie Lutton and John Oldfield, who left for Brighton and Crewe respectively.

All that remained was the completion of Wolves' quest for their first piece of silverware for 11 years. The second leg of the Texaco Cup final was on the same night as Tottenham v Arsenal. Although 3-1 down from the first leg, Hearts were encouraged by having overturned a similar deficit against Burnley in round one at Tynecastle. Apart from the first ten minutes of a very nervy night, it was all Hearts and a defensive slip allowed George Fleming in for an easy goal on 25 minutes. The Wanderers held on for a 3-2 aggregate win but, despite the healthy 28,462 turn-out, there was an understandably flat reception for Mike Bailey and his boys as they climbed the steps to the Waterloo Road Directors' Box to receive the trophy and medals from the Managing Director and Chief Executive of Texaco, Carl D Hall. Silverware won on the back of a home defeat was hard to enthuse about, summed up by the Express & Star

Hughie Curran and John McAlle arm in arm in celebration of Wolves' Texaco Cup final triumph over Hearts.

headline, 'Wolves engine stalls.'

Next day, Wolves set off for six days in Israel, where they tackled a national XI containing nine of their Mexico World Cup team. Parkin gave Wolves the lead mid-way through the first half and, after the hosts equalised, Walker and then Gould secured a 3-1 victory. McGarry enthused about the fringe benefits of the visit to Tel Aviv; "It's a glorious spot, the hotel is on the beach and the sunshine is beautiful." In 1971-72, he and his team would become accustomed to regular trips, often in less temperate climes.

1971-72: The Great Adventure

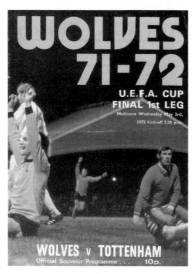

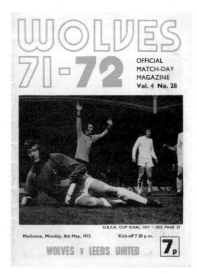

The Official Wolves Supporters' Club published its third newsletter in June, 1971 and offered best wishes to Bill McGarry and his playing staff for the new seaon. Little could they have known quite what lay ahead in a campaign that certainly rated as one of the favourites for a Pensnett lad who had made it into the fourth year (now Year 10). An unswerving interest in the Wanderers' exploits could be cited as reason for my lack of progress in Mr. Stones' Maths classes, a strange thing really because I was red-hot when numeracy skills were required to unravel the complexities of goal average in the League and away goals in Europe. A key focus of the newsletter was the loss of what it called the 'Molineux Roar'. This proved to be an interesting choice of subject given the gradual decline in gates, a trend that even the exciting experiences of 1971-72 would fail to arrest. John Ireland's message for the season struck what some may have felt was a wildly optimistic note; "We are eagerly looking forward to our games in the UEFA Cup. Our younger players should derive great benefit from the experience which, we all hope, will enable us to play in the European Champions' Cup or even the European Cup Winners Cup next season."

With injury sidelining Mike Bailey for the friendly against Groningen (it was destined to be that kind of season for the influential skipper), his replacement Danny Hegan scored twice in the second half to secure an easy victory. The visit of Tottenham attracted more than 30,000, who saw Wolves sporting trendy v-necked collars. Paul Walker was surprisingly chosen at no 4 ahead of Hegan and a goal from Bobby Gould close to half-time and a Jim McCalliog penalty with less than 20 minutes left, seemed to have secured both points. Wolves' dominance had Ian Willars reporting; "The attacking formation of Derek Dougan, Bobby Gould and Dave Wagstaffe made a horrible mess of Spurs' elegant defenders." However, not long after Pat Jennings had tipped over a scorcher from Waggy, Spurs broke away to halve the deficit. Cyril

Knowles slung in a cross that Phil Parkes dropped at the feet of Martin Chivers "rather like," according to the Express & Star's Phil Morgan, "the kid in the TV commercial who grabs at the wet soap." Alan Gilzean then snatched a very late and undeserved equaliser that had home fans shaking their heads in disbelief. Sadly this would not be the only time in 1971-72 the Londoners would have this effect on them.

Worse was to come on the Tuesday. Things were promising when a moustachioed Doog powered home a superb header after only five minutes to score Wolves' first goal at Anfield since Alun Evans first caught Bill Shankly's eye in 1967. Although John Toshack and Steve Heighway revived Liverpool before half-time, Ken Hibbitt fired a fine leveller with 12 minutes left but, with time almost up, John McAlle handled to allow Tommy Smith to win the match with yet another Liverpool penalty. The end of the first week of the season saw honour restored by a valiant 0-0 draw at Huddersfield. Leeds were the opposition, having been exiled to Leeds Road as a result of spectator misconduct during the Albion game the previous April. The back four was particularly resolute, and an injury to Dougan led to another call from the bench for John Richards, his fourth against Leeds in a fledgling Division One career. Returning home and restored to round-necked shirts, Wolves were still without Dougan and Bailey for the visit of Manchester City. The match was nonetheless notable for the debut of Alan Sunderland, another from the production line of Mark Crook's 'nursery' at Wath-on-Dearne. Hibbitt and McCalliog put Wolves in command and even a late Francis Lee penalty could not create a repeat of the opening-day Molineux deflation.

Proceeding in a southerly direction across the pitch at the Molineux football ground . . . supporters from Manchester make a pre-match sortie across the pitch which ended in a return to the terraces with assistance from the arm of the law

40 held in soccer violence
Birmingham Post Reporter

The following Saturday saw in-form Manchester United welcomed to Molineux. They had accumulated seven points and were kept off the top only because newly-promoted Sheffield United had made an unlikely 100 per cent start. Although Dougan returned, Gerry Taylor deputised for Frank Munro at no 5 and Hegan had to be brought on after just 13 minutes to replace an injured McCalliog. Before kick-off, there were serious problems as United fans in the 46,000 crowd charged on to the pitch from the Molineux Hotel end in an attempt to get among the Wolves masses on the North Bank. Police toiled to regain order and made over 40 arrests. John Roberts of Kingswinford made interesting suggestions on combating hooliganism in the programme for the next home match. These included an identity card with a photograph for all supporters aged 11-21, along with playing only on Tuesday and Wednesday evenings to effectively reduce away supporters being able to travel.

Wolves fell behind as a ball whipped across the area found the chest of George Best, who fired past Taylor from 15 yards into the corner of the net. Salvation came in the unlikely form of Bernard Shaw, the full-back leaving Alex Stepney helpless with a screamer from 35 yards. It was his fourth career goal and only his second for Wolves. Speaking out after 180 bookings and four sendings-off in the first fortnight of what had been described as the 'Ref Revolution,' McGarry lamented a Wolves - United match that he felt lacked real physical edge; "It was like a Sunday School outing. There were only two tackles in the whole game. If this continues, we're all going to be out of work. You cannot play football without tackling and physical contact."

Crystal Palace were the next visitors and, having missed the first five matches, Bailey returned for his 200th League appearance and to smash a second minute winner past John Jackson. A 1-0 win at Stoke on the first Saturday in September lifted Wolves to fifth. Munro returned and Derek Parkin turned out a day after the birth of his son. Dougan was concussed in an early collision with Denis Smith and was stretchered off but even this could not derail determined Wolves. On the hour, Hegan struck his first League goal since the Albion - Liverpool game in September, 1969.

An amazing clash with Manchester City then saw Wolves contribute to their own elimination from the League Cup, although Wagstaffe blamed it on the presence at Maine Road of his sister Val. McAlle and Hegan put the visitors two up in 25 minutes, only for Wyn Davies to reduce the arrears before the interval. Just before the hour, a Parkin penalty restored the two-goal advantage that lasted until 12 minutes from time but then what Phil Morgan described as, "a Wolves nightmare" began. Colin Bell (2) and Lee scored to "bring anxiety where once was calm." The collapse must have spoiled the enjoyment of a number of players who participated in the Harry Secombe Golf Classic later that week, and Wolves certainly still appeared to be in shock when a mediocre performance saw them only share the points at home to Everton.

Wolves' UEFA Cup adventure began on September 15 with the visit of Coimbra, a university city on the Mondego River, 140 miles north east of Lisbon. No club had ever scored more than one against them over two legs in Europe, and two years earlier they had stopped Manchester City scoring over 180 minutes. Academica had finished fifth in their league, with a miserly 24 goals against in 38 games and only 26 for. We had been told in the previous programme they would run out wearing black cloaks over their all black kit. In reality, there were no cloaks and they wore a white strip! Ten years and 149 days after the previous European tie at Molineux, Wolves faced ultra-defensive opponents, and Alan Williams of the Daily Express wrote; "Wolves started it, let's hope they land another 'first' (the first Midland winners of a major European competition)." With five substitutes available, McGarry relegated Hegan and Hibbitt to the bench and reinstated Mike O'Grady for a surprise first start of the season.

Famous Hungarian official Istvan Zsolt got the tie under-way and Wolves stormed the North Bank against a stubborn rearguard action. Just before half-time, the opening

John McAlle scores the first goal of the European campaign - at home to an Academica side against whom he also netted in the return leg in Portugal.

goal came from the most unlikely source of McAlle's left foot. Then, on 62 minutes, Richards collected a pass from Sunderland to slide past keeper Melo. Near the end, the Doog ran on from an apparently offside position to ram home a deserved third. All this on the day Gould followed Don Howe to the Albion, having scored 25 goals in 50 League and cup games for Wolves. He was only the third Wolves player to move to The Hawthorns in 35 years and left Eddie as the only Gould at Molineux.

In the first of several post-Europe hangovers, Wolves headed to the north east and tamely succumbed to lowly Newcastle. In stark contrast, the visit of Nottingham Forest on the last Saturday of September was hugely entertaining, with Steve Daley starting as substitute. Wallowing in the bottom three, Forest shocked the home crowd with a goal from Ian Storey-Moore on five minutes. A Dougan double put Wolves in front by half-time but Moore set up Martin for an equaliser. With 13 minutes left, McCalliog intercepted a back pass and took the ball round Jim Barron to score and, on 88 minutes, Dougan headed home a Wagstaffe centre to complete his third hat-trick for the club.

The front of the Forest programme had wished Wolves 'Boa Sorte en Quarta Feira' (Good luck next Wednesday) and it seemed to be much-needed on a 72-degree evening when Antonio shot in off the post after only 15 minutes. In a game peppered by petty fouls and with Gerry Taylor again deputising for the injured Munro, Wolves fought their way back on 23 minutes. A long bouncing kick from Phil Parkes beat a couple of defenders, allowing the Doog to collect and round Melo in the Coimbra goal. Soon after thwarting Gervasio with a fine challenge, McAlle volleyed in a Wagstaffe corner. Having not scored in any of his first 57 games, he had now slotted three in six, all in cups. The unlucky dismissal of Hegan could not stop Wolves and Dougan completed the rout and a second hat-trick in a week with a skimmed header and a left-foot shot. Wolves were in round two amid a cascade of cushions from disenchanted home fans.

A return to League duty resulted in a 3-1 setback at Chelsea, a display summed up by Reg Drury's headline, "Weary Wolves go crashing." A week later, Southampton came to Molineux for a game watched by Eddie Hartman, the manager of Wolves' next European opponents, Den Haag. The Saints, deprived of Ron Davies, had lost at home to Arsenal after their UEFA Cup elimination against Ronnie Allen's Atletico Bilbao. Munro was again absent and Daley made his full debut at the expense of O'Grady, with substitute Hugh Curran seen for the first time that term. Daley recalls the build-up to his first full start; "After training on the Friday morning, we always had a bit of a team meeting and five or ten minutes after this, the team sheet went up, no numbers alongside. I was in the squad. Sammy said to me, 'You're in tomorrow, you've got a chance.' I phoned my mam and dad and said, 'I'm in the squad but I wouldn't come down. It'll be a wasted trip cos I ain't going to play.' Quarter to two on the Saturday and Bill comes in, names the team and I'm no 11. Mam and dad weren't there but it was still great to get changed with Mike Bailey, Derek Dougan, Frank Munro and John McAlle, and to go out in front of all those people. It was incredible."

Daley was nursed through by experienced colleagues; "They looked after me and big Phil still does! I can't remember being nervous but all the lads were saying, 'Take it easy, just make sure your first touch is a good one, make sure you win your first header and your first tackle. Get off to a good start and get the fans on your side.' I remember in the first five minutes, I was on the right for some reason, got the ball and came inside. I shot from 25 yards, not far from the post, and thought, 'That's a good start.' It gave me confidence and I went on from there." About 25 minutes later, Hegan slid Dougan in to open the scoring but Joe Kirkup soon equalised. Just after half-time, Mike Channon headed in from a quick Terry Paine free-kick, only for Dougan to level on the hour. With Curran on for the last quarter, Wolves laid siege to the Southampton goal and won a penalty when John McGrath handled with under ten minutes left. Derek Parkin hit the post but fortune smiled when referee Styles ordered a retake. This time 'Squeak' made no mistake and Daley was fed by Dougan and Hegan just before the final whistle to make it 4-2 and crown a dream debut.

Daley admits the early success was followed by frustrating periods out of the team; "Bill used to put you in and bring you out, not giving you too much of it. If Waggy was fit, I wouldn't get in on the left wing. He had an abundance of midfield players and the break for me didn't come until a few years later when we played a friendly in Belfast and Mike Bailey was injured. I stormed it in Mike's place and Bill said, 'You've saved me a lot of money, I don't need to go and buy anybody now."

In mid-October, acting manager Tommy Docherty called Munro and Curran up to the Scotland squad for the home match against Portugal but the helter-skelter season continued as weakened Wolves were soundly thrashed 4-1 at Tottenham. With Munro,

Dougan and Wagstaffe out injured, Taylor, Walker and Richards stepped in as a Bailey goal was the only cause for celebration as Wolves set off for The Hague and their UEFA Cup second-round tie. A few fans took advantage of the Wolves Development Association trip from Birmingham to Rotterdam on British European Airways at a cost of £26. The team flew on a World War II Dakota that was forced to land in the teeth of a 45mph gale. The crowd at a Zuiderpark filled to just over half of its 30,000 capacity were treated to a tense but goalless first half in which Wolves defended against a strong wind. Everyone hoped there would be no repeat of the game against the team then known as ADO on the 1967 USA tour. Although both managers then agreed the referee was hopeless, it didn't prevent Wagstaffe and his replacement Paddy Buckley being kicked out of the game in the first five minutes, and both Ernie Hunt and Dougan being sent off. A free-for-all ensued and the trainer's bucket ended up on Les Wilson's head and the game was suspended for ten minutes.

Above: Flashback to 1967 as white-shirted Derek Dougan meets his counterpart at Wolves' game v Den Haag in the USA. Below: He nets against the Dutchmen in the 1971-72 UEFA Cup.

In 1971, Richards won the ball on 61 minutes and played Dougan in to break the deadlock by rounding the keeper. Ten minutes from time, McCalliog shot against the bar and the Doog netted the rebound, then Hibbitt went on for the Scotsman and soon converted a Dougan cross, as he recalls; "One of my first kicks was to put away a pull-back from the bye-line." The home team were given faint hope when Shaw handled and Hastad converted the penalty but Wolves had a valuable cushion.

The performance was typical of Wolves' style, as Richards recalls; "We were fearless, we just didn't know what to expect. It was the unknown and we didn't worry about it at all." A soft tenth minute goal at Upton Park by Clyde Best gave West Ham both points in yet another

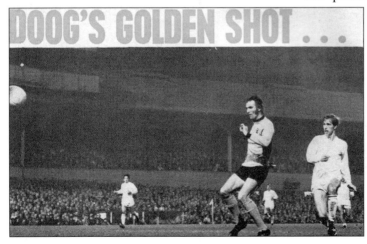

DOOG'S GOLDEN SHOT . . .

fruitless post-Europe outing and the last Saturday of October promised little better as Willie Carr gave visiting Coventry a first-half lead. The Sky Blues had Liverpool great Ian St John but ragged Wolves were saved when Munro drove into the roof of the net. Stage two of the European journey was completed on the following Wednesday with Phil Morgan reporting; 'A treble Dutch treat'. Determined at first, the visitors restricted Wolves to yet another Dougan goal in the first half but then Weimar, Mansfeld and Van Den Burch found the North Bank net in a second successive 7-1 aggregate win. A long trip to Ipswich then resulted in a fourth League defeat straight after UEFA Cup duty, this time 2-1 despite the Doog's 13th of the season.

When Derby arrived at Molineux, they sat proudly in second place with just one defeat in 16 games. Although Wolves were unbeaten at home, six away losses had kept them down in 14th. Mid-way through the first half, a familiar pattern seemed to be emerging as John O'Hare pounced to open the scoring. A hopeful cross was destined for the gloves of Parkes but McAlle unwittingly diverted the ball to O'Hare, who took an easy chance. Attacking the North Bank, Wolves mounted a comeback that promised to transform their season as, a minute before the interval, Colin Boulton spilt the ball under challenge from the Doog and Richards fired high into the net. In an exciting second half, Munro stormed forward to set up Hibbitt, whose fierce drive was parried by Boulton. A terrific scramble on the ground between Dougan and Colin Todd saw the ball squirt clear for JR to prod over the line and spark ecstatic celebrations.

Seven days later, momentum grew in a game that was my 1971-72 favourite. Although double-winning Arsenal were below Wolves in the table, they took the lead on 37 minutes courtesy of a Ray Kennedy strike. However, in a 20-minute spell after the break, they were simply taken apart by a flurry of goals that perfectly matched a November snowstorm engulfing Molineux. In Phil Morgan's words, it was; "the gayest goal spree on the ground since the 1960s." Wagstaffe set things off on 53 minutes when he cut in from the right and from 30 yards unleashed Match of the Day's goal of the

The season takes off - Richards and Wagstaffe score the opening goals against Derby (left) and Arsenal (right) respectively in November, 1971.

month. But he modestly recalls; "You don't aim for the top corner, you just aim to hit that target of 92 sq ft. How the hell Bob Wilson injured himself going for it, I'll never know. He was that knackered he must have belly-flopped and winded himself!" Wilson had to pick the ball from the net four more times thanks to shots by Hibbitt and Dougan (2) either side of the Irishman being brought down for a penalty McCalliog converted.

For Munro, it was a great achievement to keep Arsenal's strikers quiet; "Talking with John McAlle recently, we think the only pair who really got the better of us were Radford and Kennedy. I think players like Chivers and Osgood were probably better but, for some reason, I found it difficult with Radford in the air, on the ground, everywhere. To make it doubly difficult, John found it hard against Kennedy." Percy Young sums up the main elements of a glorious afternoon; "To some extent, it was a three-sided contest, with two courageous teams pitting their skills not only against each other, but also the elements. There was swirling snow throughout." Mysteriously, the Beeb resists ever showing this match, clearly a conspiracy in its determination to show London teams victorious over Wolves at every available opportunity.

Looking back, Richards fully appreciates Waggy's contribution; "On his day, he was the best winger in the country. You gave him the ball, ran and knew it was going to drop in a space in front of you. He could beat people easily and his crossing was superb. The Doog and I had the success we did because of Dave on the left and Ken Hibbitt on the right." Dougan wholeheartedly agreed; "Waggy was phenomenal, he made all the bullets. I just told David where to put it and he did. In the last 30 years or so, I haven't seen anybody in British football do what Waggy did. To go down that wing at speed, stop so quickly that the full-back almost went into the crowd and then cross. There were things he did on a pitch that nobody could emulate." Carr greatly admires Waggy's work; "He was built like a stick but could strike the ball 60 yards. He was one of the best left-sided players in the game." Barry Powell agrees; "Waggy could be facing the touchline and look as though he was shaping to bend the ball down the line. But then he would chop it back across the width of the pitch to Kenny on the right. How he did it, I'll never know. There was nothing of him but he was a superb striker of the ball with his left foot." Daley mirrors this; "Can you imagine a player with Kenny's right foot and Waggy's left? There was Waggy ten yards inside his own half on the left and pinging it diagonally straight to Ken's feet. Kenny would do the same from right to left. It was unbelievable to watch." Dave is less effusive; "People say, 'You used to put the ball on Dougan's head.' I didn't. I looked at him and he looked at me. There were five or six yards in front of him and I knocked the ball into that space. He read what I was going to do, I read what he was going to do and he'd run on and get in a header. It was the same with John Richards when he came in."

Unchanged Wolves headed to East Germany to face Carl Jeiss Jena in the UEFA Cup on the last Wednesday in November. Accompanied by club historian Dr. Percy Young, the party landed at frozen Erfurt airport to find an inch of snow covering the pitch at the Ernst Abbe Stadium 25 miles away in the shadow of the Kearnberg Mountains. Parkes recalls a less than welcoming side to the locals on a pre-match shopping expedition; "I'd seen these German goalkeeping gloves on TV (Sepp Maier was the first to wear them. Big gloves, long shorts, everybody laughed). I went into a shop and they wouldn't sell me any. They knew who we were and wouldn't even show us them!" But this gamesmanship couldn't save the home team from defeat and, in the days well before Sky Sports and Radio Five Live commentaries, I relied on a combination of radio updates and Express & Star telexed reports to confirm that, "Ice cool Wolves skated it." Things were settled on 12 minutes with another goal from Richards. McCalliog crossed for the young striker to direct a header goalwards that Hans Grapenthin could only palm out but Richards reacted first to squeeze the rebound inside the post. Hibbitt recalls that he almost doubled the lead; "I scored with a header, believe it or not, but it was disallowed for offside. I've got a picture at home of me climbing to head it down. In those days, you didn't get the benefit of the doubt, second phase and all that. It was the right decision but I did score at home against them."

John Richards sets off in celebration of his winner in Jena.

THE HAPPY WANDERERS RETURNED FROM EAST GERMANY WITH SNOW ON THEIR STUDS AND GIFTS OF SLEDGES FOR THE YOUNGSTERS

For the fifth time, Wolves returned from Europe to League action and, for the first time, they won. Against an Albion team including Gould, an unchanged team prevailed 3-2 at The Hawthorns to end a run of five away losses and climb to ninth. The Evening Mail's Bob Blackburn wrote; "Wolves may not be the most consistent team in the League but in these parts at least they are the most successful and certainly the most colourful." In the build-up, several players had been laid low with stomach problems, with Parkin, Shaw and Taylor bed-ridden. But McCalliog put Wolves ahead on 31 seconds and, when a

Richards shot was beaten back out by John Osborne, Waggy drove in a second. Although a Tony Brown penalty brought the Baggies back into contention, a brilliant run and shot from Richards made it 3-1 before a Gould goal made for an uncomfortable last ten minutes. It was Albion's fourth successive loss and they fell into the bottom two with Crystal Palace.

The good run seemed to be continuing when Dougan and Richards combined after half an hour to put Wolves one up at home to Huddersfield but the display dropped off so alarmingly that First Division debutant Terry Dolan levelled with four minutes left. As Phil Morgan wrote; "Carl Zeiss would not have recognised them in this mood." Waggy revealed that ten squad members won £47 on the pools that weekend and might have won the jackpot had they backed themselves for a score draw. Richards' reward for his excellent November performances was the Midland Footballer of the Month award. A return to UEFA action saw the team's fine form regained as a Hibbitt volley and Dougan header within 35 minutes effectively killed off the tie with Jena. The Irishman fired in a cross-shot just before the hour for his eighth goal in six games, overhauling Peter Broadbent's club record seven in 12 from 1958 to 1961. Wolves had also equalled the British record of six straight European wins but this counted for little as they squandered another point, this time at Bramall Lane. An Eddie Colquhoun own goal and Richards shot gave them a 2-0 lead but they let Sheffield United off the hook.

The pre-Christmas home game was against Stoke City, who kept Wolves out for almost an hour, due largely to the genius of Gordon Banks. A goal from Dougan and an Alan Bloor concession eventually saw the Molineux men home but the match is probably best remembered for the compassion shown by the PFA chairman to spare his opponent a caution when Terry Conroy tripped him from behind. The last game of 1971 was at Leicester on Boxing Day in front of almost 38,000. Mum, dad, uncles, aunties and I were among the many locked out of a 2-1 victory, set up by goals from Munro and Dougan. The Foxes were then drawn as Wolves' third-round FA Cup opponents and were to avenge this loss more than once later that season.

New Year's Day saw Wolves rise to sixth with goals by Parkin and Richards in a win over Newcastle. Impressive though this was, it paled into insignificance compared with what followed. Although table-topping Manchester United were without George Best after Frank O'Farrell's decision to punish him for 'extra curricular activities,' Wolves were simply irresistible. In the United Review, Peter Slingsby credited Bill McGarry with trigerring; "a new and exciting era in the history of Wolverhampton Wanderers," and, as confirmation, the Doog put Wanderers ahead on 20 minutes when hesitant defending allowed McCalliog to break away on the right towards the Paddock End. Although the cross was overhit, Hibbitt retrieved it and lofted into the box for Dougan to leap highest and power a perfect header into Alex Stepney's top right-hand corner. Nine minutes later, Munro took a free-kick well inside his own half and found Dougan 20 yards out. Richards seized on the flick, shielding the ball from his marker

WOLVES BURST CHAMPIONSHIP RACE WIDE OPEN

WOLVES burst the First Division championship wide open on Saturday, beating Manchester United 3-1 at Old Trafford.
The Wanderers are now only four points behind the league leaders

before clipping a marvellous rising half-volley into the home net. Although the Irishman had to be carried off on 51 minutes, substitute Curran was brought down in the penalty area and McCalliog converted the kick. A Sammy McIlroy consolation could not prevent Wolves' first win at Old Trafford since 1961-62 and they were now just four points off the top and beginning to be seen as genuine title contenders. The big-time dream continued with the UEFA Cup draw pitching them against mighty Juventus.

In the League, this was as good as it got. For Richards; "playing-wise, results-wise and success-wise", this was the start of the best three or four years in his career. He adds; "If just nine of our team played to their capacity, we could beat anyone. We had very good players in key positions." Parkin agrees; "In a way, it passed me by. It was a great experience because we were playing against big opposition but we had some really class players." In trying to fathom out why greater success eluded them, JR argues that half a dozen teams at that time could win something, and Wolves needed just one or two quality additions to give that extra edge. Some bad luck with injuries exposed the lack of quality cover at key times, especially when the inspirational Bailey was lost for long spells, as in early 1972.

Parkin summarises his absence; "Mike was the best skipper I ever played under. He was very under-rated and very unlucky with Alan Mullery in the England squad. I thought Mike was far better." Carr, signed later, agrees; "Manny should have played more for England." Parkin continues; "Mike wasn't dirty but he was a barrel-chested guy and, when he hit you, he hit you. He simply accelerated into everything, there were no half measures and if the ball was there to be won, he'd win it. I'd say that with Mike out, one or two players didn't play. He inspired players." Munro agrees; "Mike was special, a top, top player. I hate it when people say he was a tremendous captain. He was but he was so much more. He was one of the best I ever played with, a good passer of the ball." Powell agrees; "Mike was out of the McGarry mould and would let you know on the field. His tackles were frightening. Forget about Frank and John McAlle, Bailey was the one. When Bailey hit you, you knew it. Everything went into the tackle. He was a superb captain and he'd organise on the field and off, let you know exactly what you were doing." Steve Kindon agrees; "Mike was the best midfield player I ever played with. Everyone says, 'What a great captain' but first of all he was a fabulous player. Mike Brearley was a fabulous cricket captain and that got him his place in the side, not his batting. Don't make that mistake with Mike Bailey. Bobby Moore was a great player then a great captain and I use the word 'great' very sparingly. Mike was a fabulous player, full stop. By the way, he was also a great captain!"

Another young midfielder, Daley, confirms what it was like to play alongside him; "I don't think he's ever been replaced as captain. He was always very professional, a hard worker, disciplined and he'd give you great encouragement. He wouldn't ask you to do something he wouldn't do. He'd always lead by example. Whether or not he was having a bad game didn't matter, he kept on to the lads to keep going. He'd never think, 'Sod you mate, I'm having a bad game, I've got to concentrate on myself. I remember playing Leicester at Molineux and Keith Weller was taking the mickey out of a few people on the right wing. Mike said to Waggy, 'When he gets the ball around the half-way line, show him inside because he'll not come inside again after that.' Waggy stopped him going down the line and Weller came inside. He must have gone 6feet in the air and came down and landed flat on his back. Mike got up and just walked away. I thought, I'm glad I'm playing with you, not against you.'"

Hibbitt also remembers Bailey with the greatest respect; "He had a presence about him in midfield. I always felt that because I was a youngster, he was protecting me. He was my bodyguard, gave me great cover and allowed me to go forward. He covered and worked across midfield, up and down and he could pass. He had this pigeon chest, so he could put his whole body weight into tackles. I know because when I was in the reserves, I used to wear no 4 - Mike's shirt in the first team. He saw me as a threat and at Castlecroft in one practice match when it was frosty, he came in and the next thing I knew, I was on the floor. I was seeing stars and he picked me up, saying; 'If you want my shirt, you're going to have to get it from me.' I didn't really know what he meant but we got on really well after that. He was a magnificent captain, the presence he had. He was the best captain I played under and I told him that."

Carr recalls that Mike never suffered fools gladly and was even told off recently at a golf tournament for getting his drink wrong. Dougan wrote at the time; "Wolves had the potential for the championship, which has been denied not through lack of effort or imagination but through injuries to key men at crucial times. Remember our unbeaten run of 12 or 13 games in 1971-72? We might have gone for the championship but for Mike Bailey's injury against Leicester in an FA Cup tie and my hamstring injury at Manchester United." However, his later reflections were more critical of other players and the manager; "One player doesn't make a team but one player can make a hell of a difference. Tragically, ten guys can carry one bloke for one game or a few games but not for 40 games. A football team is made up of two ingredients, workers and players, and a manager should be able to get workers to play and players to work."

A week after Old Trafford, Wolves took on Leicester at Molineux in the Cup, the afternoon beginning promisingly when McGarry reeived the Bell's Manager of the Month award. In congratulating him, Billy Wright argued that the boss had been right to remove "ancient relics" from Molineux; "Never mind how sentimental you may feel about the golden days, I can tell you of the effect the constant reminder can have on the current players. I went through it all at Highbury, confronted by the glorious deeds of past Arsenal teams." On the pitch, McCalliog scored after 14 minutes but, already deprived of Dougan, Wolves lost Bailey mid-way through the first half to a groin injury that would keep him out for much of the rest of the season. An inspirational performance from Peter Shilton prevented any further addition to the score and John Farrington returned to haunt his ex-employees with a 76th minute leveller. The replay took place the following Wednesday and Farrington scored again to snuff out the Cup dream. In examining the way Wolves fell away that season, Percy Young cited; "An inconsistency bred from a marriage between joie de vivre and fearful carelessness."

Although the Doog returned, he was unable to influence a 0-0 draw with Liverpool and, a week later, Francis Lee scored a hat-trick to set up a 5-2 thrashing at Manchester City. Neither a Richards double nor the news the Social Club had been awarded the Club of the Year title for the second time in three seasons could lighten the gloom suddenly descending. It seemed to match the fact that industrial action by miners brought black-outs lasting of up to nine hours in parts of the country. The weather saw to it that no League games were played between the end of January and February 12 and, in addition to fielding a full-strength team in the reserves against Aston Villa, Bill McGarry took his team away for some match practice.

At the end of January, Wolves won 9-0 against Jersey on a near-frozen pitch at St. Helier's Springfield Stadium. McCalliog struck four and Dougan two, with Curran and Hegan loaned out to the opposition for the second half. The Doog then earned a draw against PAOK in a rather warmer Athens. The visit of West Ham brought the first home win since New Year's Day and the first in all since the glory day at Old Trafford. Richards volleyed the only goal on 63 minutes and, two and a half years after taking his 'A' levels in Warrington, was reckoned by McGarry to be rated in the £100,000 class. Two draws then followed, the first scoreless at Coventry, the second 2-2 against Ipswich in which the unbeaten home record was preserved by a last-minute McCalliog

Award time for Bill McGarry - but it seemed fewer fans wanted to see his Wolves team.

penalty. A 2-1 loss at Derby completed a miserable run and, in a season that saw the last but one 50,000 crowd at Molineux, a local newspaper reported that average home crowds compared unfavourably with previous seasons or even those of Third Division champions-elect Villa. Only 26,852 saw the home game against West Ham while Villa attracted 48,110 for the visit of Bournemouth the same day.

In early March, Wolves put their miserable form behind them and flew to Turin to continue their UEFA campaign. Richards sees the early rounds as; "fairly low-key but, after Juventus, people began to take note of our achievements. Interest was growing and growing." Daley recalls wonderful times; "The trips to Italy and Hungary were fantastic. The older players, Jimmy Mac, Mike O'Grady, Bernard Shaw, Parkes and Munro, looked after us." John Charles travelled to Turin as 'guide, philosopher and friend' to share his knowledge of the players, language and city. Fondly known to the locals as Signor Charlo and warmly applauded wherever he went, he proved invaluable as an ally. Parkes recalls McGarry's inspired idea of taking the great Welshman; "He pulled a masterstroke. No-one gave us a chance over there but John was a God in Italy, especially at Juventus. Bill took him as a goodwill gesture and they idolised him. He took us shopping and we even got discount in the shops."

Daley remembers he and Sunderland accompanying Charles on one outing; "He took us into town. We were only young kids and wanted the gear, some Italian shoes. Everywhere we went, people were coming out of shops, putting their bags down in the street and clapping him as he walked by. He was so unassuming but, if he'd wanted, he could have had anything in that town. I was going to say, 'Can you get us two suits please?' I was only joking." Bailey agreed; "Mr McGarry's idea to take my idol as an interpreter was inspired. When we got to the stadium, the fans couldn't believe their eyes. I haven't seen hero worship like it but, modestly, John just waved his hand as the Queen might and walked through the crowd. We went into the dressing room, where the kit man who had looked after John's boots when he played there bent down and kissed his feet. The affection was so great that when we went on the pitch, the whole crowd rose chanting 'Carlo! Carlo!' We felt like the home team and it lifted us so much. I was injured and couldn't play but it was a privilege to sit on the bench with him, a wonderful man and a great, great player." Home officials presented Wolves players with a 'Juventus Primo Amore' (First Love) book containing photos and long-playing record as well as a leather-bound case. McAlle showed me his copy, signed by Charles, and comments; "We played so well in those games. The players were very together on the trips and knew we would give anyone a good game." Hibbitt adds; "Name-wise, Juventus was the best match in that run. Playing against the likes of Anastasi and the blonde bombshell Haller was a remarkable sensation."

Top of the Italian League and losing Fairs Cup finalists to Leeds in 1971, Juve had beaten Aberdeen in the previous round. As well as Bailey, a knee injury robbed Wolves of Parkin and there was a doubt over Dougan. Parkes and Daley recall an amusing incident involving Charles on match-day morning; "We were training. Juventus had one half of the pitch, we had the other. A lot of people were watching, as they did every day there. The Doog got a slight strain and John said, 'Come on, I'll walk you back to the treatment area.' They passed these supporters and everyone stood, clapping and shouting. Derek waved but Big John said, 'I don't want to embarrass you, boyo, but they're clapping for me, not you!' They were probably thinking, 'Who's that skinny bloke with John Charles?' " Although Juve lost Roberto Bettega through illness, West German World Cup star Haller still bestrode their midfield and £440,000 striker Pietro Anastasi led the line. Another notable absentee as a result of illness was the Express & Star's Phil Morgan, so John Dee stood in to report from the Stadio Communale that Juve shared with Torino. Munro still considers it; "The best game we ever played. We all did well and drew 1-1 but should have won easily. They'd just bought an expensive centre-forward, Anastasi, but we played as a team."

After 37 minutes, Furino took the ball to the bye-line and his cross deflected off McAlle in the direction of Taylor. Unfortunately, the defender slipped and allowed Anastasi to sweep past Parkes. McGarry soon found himself taken to task by Belgian referee Loraux for touchline coaching and, despite a protest from John Charles, had to watch the rest of the game surrounded by policemen on the perimeter athletics track. On 66 minutes, Wolves stunned the 45,000 crowd by equalising. Furino headed Taylor's centre straight to McCalliog, who struck an excellent left-foot volley from the edge of the box past the despairing Carmignani and into his left-hand corner. Munro and McAlle were particularly heroic in a staunch rearguard action and, though Wolves failed to record a seventh straight European win, McGarry described the performance as their best; "Juventus are a fine team but we outran them and never allowed them to get on top." The Italians did not take it well, with 'Lofty' Parkes facing the full fury of Fabio Capello; "Gerry Taylor passed back to me and, as I picked it up, Capello spat at me, a big green one down the side of my face, and said, 'Wolverhampton, Wolverhampton!'" McGarry was so happy with the night that he allowed the players a few glasses of wine and John Charles was quick to remind them of their achievement; "You know you've won. I guarantee half of them won't go to England now. When they play at home, they spit, kick, punch, anything. If they get a good win, 3-0, 4-0, they'll all go. Otherwise they won't. Big John, God rest his soul, was right. I'll never forget that night. Me and Frank put John Charles to bed, a great man."

The Italian heroics set Wolves off on a mini run and, although McCalliog missed a penalty, he and Taylor later scored to set up a 2-1 win at Southampton in a match that marked Wagstaffe's 400th League game. His form was rewarded by a call-up to Sir Alf Ramsey's Football League team against Scotland; "I never thought about the England squad. If it happened, it happened. All I did was go out and play every Saturday." Around this time, The Doog accepted my invitation to Brierley Hill Grammar School, an event reported by Jean Bennett (5N) and me in 'The Bromlian' of 1972; "Doog's 'ere!" shouted a fourth year from a window of the mobile classroom. A few minutes later, I found myself standing amidst my classmates, who were looking unusually well groomed. As the tall Irish gentleman, wearing a moustache and a large grin, brushed through the door, it was almost possible to hear 25 hearts booming in admiration. Our star visitor soon made the class comfortable in his presence. We realised Mr. Dougan's skill on the football field was more than matched by his deep insight into the problems of today. He talked about the pressures placed on superstars. With reference to a good friend of his, George Best, he said his actions of late had been natural but that everyone in a position such as his should realise their responsibility to the public and set an example for others to follow. His advice to us was to take nothing for granted and to take advantage of every opportunity given us."

A week later, Dougan and McCalliog (netting for the fifth successive game) sealed a 2-0 win at relegation-threatened Crystal Palace to push Wolves back to fifth. Talking on the day of Dougan's funeral, McCalliog clearly still had great admiration for him; "Derek was our leader and, as for what he meant to us, just look at everyone who is here today. If there was ever going to be a bit of fun or high jinks, you never had to look too far to know who was behind it."

Unfinished business was attended to on March 22 when the Express & Star greeted the Italians with the headline 'Piacere Juventus!' Having fielded their best available team in Turin, Juve, surprising all but John Charles, rested Causio, Anastasi, Capello and Furino to keep them fresh for a key league game against second-placed neighbours Torino, not that this offended many in the season's first 40,000 Molineux crowd. On 34 minutes, Hegan chipped a perfect shot that dipped just inside Piloni's near post to put Wolves ahead. Almost immediately, Waggy was booked, the winger recalling losing patience with the disgraceful treatment meted out by his marker, Longobucco; "I came in for a few body checks and some shirt-pulling and afterwards my body was a mass of bruises and scratches. Italians always had lots of tricks, you expected it." Daley remembers the warnings; "It was just the way they were. The manager told us it was going to happen, so we had to get used to it and just get on with it. He told us, 'Don't retaliate, they only want to antagonise you and make you come back at them and do something to get you booked or sent off and miss the next match.'"

Soon after half-time, Dougan flicked in a header to make it 2-0 and equal the record of nine European goals in a season by a British player that belonged to Dennis Viollet and Denis Law. Near the end, Munro handled to present Haller with a penalty

John Richards starts to celebrate Danny Hegan's goal against Juventus at Molineux.

that forced home fans to endure a tortuous last six minutes but Wolves hung on to allow the 'Express & Star' headline, 'Phew, that was close!' Munro recalls Hegan's humour during the heat of battle; "Danny had tremendous ability but was also so funny, the funniest bloke I ever met. During the match, he kept looking in the pocket of his shorts and saying to Haller, 'Helmut, do you fancy a drink?"

Back in the League, Hibbitt scored twice in a draw at Everton while Curran, due to move to Huddersfield, was sent off and injured an ankle in a Central League match against Burnley. At Goodison, McGarry gave Geoff Palmer early experience with the first team; "He always used to take a youngster away to help with the kit. You'd have a meal with the players to bring you into what it would be like when you got in the side. I had to get the kit off the bus but he put some out for me so I could have a kick around in the warm-up. Then I sat in the stand with him and, if he wanted word passing down to Sammy, he'd give me a note or tell me. I'd be off down to the dug-out and back up because they only had phones for the home team then."

The UEFA Cup semi-final draw paired Wolves with Ferencvaros - an event Jimmy Mac marked with the opening of his Wolves Service Station on the Penn Road, where 8p off four gallons of petrol was offered for several weeks. The honours were done by Miss ATV 1972 but, on the same day, Wolves lost their proud unbeaten home record of nine wins and seven draws. Leicester ended it as a dominant home showing was undermined by a great display by Shilton and a Shaw own goal. The scheduled Easter Monday and Tuesday matches against Chelsea and Nottingham Forest were then called off to accommodate Wolves' trip to Budapest, where Bailey's understudy Hegan asked to be taken off the transfer list on which he had placed himself the previous November.

Hardy supporters were prevented from travelling because of a smallpox epidemic but, apart from the missing captain and Parkin, Wolves were at full strength in the cavernous Nep Stadium against a

Hibbitt, McAlle, Richards, Chung and Taylor relax before one of the 12 games that made up Wolves' 1971-72 UEFA Cup run.

team who contained 1966 Hungary World Cup star Florian Albert. Parkes says he felt unease at the Iron Curtain experience; "In Hungary, they followed you everywhere. You always felt there was somebody watching you."

Dougan was seeking the goal that would make him the first English club player to score ten in Europe in a season but it was Richards who put the Wanderers ahead after 19 minutes with a goal created by McCalliog and Dougan. Ten minutes later, Istvan Szoke converted a spot-kick awarded for hands against Shaw, then Albert put the Hungarians ahead just past the half-hour. Things remained close until 15 minutes from time when Shaw conceded another penalty, Parkes this time saving Szoke's effort with his feet; "He sent me the wrong way with his first kick, so this time I waited. But again I went the wrong way and just managed to get my foot to the ball." The save enabled Munro to head a precious equaliser from a corner as time ebbed away and, with two vital away goals, Wolves' day was spoilt only by cautions (green cards in those days) for Shaw and Wagstaffe that made them unavailable for the second leg.

Wolves' wilting League form continued with a 2-1 defeat at Arsenal, where Peter Eastoe made his full debut due to Dougan's muscle strain. The following Wednesday, Chris Garland struck within 55 seconds to set Chelsea up for a 2-0 Molineux win and a miserable week was complete when Parkes spilled Ally Brown's shot for namesake Tony to score the only goal a minute after the start of the home clash with West Brom. With three League defeats in eight days, two at home, a big question mark hung over Wolves' bid to see off Ferencvaros, especially with the inexperienced look to the side. Sunderland and Taylor were the full-backs, Daley played at no 11 and youth-teamers Rod Arnold, John Rutter, Eastoe and Mike Stephens joined Curran on the bench. There was a timely boost, though, with Richards chosen for England under-23s' summer tour of East Germany, Poland and Russia.

Greece's Christos Michas was in charge and, for the third successive Molineux game, there was a goal within 60 seconds, this time to Wolves. Munro's right-foot punt towards the North Bank was met by Richards inside the box. A defender scrambled the ball clear via Hibbitt's chest but only as far as Dougan, who laid off to Sunderland near the half-way line on Wolves' right and, under severe pressure from Richards at the near post, keeper Bela Voros missed the cross. The ball ran free to Daley, who fired home jubilantly from a tight angle - a finish he remembers with relish; "My favourite game was against Ferencvaros. Until Benny McCarthy scored for Blackburn recently, I held the record for the quickest goal in European football (22 seconds). Alan found himself on the right and crossed. I'm coming in at the far post, beat everyone and could have put it anywhere. Fortunately, it went into the top corner."

Despite falling behind, the visitors were full of menace. They almost levelled when a Lajos free kick was deflected past the wall to Ku, who unselfishly slid through for Florian Albert to net, only to be judged offside. Soon after, Branikovits hit a left-footer that Parkes deflected on to the bar and, as Ku closed in, Lofty's raised feet put him off sufficiently to allow McAlle to tidy up. Wolves became relatively comfortable just before half-time with a second goal. A left-wing corner eluded Dougan but McCalliog retrieved the ball and crossed for the totally unmarked Munro to power a header off keeper Voros into the roof of the net from the left edge of the six-yard box. However, just after the restart, Ku brought Ferencvaros back into it when put in on the left of the area almost exactly where Daley had been 45 minutes earlier. Ku passed the ball left-footed across Parkes and into the far corner.

There was more unwelcome excitement when Szoke passed up the chance to take

the tie to extra-time when he tamely tapped a penalty to the middle of the goal. 'Lofty' was again the hero as he stood almost still to left-foot it away. As McAlle ran to congratulate his keeper, several Hungarians collapsed in despair. Their demoralisation was clear and it was apt that almost the last action was Parkes' towering interception of a right-wing cross. Having qualified in front of a disappointing 28,662 crowd on the night Aston Villa sealed the Third Division title, Wolves' opponents in the first-ever UEFA Cup final would be Tottenham or AC Milan.

If the semi-final win was heartily

celebrated, there was no obvious hangover when the rot of three straight League defeats was ended at Leeds Road, where Geoff Palmer was again taken for the ride; "I remember the trip to Huddersfield because they were all on about the UEFA Cup." Daley's 78th minute winner all but relegated the club McGarry had played for and victory was no surprise given Wolves' post-war record there of nine wins and a draw out of 13 played. Daley remembers the effect upon McGarry; "They had to win or draw to stay up and I went into the dressing room giving it 'yeah.' Bill sat in the corner with his head in his hands. His old team were relegated and our dressing room was so quiet you'd have thought we'd got beat."

Another victory, 3-1 at Nottingham Forest on the following Tuesday, came when Hegan, Richards and Hibbitt scored to virtually put the East Midlanders down as well. The penultimate League game was against Sheffield United on the last Friday of April in front of a meagre 17,041. Richards was on the mark after five minutes but the Blades recovered to inflict a fourth straight League defeat on Wolves at Molineux. There was little excuse for such a poor performance despite the eye on the next home game, on Wednesday, May 3 against Spurs in the UEFA Cup Final. It was somewhat disappointing that a journey via Portugal, Holland, East Germany, Italy and Hungary would end in a European final against an English club.

McAlle sums up the players' feelings; "We were so disappointed it was not a real European game" - a reaction Richards agrees with; "It just lost all of its attraction. We'd gone all over the place, East Germany, Italy and Hungary, and played some of the best football the team had ever played against really top sides. Then suddenly it ends up being like another domestic cup clash." Waggy shares this view; "It was a big anti-climax. We had the best defensive record in Europe that season and it was no mean

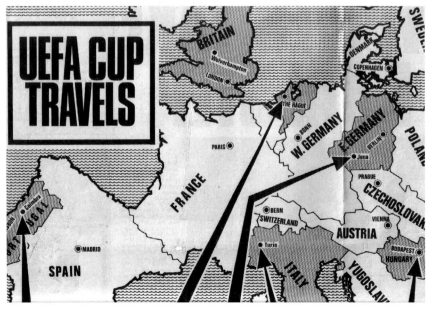

Route planner - from Coimbra to White Hart Lane

feat after going to all those places," as does Munro; "After travelling all over Europe, having two English teams in the final was a real disappointment." Parkes would have preferred a one-off game; "If it'd been like now, one-off, it wouldn't have been so bad," and Parkin chips in; "I think that's why there wasn't any media interest really." Hibbitt feels the team consequently got little credit for their achievement; "The fans knew but not much was mentioned nationally about us going to the final, knocking all these teams out without getting beaten. Why don't they ever mention it? They'd go wild about it now. I find that sad." Daley agrees; "It didn't seem a big issue at the time because we were in the final but it would have been nice to have played a foreign team. You look back now and realise it was not as big in the 1970s."

In an interview in the match programme, McGarrry was upbeat, praising superb team spirit and the fine way some of the youngsters had come through. As for the final, which had a late-night highlight slot on Sportsnight with David Coleman as the commentator, the boss expected 'two exciting, attacking matches. We can't play any other way.' Richards agrees; "McGarry realised what we could and couldn't do, and the only way we could play was to attack." Officiated by Tofik Bakhramov, the Russian linesman from the 1966 World Cup final, the game was watched by more than 38,632. The first half was goalless but full of incident, the most exciting of which came when Pat Jennings cleared to just over the half-way line. Danny Hegan spotted his compatriot off his line and, in the style of Pele in the 1970 World Cup finals, lofted towards the South Bank goal. Jennings recovered just in time to tip to safety, as Parkes recalls; "Pat was lucky, Danny's shot went to the side he was running back to. If it had gone to the middle of goal or the other side, he wouldn't have got it. He just managed to tip it over."

Spurs then went ahead on 57 minutes when Martin Chivers beat Munro to the ball to head a Mike England free-kick past a keeper caught in no man's land. After a quarter

Martin's two killer blows

The goals with which Martin Chivers killed off Wolves' hopes in the first leg of the UEFA Cup final at Molineux last night: Left, the big Spurs' striker beats Wolves defensive king-pin Frank Munro to head home Mike England's 57th minute free-kick past a flat-footed Phil Parkes and, right, the diving Parkes is helpless as Chivers' 25-yard shot crashes into the net in the dying minutes. The goals brought Chivers' total in Europe this season to eight and his total for Spurs in all games to 42.

Chivers the difference

Wolves pressed
— Spurs struck

Wolves are not out of the UEFA Cup yet, but, my goodness,

of an hour of pressure, Wolves levelled. Hegan took a free-kick while Alan Mullery was arguing with the referee and McCalliog planted it skilfully under Jennings. But with two minutes left, Wolves' hearts were broken by Chivers as he crashed home an unstoppable 25-yarder to notch his 43rd goal of the season and give his team a vital lead for the second leg. Waggy remembers how the big keeper was unfairly saddled with the blame for the winner; "Poor old Phil got some stick about that Chivers' goal." 'Lofty' says; "They still do! If you get beat from that far, it's always your fault. When you play in goal, you're the one to blame." It was not a Parkes error that made the difference that night, though, it was the performances of Jennings and Chivers. Daley adds; "We didn't perform. If you play on the night, you have a chance."

In any other year, the first Saturday in May would have marked the end of the domestic season with the FA Cup showpiece. On this day in 1972, the final was played but Wolves still had two huge games to contemplate. Leeds overcame Arsenal to win the centenary final with an Allan Clarke header from Mick Jones' cross before the latter fractured his collarbone and left Wembley in a sling. Richards was at the game and departed the stadium among Leeds fans all talking about going to Molineux and beating Wolves; "Unrecognised by the jubilant supporters, I was advised by my wife to keep my head down!" With the League and Cup double at stake and safely lodged in the Mount Hotel, Tettenhall, Leeds celebrated Jack Charlton's 37th birthday on the Sunday. Derek Dougan made a fleeting visit to present the golden boot for the season's top League scorer to Allan Clarke and said to Big Jack; "Seven out of ten times, you'd beat us but, tomorrow night, sorry, there's nothing for you." Charlton replied; "F*** off, it's a meaningless game for you." "A meaningless game in front of nearly 60,000?" asked the Doog; "I dreamt we would go two up and hang on to win 2-1." Waggy insists there was no antipathy with the Leeds players as individuals; "Everyone hated Leeds, not the players but as a team because they were so good, so ruthless and so successful." Parkin agrees; "I certainly admired and respected Leeds. There were some great players and what Don Revie did was fantastic but they were never liked. They believed in each other so much and they must really have believed in Revie."

Despite only 48 hours' rest, Leeds were able to field a full-strength if exhausted team, apart from Mick Bates for Jones. On a balmy evening Young called; "almost a midsummer night's dream," a crowd officially given as 53,379 packed into Molineux, although it is likely the real figure was much greater given the kicking-down of a South Bank gate and the numbers clinging to any available vantage points such as floodlight pylons. What is known is that 5,000-10,000 were locked out when police ordered the gates to be closed half an hour before kick-off. Richards remembers; "You sensed it as soon as you got a mile from the ground. The traffic was huge and you thought, 'God, what's going on? I was planning to get there two hours early and I still got held up." Wagstaffe adds; "We were under pressure to get a result because of the allegations and, before the game, Bill McGarry said, 'Anyone who doesn't try, I'll make sure you're investigated'. Normally, you'd be on holiday but the atmosphere was tremendous." Parkes felt particularly vulnerable; "If I'd made a mistake, I'd be the first they'd point the finger at. We won 2-1 and I got man of the match and was quite relieved." Richards agrees; "We played out of our skins because of the accusations. It was probably the best we played all year, we were playing for pride." Hibbitt says; "It was a magnificent night. I remember Leeds walking into Castlecroft for training. Allan Clarke was in his slippers because his feet were so sore from the final. Don Revie had a massive job picking them up for the double, almost unheard-of in those days. We were up for it with 55,000 in and probably 10,000 locked out. As an occasion, it was as good as a cup final, it just wasn't at Wembley. It was tight and we did them! We all know what went on in the game. Years later, we had national papers knocking on the door asking questions but youngsters like me and John Richards never heard it. I remember Johnny Giles telling me what they were on. I tackled him a little bit hard and he said, 'What are you doing, you little b*****d? Don't you know we're on 15 grand a man to win?' I said, 'I'm on £40, mate!' Being a kid, it didn't really register with me."

While desperate Leeds fans broke into the Polytechnic building to try to gain a vantage point, other interested parties in the title-race denouement were represented inside, a number of Derby and Liverpool fans managing to gain admission. Spectators had to park miles from the ground as the town was grid-locked. A crush barrier on the South Bank gave way, injuring 32, and it was later discovered five other barriers had been bent. As I watched from this terrace, I can honestly say I have never been so packed in. It was a struggle to get your hand up to scratch your nose. Although the game was immaterial to Wolves in terms of League position, it was one of unbearable highs and lows. Parkin, kept out by injury, remembers watching in the company of

No points -

no double

It's arms raised in triumph (above left) for Derek D
and John Richards after the Doog had cracked in
second goal. But Leeds goalkeeper David Harvey w
beaten by the effort from John Richard (above), g
down to smother the centre-forward's shot. Left, th
ture almost tells the story . . . the huge crowd
Wolves, the fans begin to invade the pitch, and the
players head for the dressing-rooms foiled at the
hurdle in their bid for a league and cup double.
tension of the last few weeks is gone, and the reali
that all their efforts have not quite earned them a
in the European Cup will come a little later as the l
eux delight at Wolves' success is tempered by more
a little sympathy for Don Revie and his Leeds me

Leeds full-back and ex-Huddersfield colleague Terry Cooper; "He had broken his leg so we both sat in the box in the Waterloo Road Stand, Terry with his leg in plaster. Even there, the tension was unbelievable." What a match this was to mark the last at Molineux for Phil Morgan, the Express & Star's Wolves correspondent for 24 seasons. He first reported in the 'Pink' in August, 1948, so it was fitting his final two matches were a League championship decider and a European final.

On 23 minutes, Shaw appeared to handle in the area but nothing was given and, four minutes before half-time, Wolves took the lead. Wagstaffe took a short corner to Shaw and his deflected cross fell to Munro who stabbed the ball past Paul Reaney's despairing lunge on the South Bank goal-line. Frank recalls; "When I scored, Bremner called me a f***in Scottish b****rd. He was more Scottish than I'll ever be!" On 67 minutes, Hegan threaded a pass to Richards, who helped it past Paul Madeley into the path of Dougan. The Doog strode on to fire right-footed past Harvey from 15 yards - his 196th League goal and 70th for Wolves taking him closer to Peter Doherty's record of 197 for an Irishman in the Football League. An exhausted Clarke was replaced by Terry Yorath and Bremner changed positions with Bates to move up front. As Munro remembers, everything but the kitchen sink was thrown at the Wolves defence; "All of a sudden late on, Norman Hunter and Jack Charlton were playing up front as well!" Although the surge brought the Leeds skipper one goal, Taylor headed another effort off the line and Leeds subsided despite four minutes of injury-time played by referee Gow. The view of Randall Northam was probably fair, although it did scant justice to a terrier-like Wolves display; "Leeds were destroyed not so much by Wolves, although they delivered the fatal blow, but rather by the Football League's insistence that last night's game be played 48 hours after the Cup Final." Bailey, again out injured, agreed; "Watching from the bench, I felt sorry for Leeds having to play such an important game just two days after a final." This was a sentiment Munro shares; "They were the best team. I don't think it should have been played on the Monday night after the final. It was a good game, played at 100mph." As a result of this and Liverpool's 0-0 draw at Arsenal, Brian Clough's Derby won the title, and outraged Leeds players, including Charlton and Reaney, apparently threw their stocking tags at the referee's door.

After this encounter, Wolves had to lift themselves for the second leg of the UEFA Cup final, to be played nine days later on Wednesday, May 17. Although Bailey was on the team sheet for the first time since January, it was only as substitute in a game that saw Spurs installed as 6/1 favourites to lift the trophy. The odds appeared accurate when Mullery headed home after 31 minutes but Wolves refused to give in and Waggy evaded his marker, Cyril Knowles, to crash in a fine equaliser close to half-time. Flying in off the post, it remains one of his favourites. In the second half Wolves laid siege to the home goal, Munro going close with a header and Dougan having a goal disallowed. The Doog was frustrated in his quest for a tenth goal; "I was robbed of that goal and the European record. I tussled with Mike England and headed a very good, legitimate

Wolves force a draw but it's Tottenham's UEFA Cup

By RANDALL NORTHAM

Spurs 1, Wolves 1

(Spurs win 3-2 on aggregate)

Tottenham kept their remarkable record of never having lost a Cup

goal to make it 2-1." Bailey and Curran came on near the end but it was Mullery, on loan to Fulham as the season started, who lifted the cup. Spurs maintained their proud record of never having lost a cup final and became the first English team to win two European trophies. The headline, "Wolves bow out, but not so meekly" was an appropriate one as Bill Nicholson admitted, "You've got to give Wolves a lot of credit. We never really had control." McGarry lamented; "I still can't work out how you can be the best side in both games and still lose."

Munro still shares his manager's disappointment; "The annoying thing is that we never lost an away game." Hibbitt adds; "We didn't get beaten once until the bloody final. We'd been all over the eastern bloc and were magnificent away. It was a terrific time for us kids. The final games were great and Waggy was outstanding. We didn't play particularly well at home when we lost. Phil made an error but I suppose he had saved us so many times. We just weren't able to get over the final fence but I thought getting to the final was an achievement in itself. We didn't get the publicity they get now, TV, radio and the rest." The still-absent Parkin recalls a big-hearted gesture by McGarry; "I remember afterwards Bill gave me a medal. We were allowed so many extra and he found me one." Percy Young's final word on the end of Wolves' European dream was typically poetic; "After a Grand Tour in the classical style, the sought-after UEFA Cup was dashed from the lips at the last stage."

The month ended with uncertainty over the manager's future. He had reputedly been offered £17,000 a year by Coventry but a three-hour board meeting resulted in a five-year Wolves offer that he accepted. Dougan and Hegan departed for duty with Northern Ireland in the Home Internationals and Richards joined the under-23s' East European tour. Wolves set off on an American and Australasian jaunt that would take in games in San Francisco, Seattle, Vancouver, Los Angeles, Wellington, Auckland, Sydney, Queensland, Adelaide and Perth. And glorious failure in Europe meant qualification for the Watney Cup - and a trip to Bristol Rovers' Eastville Stadium.

1972-73: Double Cup Heartache

Incredibly, four days after the UEFA Cup final, Wolves were in action against old stateside adversaries Aberdeen. In the first of an energy-sapping four games in eight days, Jim McCalliog netted on 15 minutes but the rigours of a 24-hour flight to San Francisco caught up with the players and Wolves succumbed 3-1. With Derek Dougan and Danny Hegan on international duty, things were no better on the Wednesday night in Seattle when the Dons scored three again, this time without reply. Two nights later, the venue was the Empire Stadium, Vancouver, and on this occasion English pride was restored as Kenny Hibbitt, John Richards and Hugh Curran turned the tables. Wolves went one better in Los Angeles on the last Sunday in May when former Aberdeen player Frank Munro added to a Richards hat-trick and sealed a 4-0 win. Steve Daley couldn't believe his luck being on tour; "It was fantastic to see different nationalities and the way they lived, people couldn't do enough for us. We played in the King Dome, a 60,000 indoor stadium." Steve Kindon still laments signing too late to go; "I regret the fact Jimmy Adamson didn't sell me earlier because Wolves went on a tour half way around the world, and I missed out."

As Richards flew back to London with director Wilf Sproson to join up with the England under-23s, Wolves set off to Australasia. Richards reveals that Bill McGarry broke the news of his selection by telling him he would be touring America but not Australia due to his participation in East Europe. Those that remained were joined by a Northern Irish contingent flushed with the success of a Terry Neill-inspired win over England in the Home Internationals at Wembley. The Doog boomed; "England played only as well as we let them. Their style is obsolete and outdated." Hibbitt remembers meeting up with the Irish duo; "Danny had a hand in the goal that beat England, he took the corner. We were on the way to Australia and met him and Dougan somewhere. They were legless and we were delayed for about four hours because they were so gone. Danny was carrying a Northern Irish flag through the airport, he was hilarious."

Six days after leaving LA, Wolves were in action in New Zealand, overcoming Auckland 3-2 courtesy of Dougan (2) and Curran. On the following Monday, Dougan doubled up again in a 6-0 thrashing of Wellington, with Jim McCalliog and Peter Eastoe and joining the fun. The last match in New Zealand saw Eastoe and Munro combining to see off South Island. Heading west, Wolves made unenviable history in a double-header against an Australian National XI. At the time their cricket team were struggling in the Old Trafford Test, the 1970s 'socceroos' won 1-0 to record their first ever win over an English team. Daley comments; "They were mainly exhibition games and woe betide us if we ever lost. They were brilliant lads, the togetherness of the squad and the camaraderie were fantastic." A local paper trumpeted; "An amazed crowd of 13,000 saw a side worth £35,000 humble a famous football team with nearly £2m of talent." In the re-match, Wolves drew 2-2 on the back of a Curran equaliser, although his day was spoiled by a sending-off. The rest of the tour brought routine wins over Queensland, South Australia and Western Australia at a time when Curran disobeyed instructions with unfortunate results. Munro, who later had a successful spell as manager of Melbourne Victoria, recalls; "Hughie was told not to but took out a car and wrecked it." Daley adds; "He took everything without permission!"

Representing England in Eastern Europe, Richards broke a bone in his hand in the opening 2-2 draw in East Germany that saw strike partner Kevin Keegan dismissed. The two players had earlier been trapped in a lift with Richards' room-mate Mike Pejic for around half an hour on their way down to training. However, a plaster cast could not prevent Richards from scoring in the Poland game, a strike that proved to be his only international goal. Playing alongside Frank Worthington, Richards was put in by Keegan to slot home the second in a 3-0 victory. He performed well again in the final 0-0 draw with Russia but, apart from the goal, it is not a tour John remembers with great affection; "It was quite austere in terms of the countries visited and the styles of play. We found ourselves against a type of opponent that was really hard and tough. It was dour in many respects and even the food was meagre. But it made us appreciate what we had at home." Richards admits it was daunting to join up with big names like Malcolm MacDonald, Mike Channon and Peter Shilton but he and other newcomers Pejic and David Nish were made welcome. It was successful preparation for the senior tour the next year as the squad had been to difficult places and returned undefeated. Reporters and fellow players had equally positive memories of Richards' contribution. The Sun's Peter Batt wrote; "The biggest surprise package has been Wolves striker Richards. A player's player, he looks like vintage Geoff Hurst and Roger Hunt rolled into one and earned rave notices from the rest of the team." Liverpool's Kevin Keegan agreed; "He was, for me, the no 1 success of the trip."

Back in pre-season training, Wolves were seen pounding round Castlecroft and Wolverhampton racecourse in a schedule The Doog argued was, "geared to take us to the top." New signing Kindon relished it; "The likes of George Best and Waggy didn't have to be fully fit to be brilliant but what great feet! But my whole game was based around fitness. I needed to be fit and to be able to run wholeheartedly to contribute. Although it sometimes hurt me, I knew it was doing me good. Of course pre-season was always hard since I've never been a cross-country runner, although I wouldn't be at the back. Over four or five miles, I struggled but, if we jogged for four and a half and then it was 'last one home,' that last half mile didn't bother me." Derek Parkin also remembers the sessions with an affection born out of his love for the physical side; "We did a lot of running. I just followed people like The Doog, who was a great trainer. I looked at this guy who was nine or ten years older and I'm thinking, 'If he can do it, I'll follow him'. Bill liked that. I came in, did the business, worked hard and loved it, first in, last out. Someone was paying me to play football so I kept fit." However, 'Squeak' appreciates that the approach did not suit everyone; "You were unlucky if you didn't like it. You get a lad like Phil Parkes, who used to train really hard but was so big and not a natural runner. He tried bloody hard but couldn't keep up with the smaller, thinner element. The lads who were bigger, like Frank, didn't like the running but, if you were into running, it was very enjoyable - and it suited me." Willie Carr adds; "He used to take us to Cannock Chase. There was a hill full of sand, shaped like a pork chop. We had to go up and down. It was a killer, although you expected it." Barry Powell has similar memories; "I never had pre-seasons like I had with McGarry. He would take us over Brocton and run us up hill and down dale. He'd take us so far and we had to make our own way back. Waggy and Frank didn't like running and once got a lift on the back of a lorry. He punished them with a fine or extra work. That's how he was, very much a disciplinarian."

Daley outlines the fearsome regime; "Tuesday was D for Dedication day. We'd have a full-scale match in the morning, then he'd say '2pm for a 2.15 start.' You'd come back for a weight circuit in the lower gym, 25 exercises, then you'd swap with the squad on the track. When you finished, your legs were shaking, it was horrendous. But didn't you feel good when you'd done it! As a professional, you knew you needed it and we still did it under Sammy." Parkes agrees; "If we didn't have a midweek game, Tuesday was always the hardest day. We had the first team against the reserves for about an hour, then we went back for a fitness circuit." Powell adds; "On Monday, you just got Saturday out of your body but you knew what you'd get on a Tuesday. It was all set up with weights and everything, shuttle runs and the big South Bank. He'd really put you through it. Then you had bell weights. My arms would be hanging off."

Geoff Palmer, yet to break into the first team, elaborates further; "On Tuesday afternoons, the physical exercises were just murder. McGarry had two groups, the first running on the track and he took that. The second that Sammy had used a weights machine with different exercises on it down in the pen underneath the Waterloo Road Stand towards the North Bank. It had been used for shooting when Stan Cullis was there. It was as wide as this room but a bit longer and had wooden flooring and was dusty. But it also had the drying room where the training kit was hung. Ten of us worked on the different exercises on this machine, then you'd go into the drying room. There were two exercises there, a skipping rope and a big bar bell that you did sit-ups with. Once, I was with Danny Hegan. I was doing sit-ups and he had the skipping rope. He was doing nothing but making the noise of the rope on the floor!" Daley agrees; "You could hear the rope hitting the floor and thought, 'He's skipping' but Danny was sitting on the end of the table and letting the rope hit the floor. He was brilliant."

There was no respite for those running with McGarry, as Parkes recalls; "It was one lap round the ground in a minute, two laps in two and a half minutes and four in five minutes. Then we used to run up and down the South Bank. It was three to the bottom, three to the middle and three to the top. All that was condensed into about 45 minutes and, when you finished, your legs would be shaking." Hibbitt adds; "We used to come down the tunnel and up the little ramp on to the track. Bill would say to Peter Withe, a great runner, 'Take them round, Peter, fast lap'. No warm-up, no stretches, nothing, it was Bill's way of getting us into it straightaway, getting a sweat up. Jim McCalliog used to jog round, he thought McGarry was a stupid pillock for making us do that. Peter was off and we all followed him but Jim wouldn't. Bill was a fitness fanatic, he made some good young players play and I was one of them. I had a lot of respect for him." Palmer continues; "McGarry made you do four laps of the cinder track in four minutes, then you walked a lap, then he made you do two in under two minutes, then you walked a lap, and then he made you do a lap in under 60 seconds. Then it was running up the South Bank. There were three levels and he used to have you going to the top and down again, then he'd bring you up to the second level and you'd do three of each. I've even seen Micky Bailey throw up at the top of the South Bank. It was worse coming down because your legs were just like jelly, thinking 'I'm going too fast here, I'm going to break my neck coming down'."

As Parkes is quick to add, it wasn't finished there; "Next it was 'doggies' with weights." Palmer chips in; "It would be ten yards, the next 20 and then 30. You'd fetch the far one in and do it six times. Sixty yards then back, then 50 yards more. Then you had to do a double one to finish, fetching and taking them out again. That was really hard." Hibbitt says of this torture; "They don't know they're born now! We used to run up the South Bank with weights, getting to the top and banging the back of the stand. Bill Pilbeam was the long-time groundsman and a big guy. He came round with his Wellingtons on, saw us and said, 'That's easy', so we said, 'Come on then, you do it'. He went up and it took him ten minutes and two hours to get back down. We got in, had a shower, got dressed and went out to see where Bill was. He was still at the top of the steps and hadn't moved. That's how hard it was. We were fit."

Daley appreciates the rest they were given; "Nine times out of ten, we'd all play golf the next day, Oxley, Beau Desert or South Staffs, great." Parkes comments; "We

John Ireland hits at UEFA disinterest . . .

Wolves' chairman, John Ireland, after hitting out at the lack of support at Molineux for UEFA cup-ties, revealed at last night's annual meeting of shareholders that the club made nothing out of the home final tie with Spurs.

He added; "In fact, we probably incurred a loss. We were bitterly disappointed not to have won the final, but worse still was the apparent lack of interest in Wolverhampton.

"For the semi - final we had an attendance of around 26,000 and the final, 38,000, yet anywhere else in Europe, there would have been a capacity crowd.

"We were entitled to some credit on reaching the final, but how disappointing it was

EUFA Cup-ties. He pointed out that playing in Europe had also increased expenditure.

Players salaries and bonuses had increased by £30,000, travelling costs by £12,000 and hotels by £5,000. "When every-

Happy to be back in training but all is not well with the chairman

Wolves chairman JOHN IRELAND — hit out at the shareholders fans at the shareholders

used to have Wednesday off but had to play golf or squash. Most of us played golf at Beau Desert." Palmer adds; "Bill McGarry was a golf nut and he'd arrange it. Those who didn't play had the day off. Hibby, big Phil, Waggy, Mick Bailey and me all used to play. We always loved midweek games because we didn't have to do this running. It was an incentive to do well and stay in the cups!" It's no surprise Waggy also loved midweek games rather than training; "If the truth be known, the players would have played Saturday, Wednesday, Saturday, Wednesday all season 'cos there would be no long training slog." 'Lofty' recalls a day at Cosford; "Waggy wasn't the best trainer, especially if it was hard. The weather wasn't nice and McGarry organised training on the indoor circuit. He had us doing laps on a track that was banked at the ends. Waggy got to one end and fell over. He thought he was having a heart attack! Bill said, 'Tell him to f***in' get up or I'll shoot him and pay for the funeral!" Hibbitt remembers the winger's discomfort; "He didn't like the hard sessions. He had some Vimto one day and told the physio Toby Andersen he was coughing up blood. Toby told him to go home and see a doctor. That was his way of getting out of a hard day."

At the annual meeting, John Ireland hit out at the poor UEFA Cup crowds; "How disappointing it was to realise the supporters didn't want to know or showed an alarming lack of interest in something so difficult to win." Ireland also admitted he was embarrassed by the state of the Waterloo Road Stand. Wolves began their build-up in Sweden, competing in the Sir Stanley Rous Cup. Having defeated local team Gais 4-3 on penalties, they beat Everton 2-1 with goals by Richards and Hibbitt, Munro being voted man of the tournament. To complete three games in three days, they flew back for a Watney Cup tie. I made the mistake of persuading my family to stop off en route home from a holiday in Devon to watch the game against Division Three Bristol Rovers. Their manager Don Megson was confident; "We have everything going for us. The team are in top shape and we have ground advantage." In sweltering conditions, Wolves could manage only two direct shots on goal in what John Dee described as; "a performance bordering on the ridiculous". The Eastville pitch was separated from the crowd by a dog track and I recall leaning in disbelief on a barrier behind Parkes' goal

As good as it got for Wolves at sunny Eastville.

as Bruce Bannister tucked away a first-half penalty. The keeper tells how he played in pain; "McGarry had Rod Arnold but for some reason wouldn't play him, even in the Watney Cup. I had a broken finger and needed two injections in my hand and some strapping." As home fans chanted, "Easy, easy!" ex-Albion winger Kenny Stephens rounded the humiliation off three minutes from time. We headed for the M5 convinced Wolves had indeed only been there for the beer.

Instead of further Watney Cup participation, Wolves hastily arranged games at Oxford and Notts County, which were negotiated without further embarrassment. The only pre-season Molineux action was a visit by European Cup Winners Cup holders Glasgow Rangers. Led by Willie Waddell, their line-up included John Grieg, Scotland captain Sandy Jardine, Colin Stein (signed from Hibs for £100,000), and Scotland's costliest player, Alfie Conn. A decent crowd of around 10,000 saw McCalliog inspire a win with a header and penalty either side of half-time. With the big kick-off fast approaching, of four players transfer-listed the previous November (Hegan, Paul Walker, Gerry Taylor and Mike O'Grady), only the latter remained in dispute. Although there were rumours Derek Jefferson was about to move from McGarry's old club Ipswich, this would not happen until later in the season, making Kindon the only new face by August 12 - in a record £100,000 move from Burnley. 'The Tank' had played 105 games at Turf Moor and 25 goals; "I got married on June 3 and, on the seventh or eighth, there was a knock on my door from Dave Blakey, Burnley's chief scout. That morning, I'd read Frank Worthington had failed a medical at Liverpool with high blood pressure. Dave said; 'Somebody wants to talk to you about a transfer. I'm not allowed to say who. Get showered quickly.' That's how they treated us then, like schoolchildren. When we got to the club, Blakey said to the manager Jimmy Adamson; 'Where's Bill?' I thought he meant Bill Shankly after the Worthington story. Of course it was Bill McGarry but I was very happy to sign for Wolves."

Richards learned of the renewal of an old acquaintance when reading a paper on holiday; "We played rugby league together in Warrington when we were 11, I was on the right wing, Steve on the left." Kindon adds; "John and I knew each other quite well, we used to see each other in the queue at the Odeon on Saturday mornings, aged eight or nine. Then we drifted apart. John lived on the greater borough boundaries and, when he passed the eleven plus, he went to Bottler, the soccer-playing school. Living half a mile outside the borough, I went to Way Deacon, playing rugby. John stayed on for 'A' levels and I left at 16 to play for Burnley." Hibbitt recalls they soon picked up on their friendship; "Kindo was a good lad, a big mate of John. They used to like Monty Python which I couldn't stand. They used to come in the dressing room and laugh all day about it. They could obviously see something I couldn't." Kindon found the bright lights of Wolverhampton somewhat different to Burnley; "Burnley is a very intimate town, everybody knows your business and, if you walk down the high street, everyone says hello. At 21, I moved to Wolverhampton, much more metropolitan, much more space. In Burnley, going to the club meant going to one disco. In Wolverhampton, there was a choice of four or five. It certainly broadened me as an individual."

Commenting favourably on his 14st, 6ft-plus capture, McGarry gushed; "He is a big, powerful lad who can operate up front or at outside-left and I remember how he tore us to bits in the FA Cup at Turf Moor two seasons ago." However, as Kindon recalls, McGarry was not quite as complimentary in private; "As soon as I signed, he said, 'You're my record purchase but I'm not going to play you much this season.' I said, 'Why not?' He said, 'Because you can play on the left wing and you can play centre-forward. I've got a left-winger, Dave Wagstaffe, who's better than you, and a centre-forward, Derek Dougan, who's better than you. But they're both the wrong side of 30 and you will play because when you're the wrong side of 30, you get a bang on the leg and you might be out for two weeks, whereas when you're the right side of 30, you're playing the next Saturday.' So it proved, I did play quite a lot because of injuries to Waggy or The Doog and, when I didn't start, nine times out of ten I was substitute." Richards comments favourably on Kindon's attributes; "There's no way you would stand in front of Stevie running at full pelt. I'd hate to have been a defender against him. I can remember him scoring a lot of memorable goals running from the half-way line." Daley agrees; "He was quick. Over ten yards, you could stay with him but after that he'd leave you for dead." Carr, who would later join Kindon at Molineux, was in the Coventry team defeated by Steve's Burnley in the 1967 Youth Cup final and remembers him as a great character, "always larger than life."

Palmer also recalls Kindon's pace and how he and others struggled with their weight; "Bloody hell, he could run that kid. Always took the mickey out of himself and his lisp. He was a big lad, you should have seen the size of him when he came back for pre-season training. McGarry used to go mad. Frank was the same, struggled with his weight." Hibbitt recalls; "Kindo could eat for England. He lived in Finchfield and he'd come back to my house for lunch. He stopped off at the shop and got a pound of tomatoes and a loaf of bread. He ate it all before going back to training. When he had dinner, he'd have a separate plate for his potatoes because he had so much on his plate. He never did that in front of Bill but he was strong, a big powerful boy." Daley says of pre-season touring; "We went to Sweden and stayed on an army base, sleeping in wooden huts. For breakfast, we'd go to the canteen for a smorgasbord, all cereals, salads, hams and toast. The most we had was a cup of tea, a slice of toast and cereal. Kindo, ah, the only thing missing off his plate was a Guy Fawkes! 'Kindo', we said, 'We're training in half an hour.'" Steve defends himself; "I could run it off! All these stories are true but what they miss out on is that I haven't got a big appetite. Now Peter Withe could trough, he could eat ten pieces of Kentucky fried chicken and five lots of chips at one sitting. I'm a grazer. I could eat a bowl of cornflakes and a bacon butty for breakfast, another couple of butties for my lunch, and meat and potato pie and chips for tea. I could have changed my diet but wasn't having a lot at any time. All the lads would see was me eating a sandwich and then an hour or so later me eating another sandwich, so I appeared never to stop eating. The legend has grown."

Although entirely happy with his move, Kindon reflects on perceived divisions in the dressing room; "When I arrived, there were two cliques - I'd never experienced that at Burnley. It seemed you were either a pal of Mike Bailey or Derek Dougan, and ne'er the twain shall meet. I won't name names but certain people were't comfortable with that. I was 21, quite big and didn't suffer fools. When I was eight, I had met a lad called John Richards and, when I was 21, I said to him, 'What's all this about?' It never affected them on a Saturday but I don't like cliques, so I said, 'B****cks to all that, let's have our own clique, you and me. We'll talk to both of them.' Slowly but surely, it broke down until at the end there was Dougan on his own."

On the eve of the season's first game, John Dee interviewed McGarry, who had no time for suggestions that there was too much football played; "This is a load of rubbish. They should be able to play two games a week. I think what is wrong with players is that they are concerned, some anyway, with too many outside activities." He announced that Mike Channon was a potential Wolves target; "He is quick and can score goals. That's what football is all about." He accepted that Molineux crowds would improve only once silverware was restored to the trophy cabinet; "Wolves have to win a major trophy before gates get appreciably better." When asked if Wolves could win the championship, McGarry was bullish, retorting that they certainly could, given Derby's success in 1972.

Despite McGarry's optimism, a severely weakened team turned out at Newcastle on day one. With Wagstaffe out and Dougan struggling for match fitness, Eastoe joined Richards up front and Kindon made his debut at no 11. Bailey and Parkin had their 250th and 200th senior outings respectively and, although three goals were scored in the first 17 minutes, Wolves got only one. A well-placed shot by Kindon could not stave off another Tyneside defeat and, making matters worse, Wolves' skipper limped off with a knee injury on 25 minutes and was replaced by surprise substitute O'Grady. Kindon recalls; "I must have done well because Joe Harvey switched his full-backs at half-time. I paralysed David Craig, so he put Irving Nattrass on me. He had more pace but that didn't bother me because I preferred playing against people with pace. That was usually their greatest strength and I could nullify that."

Although Dougan returned for Eastoe, he could not prevent a 5-2 humiliation at Arsenal that had McGarry blasting his team; "It doesn't matter one bit what happened last season and the sooner some of my players get that into their heads, the better." Wolves bounced back on the season's second Saturday to be three up on Spurs after 34 minutes. With Kindon out injured, Daley came in on the left and, although Martin Peters and John Pratt narrowed the margin, there was to be no great Spurs comeback this time. The performance was perfectly summed up by the headline, 'Wolves are great, then hang on'. A London double was achieved the following Tuesday despite a crippling injury list that forced McGarry to switch John McAlle to left-back, Alan Sunderland to right-half, and 27-year-old youth coach Brian Owen to centre-half alongside Munro. West Ham kept Wolves scoreless until 17 minutes from time, then McCalliog, Richards and Dougan secured a 3-0 win. The biggest North Bank cheer was reserved for the Doog heading home Sunderland's cross to score what was thought to be his 200th League goal (it was later proven to be 199). His first had come against Wolves for Portsmouth in November, 1957 when he equalised an Eddie Clamp goal.

Next day, Parkin was admitted to hospital with suspected heart trouble, so ending a run of 233 League games, 173 of them for Wolves. He had felt unwell for a while and had tests as a precaution, believing he was suffering from a virus picked up in Australia. He remembers the shock; "There was something they picked up on. Whether it was a virus or a heart murmur, we won't ever know. I loved training and never took it for granted. I always prided myself on being fit, always wanting to play every game even when I had little niggles. I never felt bad but it was a horrible time."

Bailey and Taylor returned for the visit to The Dell, where McCalliog's 25-yarder rescued a point after Munro's own goal had put Southampton ahead. Rounding off

200 up for the 'Doog'

That's it! The ball speeds from the head of the "Doog" with the deadly accuracy of a man whose experience with head and foot has bewildered and bothered teams in the league for 16 seasons. It was goal No. 200 for the Irish international and no doubt one of the most memorable in the seven seasons Derek has been at Molineux. The Wolves' man has waited since last season for this

August with a trip to Coventry, Wolves somewhat undeservedly snatched both points with a goal at the death, their climb to seventh confirmed when Roy Barry misjudged Parkes' clearance and Richards nipped in to head over Bill Glazier. Meanwhile, it was reported Wolves had agreed to pay £89,000 for 24-year-old Ipswich defender Derek Jefferson. On September 2, newly-promoted Birmingham made their first League visit to Molineux since 1966-67 - a season in which they had done the double over Wolves. Bob Latchford and ex-Wolf Bob Hatton led the visitors' attack in front of a sun-baked crowd of 32,529 but it was Wolves who were three up in 24 minutes thanks to a Munro header and a McCalliog double. With future PFA chairman Gordon Taylor pulling the strings on the wing, goals from Bobby Hope and Kenny Burns hauled Birmingham back into the match but they couldn't get back on terms.

The following Tuesday, Wolves limped to an unconvincing second-round League Cup win in their first-ever tie against lowly Orient. This was the day a group of Black September Arab guerrillas broke into the Munich Olympic compound and seized Israeli athletes with desperately tragic consequences. At the end of the week, an incredible match at Liverpool saw Wolves lose their third away game in five. The luck of the visitors was summed up by an Emlyn Hughes' goal that entered the net via a post and Parkes' back to set up a 4-2 scoreline. McCalliog let his frustration boil over when adjudged to have fouled Peter Cormack to concede the fourth penalty Wolves had had against them in six Anfield visits. He was sent off for pushing a linesman.

Texaco Cup action then returned to Molineux and, after Bailey's early own goal, Wolves woke up in the second half to net five times against Kilmarnock. Only 8,734 attended and the night was most memorable for the cavalier refereeing of Leicester's 'Mr Pickwick', Roger Kirkpatrick. It was at this point Curran was sold to Second Division Oxford for £55,000 - and he scored on debut against Millwall on the day Wolves took on Manchester United. The Red Devils were bottom after eight matches without a win and things got worse for them as Dougan and Richards scored in either half to see off, "an appallingly weak United side." To further dent their fast-sinking morale, Jimmy Mac signed off before his three-game ban by setting The Doog up to crack past Alex Stepney and end any lingering dispute on the 200 League goals issue, although the second was somewhat dubious. Bobby Charlton was advancing towards the North Bank end when he played a terrible ball to the right that was intercepted by Taylor. He found Wagstaffe, playing his first League game of the season, and Dougan sprinted free on the left with Richards yards offside in the centre. Waggy crossed for Richards to nevertheless slot coolly home under the advancing Stepney.

The next day, Britain was stunned by Sunday newspaper reports of alleged bribery in the Wolves v Leeds game of the previous May. In a Sunday People world exclusive, David Farr and Sydney Foxcroft reported a 'Soccer Bribes Sensation' in which Wolves stars had supposedly had offers to 'fix' the match. Wagstaffe, Shaw, Munro and Hegan were all mentioned in an article claiming that up to £1,000 had been unsuccessfully

A massive story - broken by the Sunday People - about Wolves' 1971-72 game with Leeds.

offered. The key elements of the report alleged; "Damning evidence can today be made public of a brazen series of attempts to fix one of the most crucial soccer games for years. All bribe offers, and these may have been more than three, were rejected. The big fix had failed." John Dee quoted McGarry in the Express & Star as confirming that Shaw had taken a phone call 24 hours beforehand asking him to sell the game; "From what Shaw told me, I immediately called the players together to inform them. With this in mind, I warned all the team that they too might be approached during the day. Of course, all offers were rejected." McAlle recalls McGarry's warning while Dougan believed the claim that Billy Bremner tried to persuade Danny Hegan to concede a penalty was 'sheer fiction'. Wagstaffe confirms there was no impropriety; "I can assure you nobody had taken a bribe." Munro remembers that around ten years later, when he was in Melbourne, the affair was rumbling on; "Four separate Sundays, a reporter from The People knocked my door and asked me to come back and appear in court."

The bribes bombshell came amid continuing concern over Parkin, who was now ruled out for at least two months following cardiac tests, a sadness compounded by the death at only 47 of late 1940s Molineux full-back Laurie Kelly. Wolves' tepid late-September form continued with dull draws at Leicester and Kilmarnock, the tedium at Firs Park summed up by an electrical fault that blacked out the stadium for 20 minutes. The last Saturday of the month saw Molineux lit up by an eight-goal encounter with lowly Stoke. Eliminated from the UEFA Cup by Kaiserslautern in midweek, injury robbed the Potters of Gordon Banks and, although Geoff Hurst converted a penalty in two minutes, Wolves ran out 5-3 winners. Ignored by Sir Alf Ramsey for an up-coming match against Yugoslavia, Richards netted a hat-trick to become the division's top scorer and send Wolves to fifth. Hegan paid tribute to the part played by Dougan in Richards' blossoming; "He's older than Father Christmas but, today, he was running round like a two-year-old." Dougan recalled the energy for the game he still felt; "I

Richards 3-goal nudge to Sir Alf!

A goal down after only three minutes—the result of a typical Geoff Hurst penalty blockbuster—Wolves climbed dramaticall;

Sir Alf takes the hint and calls up JR

READY TO GO.. ALF'S NEW BOYS HIT THE TOWN

THREE of the England new boys — John Richards, Mick Mills and Frank Worthington. And for them now the big question is . . . will they be chosen to play?

could waste the second half on my own by getting throws or corners with my trick of knocking it off an opponent's foot. I was trying to drive the opposition to desperation so they would make wild tackles and perhaps concede a penalty."

As Parkin remembers, this match summed up the team's approach; "We often won because, although we let in three, we scored four or five. We had some really good players. A talent like Waggy who could put a ball exactly where he wanted; The Doog and John Richards terrorising defences; Ken Hibbitt and Jim McCalliog, they all did a good job." Dougan remembered a good-natured clash with Hurst in the Stoke match. He had previously kicked Hurst, who later clattered into him off the ball; "I just looked at him and said, 'Geoff, if you want to do it, do it with a bit of subtlety', to which Geoff responded with that wonderful smile with the missing teeth." In the Sporting Star soon after, Richards was hailed by 1950s great Roy Swinbourne as the new Molineux idol; "He is quick and has great positional sense." He also received praise from managers Joe Mercer, Tony Waddington and Frank O'Farrell and modestly calls 1972-73; "just one of those seasons. I was young, a lot of people were not aware of me and I benefited from the surprise element. I just played naturally. I don't think scoring goals can be taught. You either can or you can't. You can practice technique but not instinct. It's anticipation, it's gut, knowing where the ball's going to land and getting in front or behind someone." Richards was belatedly named for England, along with Mick Mills and Worthington, and celebrated by helping see off Sheffield Wednesday in the League Cup third round. Jefferson made his debut at no 6 and even old boy John Holsgrove couldn't stop Wolves reaching the last 16 for only the third time in the competition.

A disappointing draw at Manchester City is best recalled for Malcolm Allison's controversial comments on challenges by Jefferson on Rodney Marsh and Colin Bell that earned him a second booking in two games; "Both players have reported for England with badly scarred shins. They are lucky to be going." In October, Wolves'

League form deteriorated further as Crystal Palace's visit ended their 100 per cent home record. Martin Hinshelwood scored Palace's first goal in nine games to earn a point and, a week later, McGarry suffered his first loss at The Hawthorns with Wolves. The game also ended a run of 14 League games in which Wolves had scored. Dougan, chosen by 'Taylor and Cutter' as best dressed man of 1972, collided with Alan Merrick and broke his nose before, eight minutes from time, Bobby Gould nipped ahead of Owen to turn Tony Brown's cross into the Smethwick End net. The author 'enjoyed' the dubious pleasure of being directly behind the goal.

Tragedy struck World Cup legend Gordon Banks next day when his eye was irrevocably shattered by splintered glass in a car crash. Trying to put their miserable form behind them, Wolves returned to Texaco Cup action and lost 2-1 at Ipswich. O'Grady left for Rotherham for only £7,500, his sharp depreciation reflecting a modest Wolves career dogged by injury and also featuring a loan spell at Birmingham in their 1971-72 promotion season. On the last Saturday in October, Leeds were back in town and took revenge by going two up in half an hour. Shaw's 100th League start for Wolves was the only memorable aspect of the weekend for the Molineux men.

Before the month was out, Wolves had reached the League Cup quarter-final for the first time. Given the fact Watney Cup conquerors Bristol Rovers were the visitors, it was not going to be plain sailing and 6,000 visiting fans were almost celebrating early on as a Bannister effort flashed across the gaping Wolves goal. In the end, the home team were three up by the break, eventually gaining a 4-0 win that included only Kindon's second career headed goal. Bonfire weekend almost yielded a first League win since the Stoke match when a Kindon double put Wolves 2-1 up at West Ham, only for Trevor Brooking to salvage a point two minutes from time. Kindon remembers this visit to the capital and how Wolves attracted big-name fans; "I scored two very good goals there and was struck by the famous people who supported us. Alan Knott, the greatest wicketkeeper I've ever seen, a big fan; Bev Bevan of ELO became a very good friend of mine. Politicians and lords of the realm, we'd go to London and, in the players' lounge afterwards, you'd recognise five or six famous people who were there to watch their club, Wolverhampton Wanderers. A lot had cottoned on to the Wolves during the great era of Billy Wright, Bill Slater and those lads."

The following Tuesday, Ipswich won by the only goal to extend their aggregate lead and remove Wolves from the Texaco Cup. Successive Saturday home defeats then sent Wolves sliding to 14th. First, Richards could not prevent Arsenal winning 3-1 win, although his fine goal was a rare bright spot. Munro found him half-way in the Arsenal half and he turned with pace away from his marker. As defenders closed in, he struck a fine shot from the edge of the box past a helpless Geoff Barnett and into the South Bank net. It ended a personal drought of five games for the no 9 but he couldn't prevent Ipswich repeating their Texaco success on a snow-bound pitch. It was Wolves' seventh League defeat in 18 and their lowest home League crowd (14,888) since April, 1965.

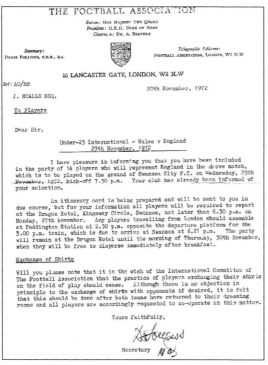

THE FOOTBALL ASSOCIATION

Patron: Her Majesty The Queen
President: H.R.H. Duke of Kent
Chairman: Dr. A. Stephen

Secretary:
Denis Follows, C.B.E., B.A.

Telegraphic Address:
Football Association, London, W2 3LW

16 LANCASTER GATE, LONDON, W2 3LW

Ref: AO/MB

20th November, 1972

J. MCALLE ESQ.

To Players

Dear Sir,

Under-23 International - Wales v England
29th November, 1972

I have pleasure in informing you that you have been included in the party of 14 players who will represent England in the above match, which is to be played on the ground of Swansea City F.C. on Wednesday, 29th November, 1972, kick-off 7.30 p.m. Your club has already been informed of your selection.

An itinerary card is being prepared and will be sent to you in due course, but for your information all players will be required to report at the Dragon Hotel, Kingsway Circle, Swansea, not later than 6.30 p.m. on Monday, 27th November. Any players travelling from London should assemble at Paddington Station at 2.30 p.m. opposite the departure platform for the 3.00 p.m. train, which is due to arrive at Swansea at 6.21 p.m. The party will remain at the Dragon Hotel until the morning of Thursday, 30th November, when they will be free to disperse immediately after breakfast.

Exchange of Shirts

Will you please note that it is the wish of the International Committee of The Football Association that the practice of players exchanging their shirts on the field of play should cease. Although there is no objection in principle to the exchange of shirts with opponents if desired, it is felt that this should be done after both teams have returned to their dressing rooms and all players are accordingly requested to co-operate in this matter.

Yours faithfully,

Secretary

An England under-23 call that the unlucky John McAlle was unable to accept.

Dougan, who returned against the Gunners from injury, moaned; "We're entertaining, too bloody entertaining!"

In the League Cup, Wolves were drawn with Blackpool, a team they hadn't beaten in two previous cup-ties. Apathy seized Molineux as just 17,000 turned out and only a headed equaliser from McCalliog spared the blushes. The replay date deprived Richards and McAlle of an England under-23 outing in Wales. 'Scouse' was particularly unfortunate not to be given a second chance partly due to the fact Ipswich's Kevin Beattie stepped up instead. A run of eight League matches without a win was ended by Richards and Hibbitt at Bramall Lane, the confidence gained setting them up to win the replay at Bloomfield Road. JR set up Dougan to drive past future Wolves keeper John Burridge with six minutes to go. The next Saturday, Richards scored yet again but in a 2-1 setback against Derby. Wolves' home record was distinctly lop-sided, the side scoring 16 times in five opening wins but netting only three times in the next five that brought four defeats and a draw. An article focused on one of the few positives, the incredible consistency of Parkes and McAlle. They had not missed a match since Ipswich away in September, 1970, and would ultimately share 145 unbroken first-team games (106 League, 12 UEFA Cup, 12 Texaco Cup, 9 League Cup, and 6 FA Cup). Indeed, of the top 30 all-time Wolves appearance makers, ten were by players of the late 1960s and 1970s, all with at least 300, namely Parkin, Hibbitt, McAlle, Palmer, Richards, Bailey, Wagstaffe, Parkes, Munro and Dougan.

Things looked up in the League as December ebbed away. First Hibbitt sealed a 1-0 win at Everton and, although Dougan was again sidelined, Sunderland came in to slam an early winner at home to Chelsea. However, little else could have been on their minds than the League Cup semi-final first leg, with cup bogey team Spurs the visitors on the last Wednesday before Christmas. If Wolves were determined to learn from the 1972 UEFA Cup final, it didn't show. Peters and Pratt put Spurs two up in 15 minutes, inspiring the Express & Star headline, "Wolves' dream faded in fatal first few minutes." Although Hibbitt halved the deficit with a penalty on half-time, Wolves could not get level. John Ireland's summer lament was borne out by a disappointing attendance of 28,327, well below the numbers that poured into White Hart Lane for the second leg. Two days before Christmas, The Doog came off the bench to save a point at Norwich and, on Boxing Day, he chipped in again with Richards to secure a home win over Leicester that lifted Wolves back into the top six. Munro completed a two-game suspension that freed him up for the Tottenham match.

A 3pm kick-off on Saturday, December 30 would decide who would proceed to Wembley. In preparation, Bill McGarry dragged his squad into ATV's Birmingham studios to watch what he felt was an unacceptable first-leg performance. Shaw was fit to return but a twisted ankle kept Munro out and pressed Jefferson into service with McAlle. Going to press with the tie still in progress, the Sporting Star headline ran; "Richards keeps final in sight." On 39 minutes, Sunderland's shot was deflected into his own net by Terry Naylor to put Wolves level overall but Peters gave Spurs a decisive advantage on 71. Parkes saved magnificently from Alan Gilzean and Chivers to keep Wolves afloat and, with just two minutes left, Richards silenced most of the 41,716 crowd as he crashed home Match of the Day's second best goal in December to send commentator Barry Davies into raptures and the tie into extra-time. This was

a real team goal, starting with an interchange between Taylor and Bailey in the right-back position. Taylor played the ball down the line for Richards, who took the ball on his chest and laid it back to Bailey. The skipper hit a probing ball towards the edge of the box, where Mike England flung himself forwards to head clear. Back on the half-way line, Taylor squared to Jefferson, who fired it towards the edge of the 'd'. Dougan leapt to find Richards, who was lurking on the penalty spot. He turned sharply to drill low with his left foot past the groping Jennings and into the

Two goals at White Hart Lane but Spurs still came out on top again despite a man-of-the-match display by John McAlle.

138

right-hand corner. In a seesaw additional 30 minutes, Wolves fell to their old nemesis Chivers, superbly marshalled until then by McAlle - chosen as both Man of the Match and Midland Player of the Month. Six minutes were left when Ray Evans swung over a free-kick and England flicked on for the striker to smash home.

Understandably shell-shocked, Wolves struggled to lift themselves for the visit of Southampton and Channon nicked the points in the 88th minute. A week later and a still-bottom Manchester United were the visitors for an FA Cup third-round tie for which Tommy Docherty could not include new signing Ted MacDougall. With only two minutes gone, Bailey had a free-kick blocked but latched on to the rebound to hammer home. However, just before half-time, the Wolves skipper was forced off for an x-ray revealing ankle damage that would scar the remainder of his season and give Danny Hegan yet another chance. Although there was no further scoring, veteran Tony Dunne was sent off for the first time in his United career 87 minutes into a tie marred by ugly scenes before, during and afterwards. A Wolverhampton boy was struck by an axe and a Shrewsbury man stabbed in the chest. Richards was later called up to the full England squad for a match against Wales but the following Saturday's League trip to Birmingham was snowed off. Several Wolves and Blues fans still contrived to get arrested after a pitched battle with fruit in the Bull Ring. Sixty arrests were made when a stall was tipped over to allow its contents to be used as ammunition.

The visit of table-topping Liverpool at the end of the month proved to be one of the season's high spots. Wolves enjoyed the early good fortune of a Hughes own goal, then Keegan equalised on 17 minutes. In a tremendous second half, the game could have gone either way but late on Richards was fed by Shaw to inflict only Liverpool's fourth loss of the season and their first since November 11. McAlle found Sunderland free on the left and his clever pass supplied McCalliog. He squared to no 4 Shaw, who charged forwards and played Richards in on the edge of the box. Richards ignored offside claims to slide the ball right-footed under Ray Clemence. Playing in midfield, Shaw said; "I always take notice of the crowd and they were tremendous to me."

February 3 was FA Cup fourth-round day and Bristol City were KO'd courtesy of a Richards strike from six yards at the end of the first half. Gould turned out for City and Les Wilson was in their squad without playing. Equally significantly, Derek Parkin scored the winner in

Well-behaved snow-bound fans en route for St Andrew's.

the 2-1 West Midlands League victory over Hereford at Castlecroft, his first game since August. Having been given a clean bill of health, he went on to make two Central League appearances against Manchester United and Nottingham Forest. Parkin remembers the relief of this long-awaited positive diagnosis; "I was very lucky they took me to see a specialist in London. He had a look inside. It's quite common now but it was pioneering then. They went through the arm into the chest area and put a camera in, an angiogram. They took me back to the ward and this specialist, Mr Gibson, came straight up. I was panicking, Norma and me and two young kids, we'd just bought a house and this was it, sink or swim. I could have kissed the guy when he told me everything was alright and I just phoned Norma straightaway. He was a lovely man and I went to see him every year after that. He became a friend, really."

Jefferson was named January Midland Player of the Month but Manchester United avenged their Cup setback when a Charlton double set them up for a 2-1 win at Old Trafford, their first victory in seven under Docherty. Hegan scored for Wolves but it was his last goal for the club and Richards had another game for England under-23s in a 2-1 win over Scotland at Kilmarnock. A home draw with Newcastle was memorable for Parkin's long-awaited return and he appreciates the coincidence of it being against his home-town team; "It's surprising how things have a habit of doing that. It was ironic really when I thought about it." The only down-side was that this game brought McAlle's proud unbroken sequnce to an end. The points were shared dint of a goal from each Hibbitt brother and the game was climaxed by a Dougan miss at the South Bank End. He rounded Iam McFaul, only to kick fresh air in front of an open goal - an incident he recalled affectionately; "I went around the goalie so easily because it was McFaul. I would nod to him before we went out and he'd dive! It was on my weaker right foot and my left gave way. What else could I do but share it with the crowd?"

In the build-up to the FA Cup fifth-round visit of Millwall, there were high hopes

Oops! An embarrassing mis-kick that became an opportunity for a laugh with the crowd....

Bailey would return but, having recovered from a broken ankle, he pulled a muscle in training. With Wagstaffe also ruled out, Daley came in at no 11 to make his Cup debut against a team who had seen off Everton in the fourth round. He had scored in his first League and UEFA Cup starts but it was Richards who, on seven minutes, netted his

20th goal of the season to earn a third successive single-goal cup win. Barry Powell appeared in the squad for the first time as an unused substitute. The rearranged game against Birmingham went the same way as the Millwall tie when Dougan put an angled shot past Dave Latchford from the edge of the area to send City into the bottom four.

The first Saturday in March brought one of Wolves' best Molineux performances of the season. With Coventry boss Joe Mercer watching, his old team Manchester City were demolished, having already been eliminated from the Cup by eventual winners Sunderland. They arrived weakened by a suspension to Mike Summerbee and an injury to Francis Lee and, with one goal from Dougan and two from Richards, the visitors were three down by the break. In the second half, Dougan netted twice more to complete his hat-trick. Parkes' 150th consecutive game was marred only by a Rodney Marsh consolation goal in what the News of the World described as "Murder at Molineux". In the Daily Express, Marsh bizarrely argued that City should have had at least a point; "Three of their goals were scored by players who were offside when the ball was played. On top of all that, one of their players handled as he dived to clear and we should have had a penalty. With my goal, it would have been 2-2. See?"

This was the time the Richards/Dougan combination was at its peak, and the latter reflected; "We were certainly the best post-war striking duo. It was a chemistry and a formula sent from heaven. We were better than Keegan and Toshack, they were not in the same league as us since Richards was that bit quicker." Powell recalls; "That team, Dougan and Richards, a perfect foil for each other, Wagstaffe, the great winger going forward changing play, and then Kenny Hibbitt. Nobody played that position as well as him. When we were defending, he tucked in and, when we were attacking, he'd give us width." Parkin agrees; "I thought then the partnership of The Doog and John was the best in Europe. They frightened the life out of the opposition." Munro agrees but argues that they rarely shone in really big games; "I've told them that individually and together they were fantastic but that in semi-finals, UEFA Cup and League Cup Finals, they never played as well as they could. Typically, the Doog said, 'We were the best players' but John agrees with me. They were still probably the best pairing in the country at the time." Daley recognises how important the partnership was; "You knew that nine times out of ten the Doog would win the ball in the air. John ran on past him and gave me or Kenny the chance to support John. It worked every time because if it was played into Doog's chest I'd still go. We got more bodies forward, more chances of scoring. The flick-ons John got from the Doog....you have to use what you've got."

They combined again to score in a 2-0 win at Chelsea the following Tuesday that lifted Wolves to sixth. Their keeper John Phillips kept a black Labrador out of his net but stopped little else. Wolves stayed in London for a Saturday trip to Crystal Palace, where Munro's goal grabbed only a point in a match that marked Powell's debut as a second-half substitute; "Somebody came in and said, 'Baz you're on the first-team sheet'. We were playing Chelsea and Palace and going to Sussex for a few days. I thought I was going because of the kit. But, at Selhurst Park, he named me as sub and I got on for 20 minutes for Danny Hegan." He remembers McGarry being typically hard but fair with him at Worthing; "On the night after we beat Chelsea, the lads were getting dressed to go to pubs and clubs and I got ready to go with them. He's sat in the foyer and said, 'Babs, where the f...in hell are you going?' 'I'm going with them', I replied. 'Make sure you're back before 12 o'clock.' I walked back in at midnight and there he was sat in the same seat. 'Goodnight.' 'Goodnight'. That was it."

The following weekend, Shaw wore no 4 in the FA Cup quarter-final with Coventry and Wagstaffe returned to relegate Kindon to the bench. The big striker almost contrived to get a start when he inadvertently flattened Dougan with a powerful shot in the warm-up. Richards recalls one of the funniest incidents he ever saw on a football field; "Dougan was doing his warm-up in front of the North Bank while Stevie was hitting balls at Phil Parkes. He hit this thunderbolt that happened to coincide with the Doog's stroll across the area and it knocked him clean out." Bill McGarry had just reached his seat in the stand and raced down to the pitch, where Wolves' talisman was being treated by Toby Andersen and Sammy Chung. The language was understandably choice and JR remembers Kindon standing by the far corner flag whimpering, "I didn't meant it, boss, I didn't mean it!" They revived the Doog but kick-off was delayed five minutes." Kindon made it sheepishly to the bench to position himself next to Chung and as far from McGarry as possible but, as JR recalls, this did not spare his old mate a verbal savaging (expletives deleted!); "Kindon, you idiot, you must be the biggest waste of money at this club. If I had a gun, I'd shoot you!" Kindo sat there, head in hands, but Sammy, always the 'good cop', calmed him saying; "Don't worry, Steve, he doesn't mean it. He's only repeating what he's heard the directors say!"

Hibbitt adds his memories; "The fans were chanting, 'Dougan, Dougan' and he

Luck of the Irish on St. Patrick's Day

always responded by putting his arms up. Steve just blasted one and hit him full on the back of the head. He's out cold, needing the smelling salts. I remember McGarry racing on ranting; "What have you done, you big fat b*****d!" Parkin chips in; "You can imagine McGarry's reaction, can't you? He went ballistic." Palmer believes the incident perfectly sums up the chalk-and-cheese nature of manager and assistant that made them such a success; "They complemented each other so well. Sammy was an excellent coach and Bill knew exactly what he was talking about." Kindon's memory of the incident begins with an understatement; "I got immense stick from McGarry. It was worrying but, when it's over, you laugh about it. Soon after, I received a questionnaire from students at Wolverhampton Polytechnic. Question one was; 'What's the worst thing you can imagine doing? A) Going to the dentist, B) Jumping out of a plane at 35,000ft, C) Sleeping in a tank of snakes, or D) Knocking out a colleague just before an FA Cup quarter-final.' Question D was, of course, linked to 20 further questions all related to knocking out the Doog."

Dougan recovered sufficiently to set up the first goal after seven minutes. Munro powered a fabulous header from the edge of his own box. The Doog, just inside the Coventry half, outjumped Roy Barry to head cleverly into the path of Richards, who was behind Bobby Parker. Richards' tremendous pace took him past the Sky Blues number 6 and into the box before he slotted left-footed inside Bill Glazier's left-hand post, as described on Star Soccer in the immortal words of the late Hugh Johns; "Richards, the speed of him. He must be in for it. He's got it!" Carr, then of Coventry, recalls the goal with less relish; "We had a decent team and were unbeaten for about 13 matches. I just couldn't see us getting beaten. All I remember is the Doog flicking on and Richards giving Bobby Parker ten yards and still outstripping him, just pushing him out of the way. It was the first time I'd seen Richie first hand and the type of player he was." In the second half, breathing space was gained when Mick Coop bundled Richards over and Hibbitt placed the penalty into the North Bank net. Although Carr scraped the upright, most of the 50,000-plus crowd could relax and enjoy the rest of the game. Molineux has never since seen a higher attendance.

On the following Tuesday, almost 20,000 fewer witnessed an easy 2-0 win over Albion, with the same scorers. At 17, Powell made his full League debut and played his full part in a victory that set the Baggies three points adrift of Norwich and Palace at the bottom of the table. They would not recover. Powell remembers his baptism of fire; "In the first couple of minutes, I got an elbow; an initiation to the game. Bang, have that, thanks very much!" He recalls Dougan's support; "They were father figures, him and Mike. I remember The Doog standing over me, waving for the trainer. When he came on, he grabbed the sponge and started treating me himself."

As so often, the fixture list threw up a rehearsal for the FA Cup semi-final against Leeds. With Clarke, Cherry, McCalliog and Hibbitt missing, the Elland Road clash gave few pointers in a dour 0-0 draw that stretched Wolves' and Leeds' unbeaten runs to nine and eight games respectively. Most significantly, Munro pulled a hamstring and was left a doubt for the semi. Wolves then produced a lack-lustre performance at home to Sheffield United. While a Pakistan v England Test match in Karachi saw police baton attacks and a stand set on fire, just 19,114 fans turned out at Molineux to see a Richards goal save Wolves in a display McGarry labelled as "rubbish".

It was at this time the management realised they had unwittingly pushed one player too far. Kindon explains; "Although I'd initially been told not to expect much, I had played quite a lot and been sub all the time. When you played in the first team, you had Sunday and Monday off if there was no midweek game, and the reserves played Wednesday and had Thursday off. I was training with the first team on Friday, sub and sometimes played an hour on Saturday, Sunday off, Monday training with the reserves because I'd only had half a game, then Wednesday playing for them and Thursday training with the first team. McGarry called me in and asked; 'You alright?' I said; 'Yeah, fine.' 'Only you're not training as hard as eight months ago.' I had boils on my face, looked run down and they thought I was burning the candle at both ends. I told him I wasn't. While we talked, Sammy was reading notes; 'Gaffer, it's probably our fault.' McGarry retorted; 'What you mean, it's our f***in fault?' 'Look at this, he's not had a day off in eight months.' 'What do you mean? Each Wednesday, we play golf.' 'Well he hasn't, he's played with the reserves.' He turned to me; 'Haven't you had a day off? Why the f***in hell did you not f***in tell us?' It was as if it was my fault but he gave me four days' break and it did me the world of good."

April 7 was semi-final day, with Arsenal favourites to see off Second Division Sunderland, and my uncles Cliff and Barry driving me to Maine Road, Manchester for another momentous showdown with Leeds. The Doog commented; "Everyone was

Buying a semi-final ticket called for patience from these fans queueing in Molineux Alley.

talking about another Leeds v Arsenal final but I said why not Wolves v Sunderland?" In the build-up, Bailey and McCalliog faced Huddersfield reserves. Crucially, neither made it, although Munro recovered enough to play and Bailey to be on the bench. Although Jack Charlton returned for Leeds, Eddie Gray and Norman Hunter were out. McGarry made what Dougan called a wrong decision by giving Powell his FA Cup debut rather than McCalliog. Munro was made to feel responsible for the decision; "McGarry blamed me for two years. I wasn't 100 per cent fit, nor was Mike, we both had hamstring injuries. He was desperate for us both to play and was convinced if we had played, we'd have won. So I sort of convinced him by saying, 'If we both play and break down, you've only got one sub. If we've both got to come off early, you're left with ten men. Against Leeds, probably the best in the country at keeping the ball, we'll never get it back'. He talked to me and Mike in his bedroom after breakfast and was desperate to play us. I said, 'If I was you, I would play one with the other as sub'. So he thought about it, made me captain and put Mike as sub. He went on in the second half and we were both ok. McGarry said, 'I knew it!'"

Powell reflects on the experience; "It had been in the press I might well be taking over. Bill saw fit to tell me early on that I was playing, instead of me thinking about it. He felt I could handle the big game. The bigger it was, the better I seemed to perform. To play in front of 52,000 at Maine Road was a big experience. You don't remember any of it, it just seems to flash by." In only the second minute, Powell was put through, only to place his shot too close to David Harvey, as the Doog remembered; "I rose like a bird and beat Big Jack, but surprise, surprise Cilla, Richards, wasn't on the end of it, it was little Barry Powell. Unfortunately, as he closed in, he hit it straight at Harvey." Barry is regularly reminded of the miss and recalls it vividly; "Every time I go to Wolverhampton, someone says, 'You're the one who missed that chance in the semi.' I wouldn't watch it in the evening and hadn't seen it for 20 years until recently. It wasn't as bad as I thought it was. The ball went out to Kenny on the right and my role in that game was to get round their ankles whenever Bremner and Giles had the ball, snapping at them. I was a fit lad, I could run and pass and whenever we had the ball, I was to run past them. I made a run, the Doog took Jack Charlton away and Reaney got dragged to the left. I went up the middle and Kenny played it. It seemed to take an age to get to me and I had a little look and Harvey, quite an experienced keeper, had started to come. I was on the edge of the 18-yard box and thought, 'I'm having a go at this'. I bent it first time, a reasonable strike, but he got down to save. I looked round and there was no-one within ten feet of me. I could have controlled it and taken it on."

Revie's gamble also backfired when he had to replace Charlton with Joe Jordan in the first half but, in a tense affair of ebb and flow, the decisive moment came on 68 minutes. Parkes pulled off a point-blank save from Mick Jones but, from the resulting corner, Hibbitt crucially failed to clear cleanly. Giles sent it back in and Bremner slashed home when it dropped fortuitously for him. How he enjoyed it! How we hated it! Parkes says; "If there was one side you always wanted to beat, it was them because of their reputation. The semi-final was the only goal we conceded all the way through." Bailey recalls; "The goal was very scrappy. We failed to clear a corner and the ball was bobbling about in our box for a while. It eventually fell to Billy, who put it in the net." This dagger to the heart is a memory that still haunts Munro; "I still have nightmares about that goal. I'm screaming to Ken to leave it. I know I can head it clear or chest it and walk out of the area with it. I can see it all now, I was screaming but Kenny couldn't hear me with the crowd noise. He tries a bloody bicycle kick, it goes straight up in the air and where does it fall? Bremner smashes it home and that was it." Hibbitt adds; "I thought Leeds were the best side in that period. We were just unlucky we got drawn against them. Every time I see Frank, he says, 'Your fault'. Nobody said anything on the day, I didn't even think about it. The ball was going out of play but I tried to kick it clear over my head. It went straight to Bremner, who smashed it into the top corner. Frank says, 'I shouted to you to leave it'. I reply, 'You should have shouted louder, I couldn't hear'. I cringe when I look now and accept the blame. We played really well in the second half and had some great chances, and Richie hit the post. I knew Don Revie from years earlier as my brother had been at Leeds and was one of those advising me to go to Wolves in the first place. I saw him afterwards and he said, 'You were the better side in the second half', but they got the goal and that was it."

Bailey replaced a tiring Hibbitt on 73 minutes and the fates were clearly against Wolves when Dougan headed inches over and Richards freakishly struck the inside of the post, the ball rebounding into Harvey's grasp. The Leeds keeper takes up the story; "When the ball went by me, I had given up. I thought it was the equaliser. I was amazed how it came off the post." McGarry persisted in blaming himself for picking Munro ahead of Bailey; "We needed Mike, not only as player but also as captain", something Richards wholeheartedly agrees with; "He was a major loss to us in that game." But, at time when only one sub was named, playing two unfit players would have been a massive risk. One national paper headline was; "Leeds trick a way past brave Wolves". Powell agrees; "You know when you've played well and I felt I'd played very well. We all did. We were the better team and were unfortunate not to win."

Richards recalls the sickening feeling of two semi-final failures, hard on the heels of UEFA Cup despair; "We were gutted and it really was a dreadful time. There were six or seven teams who could have beaten each other on the day. We were one of that group and unfortunately came up against two of them, Spurs and Leeds. Wolves had all that success back in the 1950s and early 1960s and here we'd been on the verge of getting to Wembley twice, every player's dream, and had it snatched from us at the last. I'm reminded of it regularly, mainly by Leeds supporters; 'that was a shame that John!'

John Richards hits the post - it wasn't Wolves' day at Maine Road

they say. I felt we should have won. It was very close all the way through. Even after they scored, we were the stronger team. We hit the post and put them under a lot of pressure. I wasn't over-disappointed because I was fairly young and expected we'd have more opportunities. A lot of our senior players came off upset, some in tears as we'd played probably as well as all season and ended up losing. Personally, I have to be disappointed never to play in an FA Cup final. We missed out three times (1973, 1979 and 1981) and, in at least two of those runs, we should have gone to the final."

Parkin recalls the gut-wrenching agony of falling again; "I really think we were very unfortunate. We matched a good Leeds team. There was a lot of heartache in that dressing room. I cried, I can remember. I hadn't been to a semi-final before." Though down, Hibbitt stayed positive; "I never felt I wasn't going to a Cup final. It was a great period." Although sharing the disappointment, the captain stayed proud; "We missed a wonderful opportunity to go to Wembley. With neither Frank or I fully fit, Bill could not take the chance of playing us both. I went on mid-way through the second half and almost scored. I think Leeds just about deserved it but lost in the final to Sunderland, who were managed by Bob Stokoe, my former boss. And we were again competing for major honours. We were up with the best of them."

Hegan, kept out of the semi by Powell, failed to show for training soon afterwards and started the final bout of self-destructive behaviour that ended his Wolves career early the next season for, "persistent infringement of club rules." Wagstaffe comments sadly on why he never quite made it at Wolves; "He liked his drinks, liked his nights out. He'd be joking with you on the field would Danny." Hibbitt recalls; "Danny could drink for England. You'd be jogging round the track behind him, saying, 'Bloody hell, Danny, you smell like a brewery'. He'd say; 'Swear on me babby's life I haven't had a drink for three weeks'. I went out with him once and regretted it because he got so legless on champagne. I had to get us into a taxi. We were in West Bromwich, then we were back in Wolverhampton, all over the place. I tried to get him awake to tell me where he lived and he gave me this address in West Brom. We got there and it was derelict, a row of houses that had been knocked down. Then suddenly he sobered up and told me he was living at this little hotel by the Banks's brewery where we'd started three and a half hours earlier. I never went out with him again but he was a great lad. When I went to Coventry, his son Anthony was an apprentice there. I met his ex-wife Patsy and we talked about the times we'd had. Danny was a character and a half." Parkin adds equally sympathetically; "He was a good friend. I liked him. He was a super lad and was never any trouble but had this big problem everybody at the club ignored. If he had the same problem today, things would be done."

There was still much for Wolves to play for in the last seven League games, with European qualification at stake. The following Saturday, Everton were the visitors, having recently parted company with long-standing manager Harry Catterick. Richards hit a fine hat-trick in a 4-2 win, taking him to 32 for the season, the best of the three coming when Parkin lifted the ball to him on the edge of the area. Richards breasted it down, swivelled and cracked left-footed high into the net. The win didn't prevent rumours that McGarry was Everton-bound 12 months after he seemed set for

A three-shirt day for Mike Bailey in the mud against Norwich.

Coventry. John Ireland moved swiftly, insisting that McGarry 'is under contract and stays here.'

A visit to Ipswich resulted in a 2-1 loss in which Munro and Colin Viljoen were dismissed. On Easter Monday, Wolves fared better against Norwich on a Molineux gluepot. A powerhouse display from Bailey saw him go through three shirts as Sunderland (2) and Richards clinched a 3-0 win. Unfortunately, the inconsistencies continued with a 2-0 reverse at Stoke the next day before another 3-0 win was secured in the last home game, against Coventry. Richards was presented with the Midland Footballer of the Year award, then, along with Sunderland and Powell, he netted against the Sky Blues. Wolves had taken 29 of 42 home points available with 13 wins, three draws and five losses - identical to 1970-71 and almost guaranteeing a return to Europe. Confirmation came with a second 2-2 draw at Spurs, where Richards' goal five minutes from time was his 27th in the League goal and 36th in all competitions. The last game, incredibly the 58th of the season, was an anti-climax as Derby's 3-0 win confirmed their own UEFA qualification. Fifth spot had been secured and Wolves had played a staggering 27 cup-ties in two years without tangible return, 17 of them won, five lost and five drawn. Parkin couldn't wait for more big tests; "I always felt confident, whatever game I went into. I never felt pressure. The bigger the game, the more I wanted to play."

The season was a personal triumph for Richards, crowned by his marriage to Pam at St. Bartholomew's Church, Penn, and an England debut; "It was very special for me and the club. If anyone asks me the best team I played in, I say it was definitely that one." He became the first Wolves player to win an England cap for seven years when injuries earned him a sudden call for the Home Internationals and the subsequent tour of the Soviet Union and Poland. He was one of six players added to the original 16 for games against Northern Ireland, Wales and Scotland but, in the week leading up to the Ireland game, an injury to Allan Clarke thrust him into contention. The troubles in Belfast meant the game was switched to Everton and, in a strange twist, England trained on a pitch just outside Warrington he had played on as a boy. Staying in Lymm, close to his home town, he was told by Sir Alf Ramsey on the Friday night he would be playing up front alongside Channon and Chivers.

Hibbitt reveals the pride the club felt as Richards fulfilled his dream; "We were so pleased we had a full England international playing for us." What would inexplicably be his one and only senior match saw him bemusingly posted on the left of the attack in England's 2-1 win over Northern Ireland at Goodison on May 12, 1973, Chivers scoring both. Hibbitt feels John couldn't be properly judged on the wing; "He is a big friend of mine but I think if he'd played in the right position, he would probably have scored and gone on to get a lot more caps." With typical but misplaced modesty, Richards lays the blame at his own door; "With Channon and Chivers as established right-footed strikers, I didn't have the confidence to get into it. I was very disappointed with myself." Hibbitt goes on; "He was a prolific scorer for us but unfortunate to be around when there were so many strikers. I think the press wanted to see him in, the Wolves supporters wanted to see him in and I think they forced the manager's hand to play him. The manager thought, 'I'll show you whether or not he's an England player, I'll play him on the left wing'. I just felt there were three or four in front of him and that's why he didn't get the proper striker's role. They played him there to try to prove he wasn't international class. If Alf Ramsey had played him up the middle, he would have got goals. John revelled in chances. Half a chance and he'd make it his chance. A quarter of a chance and he'd make it his chance. That's the kind of player he was. It was so disappointing to see him play out there. He was totally lost."

The night before, a Wolves side minus Sunderland and Richards humiliatingly lost 3-2 in front of 8,000 passionate Somerset folk on Yeovil's treacherous slope. With six or seven other strikers ahead of him, Richards was never given another chance but was on the bench when Bobby Moore smashed Billy Wright's record for England caps and on the June day the skipper's mistake set Poland on their way to a 2-0 World Cup qualifying victory in Katowice. Snubbed by his country, Dougan went to South Africa to play for Arcadia Shepherds in Pretoria, became a great hit and brought back a certain Peter Withe. He later played and scored for an All-Ireland team in a 4-3 defeat at home to Brazil and had further cause to celebrate when the Dudley Zoo authorities decided to name one of their polar bears after him. But when would honours come to him at Wolves?

John Richards rubs shoulders with one of England's finest.

1973-74: Nearly Men No More

The new season dawned at the end of a long hot summer during which Phil Parkes had performed with distinction for Fordhouses CC, typified when he took 3-77 in 20 overs against Uttoxeter. School football began on a bone-hard pitch in Evesham, where Brierley Hill Grammar's finest took a seven-goal hammering. Like Wolves, we struggled at first and then improved, although our only prize was a staff v pupils match kicked off by headmaster Mr. Huffer. Having had several bids turned down for Millwall keeper Brian King, Wolves' only pre-season signing was 22-year-old Bury lad Gary Pierce from Third Division Huddersfield. Joining two days before the start of the Swedish tour, Pierce commented; "I didn't like training before but I must admit that with Wolves there is so much variety, I now enjoy it." Defending the Rous Cup, Wolves began strongly to beat Oergryte 3-1 before overcoming Leicester in the final through an Alan Sunderland goal. During this same pre-season Oxbarn Social, mistaken for Wolverhampton Wanderers, had toured Germany and found themselves pitched against SVW Mainz. They duly lost 21-0 and McGarry pledged to take his team to Mainz as soon as they had a clear date, "to put the record straight." This pledge must have offered some comfort to the Sunday League players licking their wounds.

The main Molineux friendly brought Division Two Albion to Molineux for their first visit for anything other than a League or Cup game since the 4-4 Charity Shield classic in 1954. The Baggies were dispatched embarrassingly easy by goals from John Richards and Kenny Hibbitt and an unintentional contribution from future Wolves skipper Ally Robertson. Cannock-born Geoff Palmer, who had turned pro the previous August, went on for the injured John McAlle and was reported by John Dee to have shown; "a willingness and tigerish tackle that must have impressed McGarry." Derek Parkin argues Palmer was much underrated; "He was a very good player. I think had he moved early in his career, he would have been better still. Very quick, two good feet and he could tackle. He was only a young boy when he came in and he stayed in and that takes some doing. There were a lot of good left-wingers about but I don't recall him getting a roasting." Palmer made his full debut against Arsenal two days later in a match to decide third place in the previous season's FA Cup. Derek Dougan (2) and Jim McCalliog broke goal ducks going back five months and nine months respectively to secure an encouraging 3-1 win at Arsenal for a team surprisingly captained by the errant Danny Hegan. Later in the week, Richards was named Rothmans Young Player of the Year, while a Parkin own goal against Belgian champions Bruges spelt defeat in the final warm-up match. Parkin's simple aim for the season was to put his health scare behind him; "My attitude is to forget the whole business, worrying though it was." In light of the Bruges loss, McGarry issued a warning for the European campaign ahead; "I'm disappointed about the result but there's more to it. The Continentals are getting fitter and stronger all the time and catching up fast on the physical side." And his message also took in England; "If we aren't prepared to work at our game and improve the basic skills of passing and control, we'll fall so far behind it will be unbelievable."

At the club's annual meeting, John Ireland hit out at the growing hooliganism problem; "Not long ago, we were proud of our North Bank but now we are worried. With visiting fans watching from the South Bank, it can only be our own supporters causing so much worry. The situation is that a man who wants to take his wife and children to Molineux simply stays away because of the nonsense that comes from a minority who stand there." Harsh words maybe but this was also the experience of some of my family members, and the Express & Star's Ray Matts wrote of 90 minutes on the North Bank; "My brief? To get an on-the-spot view of the long-haired, baggy-trousered, banner-waving, boisterous boyos and their green, mauve and blue fingernailed molls." His findings were not positive; "It's crowded, noisy and no place for the sensitive. The few spoiled it for the majority." Ireland also bemoaned trading problems, with 1972-73 crowds down by 3,500 to 24,500 and season ticket sales of only £71,000. The Sun called Wolves 'poor relations of Midlands soccer' and McGarry moaned; "People wonder why I don't buy a big-name player every year."

In the year to May 31, profits fell to £42,262 from £68,084 the previous season, a drop largely attributable to Wolves' absence from Europe. In pessimistic mood, Ireland commented; "It is sad to reflect we are a better attraction away than at home. We are just not supported well enough to live up

THE NORTH BANK MOLINEUX BURDEN?

Wolves chairman, John Ireland, recently hit out, at his club's annual meeting, at the minority of fans, who were ringing Molineux's North Bank into disrepute. This week the Sporting Star takes a look at this unpleasant aspect of soccer in the 70s which is by no means a problem exclusive to Wolves.

The few spoil it for the majority

It's as well sardines are dead when they're put into tins — otherwise they'd go crazy. I know. I spent 90 leg-weary minutes in the Molineux North Bank "cannery" on Tuesday night.

I left the cosy comfort of the Press Box to go among the fans; to rub shoulders with the terrace terriers for a match between Wolves and Sheffield United.

My brief? — to get an on-spot view of the long-

Ray Matts

The scene on the North Bank at Molineux on Tuesday night as two policemen watch the fans filling up the controversial section of the Wolves' ground.

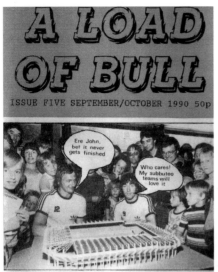

ISSUE FIVE SEPTEMBER/OCTOBER 1990 50p

An Alternative View of Wolverhampton Wanderers

with the Jones's of the football world." More positively, there was speculation that Wolves might move within five years to a magnificent new stadium ten miles away at Cannock. A 40,000 capacity all-seater ground would also provide facilities for athletics, cycling and equestrianism as part of a £100m leisure plan announced by Merrie England Ltd, a subsidiary of Eric Morley's Mecca Group.

A relatively late start to the season saw Norwich City visit Molineux for an encounter Wolves must have approached with confidence given six wins and a draw in their previous encounters. A three-match ban and ankle injury respectively deprived the Wanderers of Frank Munro and Mike Bailey. This had the skipper complaining; "Someone in the Wolverhampton area must be using me for voodoo practice! To say I am choked is putting it mildly." Hegan slotted in at no 4, assuring his boss there would be no more brushes with authority as he had; "finished with trouble." A new-look Molinews programme rose by a penny to 8p but simultaneously shrank as a result of the need to use economically viable continental-size paper. Led by McAlle, two goals from Dougan and one from McCalliog secured a 3-1 win as Wolves sported the open-neck collars that would be worn for several weeks. The match is best remembered, though, for Kevin Keelan's demolition of the North Bank posts as he tried to keep out Dougan's second-half effort. John Dee described the Doog sprinting like "a kid in a school 100 yard dash" on to a long punt by McAlle. He spotted Keelan off his line and lobbed him. The keeper chased back and in so doing hit the upright and caused a 16-minute delay as he was carried off, taking the minds of older fans back to Reg Cutler of Bournemouth in 1957.

At the other end, Parkes set a Wolves post-war record of 122 League games in a row, outdoing

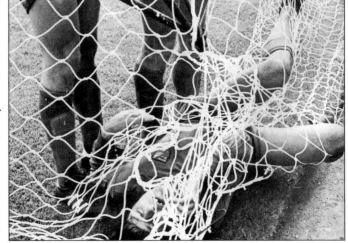

Kevin Keelan in a tangle as he brings the goal down.

Bobby Thomson, who was by now with Luton. Dougan notched his 501st League appearance at the start of what he intimated might be his last season, something belied by his tremendous energy, as the Sporting Star reported; "Dougan plans to keep those Irish eyes smiling longer." The following Tuesday, Munro returned for Derek Jefferson as Sheffield United were dispatched by a goal each from the 'MacDougan' strike-force. Even so, Dee wrote; "Wolves made too many elementary mistakes to talk about the championship. The games at Southampton and Leeds will provide a better guide to their title aspirations."

With Bailey, McCalliog and Kenny Hibbitt ruled out, they lost 2-1 at Southampton despite an early Dougan goal. Hegan had to limp off with an ankle injury on just nine minutes and, after Mike Channon had scored his customary goal, future Saints FA Cup hero Bobby Stokes hit an injury-time winner. Another blank afternoon for Richards brought sympathetic words from his manager; "I have told John not to get concerned. He will come good soon." In a week in which ex-Wolves keeper Alex Scott died on holiday in Jersey, a trip to Elland Road resulted in a 4-1 hiding. Two up in 12 minutes, Leeds never looked in danger of surrendering their 100 per cent start. Having been booked just once in 250 League games, Parkin was dismissed by referee Arthur Jones, partly as a result of Peter Lorimer's dramatic writhings on the floor. Parkin has more positive memories of the evening; "Some of their play at that time was unbelievable. I don't think we touched the ball for about five minutes."

The following Saturday, newly-promoted Burnley visited Molineux and won 2-0 to take their points tally to nine out of ten on the day former Claret Steve Kindon made his first senior start of the season. A youthful midfield of Barry Powell and Sunderland could not subdue the probings of Martin Dobson, Frank Casper and Leighton James. Very soon, it was five successive defeats as a result of 2-0 setbacks at home to Leeds and at Newcastle. Richards was belatedly presented with the Whitbread Young Player of the Season award before the former, which saw Wolves slide ominously into the bottom half. Having failed to win at St James' Park for 15 years, it was little surprise they capitulated in the last five minutes - they even faced a £100 Football League fine for arriving just 20 minutes before kick-off. The Sports Argus rated their form 'dismal' but the performance of the debutant Pierce provided a bright spot as he ended Parkes' club-record run of 127 consecutive games; a record previously held by Noel George.

To take their minds off the alarming slide, most of the first-team squad took to the studios in Stockport under the direction of producer Malcolm Rowe to produce the classic "Wolves, Wolves, Gold and Black", with "Molineux March" on the flipside. The rot was halted when Dougan matched Joe Royle's goal for visiting Everton to earn a point but Wolves still found themselves 20th with only West Ham and Birmingham below them. Having failed to hit the target in eight games, Richards was now reputedly under threat from McGarry. "Score or you'll be axed" ran the unsupportive headline. The manager reportedly mused; "I suppose it's my fault for keeping him in. I should have left him out three games ago. I can't wait any longer for him to find his form." Richards maintains it wasn't like that at all; "Training was normal and I never had an ultimatum from Bill McGarry. It's not what managers do." However, he does recall the tough start; "It became a psychological thing and the longer the run went, the more difficult it became. It was partly because people expected my success to continue. I had gone on tour with England and probably had only two or three weeks break."

The last Wednesday in September provided the distraction of the UEFA Cup first round, with fans offered the opportunity to watch the game in Portugal against OS Belenenses for an all-in £35. Wolves successfully negotiated a potentially tricky night in Lisbon's Americo Thomaz Stadium and, more importantly, Richards broke his 13-hour famine with only ten minutes gone. Running on to a through ball from McCalliog, he outstripped defender Freitas and slammed a 20-yarder past keeper Jose Mourinho. Although a leg injury soon forced Bailey off, a Dougan header on 58 minutes made the game safe. With little left to play for and just 12 minutes remaining Richards was dismissed for the first time in his career in an uncharacteristic clash with Minervino Pietera. The players exploded in a flurry of fists that saw Richards punched twice before retaliating, leaving Spain's Franco Martinez little alternative but to send both

Ups and downs v Belenenses - an early bath in the away leg for John Richards (above) and a fine goal by Peter Eastoe in the return (right) back at Molineux in a clear victory.

off. Wolves' striker recalls; "I was on the half-way line, up front on my own with their centre-halves as Belenenses attacked. Suddenly, one of them thumped me on the side of the head and, before I knew it, the other hit me from the other side. I turned round and hit the second one back, just as the linesman flagged. Me and the second bloke were sent off as the first guy got off scot-free! It was nothing I'd ever come across before and I was really upset that I'd let the whole team down."

Back in the League at Chelsea, Wolves threw away a 2-0 lead given them by McCalliog to surrender a point but, more worryingly, Bailey again limped off. On the same day, Steve Kindon was sent off in the reserves. Richards was suspended for the second leg of the UEFA tie and injuries also deprived Wolves of Bailey, Hegan and Kindon. With Peter Eastoe making his European debut, a Murca goal after only seven minutes gave the Portuguese hope - and nerves were only settled when goals in each half by Eastoe and McCalliog secured a reasonably comfortable aggregate victory. Soon after, there was some good disciplinary news as Parkin's 'exemplary record' spared him a ban. Manchester United's visit yielded a jittery first League win since August, courtesy of McCalliog and Dougan in a match covered by ATV's Star Soccer and watched by Sir Alf Ramsey. Richards' first domestic goal since April 30 came in an easy second-round League Cup win at Halifax with Sunderland and Dougan also chipping in. Five days later, JR got his first Division One goal in 11 outings but his 75-second strike at St Andrew's was nullified as Trevor Francis and Kenny Burns combined to set up Birmingham's first League victory.

Geoff Palmer, who had already deputised for the injured Parkin at The Shay, made his First Division bow at Blues while ex-Leeds keeper Gary Sprake was carried off in his first start for the home side. Palmer remembers realising his dream; "I had progressed through the youth team into the reserves and, luckily, when I was 19, I got picked to play against Halifax at the start of the League Cup run. I always remember Bill McGarry calling me into his office on the morning of the match and saying, 'I'm going to play you tonight. I've had some bad reports from the reserve team coach (Norman Bodell) but I'm going against his judgement.' So I was in and then at the weekend made my League debut against the Blues."

Geoff also felt the need to change his domestic arrangements; "I lived in Cannock rather than in digs and was catching the bus. I felt a bit alienated because I was training then going home away from the lads. I asked if I could go into digs and they found me some with Ian Cole in Jockey Fields, Sedgley, just off the main road towards Lower Gornal. It was close to where Stevie Daley and another couple of the young lads lived. It was a time when lads were given a chance at an early age unlike now, when clubs go and buy somebody. We were given the chance. Stevie was about 18 when he first played and had scored in the UEFA Cup semi-final a few years earlier." Around this time, Palmer was 'stalked' in his digs by my sister Sue and cousin Bev when my dad took them for a visit. He recalled that he had to do the bulk of the talking as the teenage girls sat tongue-tied and open-mouthed for most of the time they were confronted by their hero.

On the following Wednesday, Alf Ramsey's world collapsed as Jan Tomasevski performed like Superman to earn Poland a 1-1 draw and knock England out of the 1974 World Cup. Richards, still ignored by the national team, scored again to give Wolves the lead over mid-table Queens Park Rangers in another televised game but they meekly succumbed 4-2 in front of a Molineux crowd below 20,000, with Stan Bowles (2) and Gerry Francis among the scorers. Wolves had fallen to

Sinking feeling as QPR hit four

After John Richards had grabbed his first home league goal

TV soccer

BBC-1 (10.15 tonight): Derby v. Leicester; Fulham v. Sunderland.

ATV (2.5 tomorrow): Wolves v. QPR.

15th place in the Division One attendance table, dropping from a 1972-73 average of 29,323 to only 25,927. "Wolves hit rock bottom", wrote John Dee in the Express & Star after the team were booed and whistled off. There was particular derision for the decision to replace Dougan with Sunderland in the week the Doog had been given a new five-year deal, McGarry countering; "We were dreadful. We got exactly what we deserved, nothing."

Any optimism that Wolves might embark on another successful UEFA run was then virtually blown away on a dreadful night in Leipzig on which Palmer made his European bow. A mistake by Parkes on 36 minutes let Matoul in to put Lokomotiv ahead but, after Daley had struck a post and Dougan the underside of the bar, two goals (one from a penalty) in the last 15 minutes put the match firmly under Leipzig's control. Reflecting on a first defeat in eight UEFA Cup away games, McGarry raged; "Against such opposition, this result was pure fantasy and even when we were a goal down, I would have bet my house on us going through to the third round."

Although Parkin and Hibbitt made their 200th and 100th full League appearances respectively for Wolves, another wretched display brought a 2-0 defeat at Ipswich, their fifth in a row against the East Anglians. McGarry was reputedly striving to strengthen his midfield with a six-figure bid for Everton's Mike Bernard. In an unusual fixture twist, Wolves' League Cup campaign continued at Tranmere on a Saturday night at the end of October. The Third Division team had earlier won at Arsenal by the only goal and things again looked rosy for Ron Yeats' team when Eddie Loyden put them ahead, only for Sunderland to come to the rescue to earn a replay.

As November arrived, 29-year-old Danny Hegan was sacked by Wolves and listed at the giveaway price of £5,000. He finally got his cards after failing to report for training on Tuesday and Wednesday, and left claiming; "I'm so ashamed of myself."

Parkes knew him better than most; "Danny was naturally funny, one of the funniest lads you'd come across. He was great when he hadn't had a drink and a great player in his own right but a fool to himself. He used to go out drinking and miss training. He was a friend of mine and lived over the road. Bill McGarry used to say, 'Danny's gone missing, go and find him.' I'd make a couple of phone calls and he'd mysteriously turn up." Richards also comments sympathetically; "It was common knowledge Dan had his difficulties in life and it did affect him on the field", but feels the time had come to get someone else in. Parkin believes Hegan could have been a success in different circumstances; "He was a damn good player, very skilful, but was brought in at the wrong time and wasn't a Mike Bailey. Nobody could replace Mike. Danny brought something into the side but needed somebody like Mike around him. Mike did all the mopping up while Danny could make things happen." Hibbitt adds; "Danny was completely different. Mike was a solid tackler and captain while Danny was a footballer." Wagstaffe agrees the biggest mistake was to try to use him as a straight replacement; "He wasn't in the same mould as Mike. He was very talented with great vision but you couldn't play him in Mike's role. He was not a tough tackler."

Only three League games had been won out of 13 by the start of November and Wolves languished in the relegation zone, as they would until December. The first Saturday of the month saw Bailey return to League action for the first time since October 6 but he couldn't inspire anything more than a 0-0 draw with Manchester City at Molineux. McCalliog joined Richards in being banned for the unlikely task of retrieving the tie against Lokomotiv while Bailey failed a late test and Munro climbed off his sick bed to play a stormer. The unlikely seemed to have become the impossible when half-time was reached with no goals in front of a poor 14,530 crowd. Then, around the hour, goals by Kindon and Munro brought hope, only for it to be seemingly

snuffed out by Lowe after Parkes failed to hold his header. Within a minute, Friese dropped a Palmer centre and Dougan fired home, then, with nearly ten minutes left, a low Hibbitt shot had Wolves level on aggregate but behind on away goals that ultimately proved costly. Fans overcame their disappointment by sportingly applauding the efforts of both teams. Leipzig had become the first German Democratic Republic team to beat an English side in European competition, an indication of the creditable impact the national team would have in 1974 on their first World Cup. To add insult to injury, Wolves were cautioned by UEFA because of encroachment by a black mongrel. Portuguese referee Antonio Garrido informed the governing body the dog had twice gone on the pitch without his permission.

A visit to Anfield provided its customary misery as Steve Heighway earned both points to preserve Liverpool's 100 per cent home record. On the day Reds legend Roger Hunt presented him with the Rothmans Golden Boot as Young Player of the Year for 1972-73, a twisted ankle kept Richards out of a League game for the first time since January 29, 1971, so ending a run of 72 consecutive outings in which he had scored 35 goals. Although Wolves were once again without him for the visit of Tranmere the following Tuesday, a goal from Dougan eight minutes after the break seemed to have seen them safely through. Twenty minutes later, though, Ronnie Allen's young son Russell fired home through a crowded area before the ground was plunged into semi-darkness by a power failure. Play was allowed to go on for ten minutes in the gloom before full lighting was restored and, with five minutes left and extra-time likely, Munro found Parkin free on the left and his long pass sought out Barry Powell. Spotting Johnson off his line, the Kenilworth youngster opened his senior scoring account by holding off two challenges to lob home. He remembers; "They all took the mickey by saying it was only because we had partial lighting!"

Progress could not spare Wolves the crowd's wrath after a pitiful 0-0 draw against a West Ham team who lay bottom with just one League win. The game was the first 2.15 kick-off at Molineux in response to the growing energy crisis and protests were aimed at the directors' box after six League games without a win and four without a goal. Amid the booing were calls for McGarry's resignation, a letter to the press from Tony Jones of Bloxwich summing up concerns with what some perceived to be an ageing team; "Mike Bailey, all those injuries keep piling up and that's a sure sign of old age. Derek Dougan is amazing but how old is he? Dave Wagstaffe is batting on, too. Add a suspect keeper, Phil Parkes, to a defence without a lot of confidence, and you have a team at the bottom end of the First Division. What about it, Mr. McGarry?"

Harsh perhaps but, with rumours of a bid from Celtic for Munro, Wolves were now languishing in their lowest League position since McGarry had taken over almost five years earlier. In the Daily Express, Mike Brettell commented; "With six away fixtures in their next eight games, the future does not look bright for Wolves unless they can regain their confidence and start winning tackles in midfield." This was not a sentiment with which Richards agreed; "The team we had at the time was capable of beating anyone if nine of us played to our capacity. It was as simple as that."

With little hope of swift improvement in their League predicament, the diversion of League Cup action returned to Molineux with the visit of Exeter City. An afternoon kick-off on a Tuesday contributed to the lowest post-war home crowd of 7,623, though I did my bit by truanting from school for the first and only time. It was well worth the risk of being caught as two each from Hibbitt and Richards and one from Dougan saw the Devonians thrashed 5-1. The margin of victory probably flattered Wolves who laboured for over 70 minutes to cling to a 2-1 lead but Hibbitt remembers a vital goal from him just before-half time that brought an unexpected

Things improve as Exeter are sent packing from Molineux. The Doog plays his part on a day that Richards and Hibbitt doubled up.

response from his manager; "McGarry was a b*****d but he was respected and made me a player. In seven years, he only praised me once, I'll never forget it. It was at half-time against Exeter. It was a sticky game in more ways than one. The pitch suited them more than us because we were a good football side. Playing in the afternoon, it was a real banana skin. We were terrible but I scored a minute before half-time and took all the tension out of it. I walked in and the boss came up, tapped me on the shoulder and very quietly, and not in front of anyone else, said, 'Well done, son'. I thought 'great'! The goal just changed it and in the second half the lads went on from there."

Reaching the quarter-final for the second time in three years spurred Wolves on to greater things in the League, with a 3-1 win over Tottenham inspired by a super display by Wagstaffe, who "led Spurs a merry dance" and had the Sports Argus recording a form rate of 'Brilliant'. As Bailey had predicted; "A few goals will soon put us right", and they overcame the shock of Chivers' early goal to reply in style through Powell, Palmer and Hibbitt. Although the scheduled Derby game was postponed due to frost, the momentum was maintained by goals from Dougan and Richards in a 2-2 draw at Highbury. Arsenal maintained that a 2pm kick-off on a Tuesday that attracted only 13,000 cost them £10,000-plus in gate receipts. McGarry agreed, calling on the League to end 'the midweek madness' by extending the season by a month; "afternoon midweek football is ludicrous", he said. At the end of the week, Wolves' fine progress was halted by a Colin Stein goal at Coventry, where Munro was stretchered off.

As the energy crisis deepened, Midland managers met at Wolverhampton Racecourse, with McGarry joined by counterparts from Coventry, Birmingham, Stoke, Aston Villa, Nottingham Forest, Notts County and Albion. The gathering urged the Government to waive the ban on using normal power supplies for floodlit games. In light of a ten per cent drop in First Division crowds alone since 2pm kick-offs were introduced, even the possibility of playing on Sunday mornings was considered. In the end, the clubs unanimously decided not to ask the League for a month's shutdown or for Sunday soccer, choosing to carry on with midweek games and continuing with strong representations to get the floodlight ban lifted. The Saturday after Gordon Banks' testimonial game, Wolves visited Stoke, where Munro and Richards gave them

Whatever Wolves manager Bill McGarry (right) has said, it has brought a smile through the soccer gloom from managers Tony Waddington (Stoke), Freddie Goodwin (Blues) Don Howe (Albion) and Jimmy Sirrell (Notts. County) at the "clear-the-air" meeting yesterday.

Blow for soccer chiefs

Midland clubs decided in Wolverhampton yesterday not to ask the Football League to shutdown for a month, not to give Sunday soccer a chance and to carry on with midweek games.

By a unanimous decision from the four First Division and four Second Division clubs in attendance, they agreed to ask the League to make further and stronger representations to the Government to lift the ban on floodlighting.

Report by
JOHN DEE.
Pictures by
GORDON JONES

But at about the same time as Wolves chairman, John Ireland was announcing the club's feelings, the Government, in their latest drastic emergency action were providing the answer to Wolves' floodlight plea from the League.

a half-time advantage. Although two goals in two minutes brought Stoke level, Hibbitt soon sealed a 3-2 victory that saw Wolves leapfrog their hosts.

The big League Cup crunch came at home to Liverpool at 2pm on the last Wednesday before Christmas, the end of the school term fortunately negating the need for another sick note. I was already in my holiday job with the Post Office and simply had to hop on the bus in Wolverhampton Street, Dudley, to join the crowd of just over 16,000 who saw Richards score on 47 minutes to put us through. Bailey recalls; "The first half was fairly even but, playing towards the North Bank in the second, I felt us move up a gear. We were very patient, very focused, waiting for a chance and it came through John Richards. He latched on to a ball in the left channel, showed great strength in holding off very determined defenders before shooting past Clemence. It was well deserved for a player who took lots of knocks but never gave up. I was always pleased to be on his side." Munro was equally effusive; "John was fantastic, I think he put four years on Dougan's professional life. He was so quick and brave. I think the best goal he scored, and I've told him so, was the one against Liverpool in the League Cup. Larry Lloyd had three yards start on him but John's power and bravery got him there and he smashed it with his left foot, a fantastic goal that showed what he was all about."

The goal was born out of a long left-foot clearance by McAlle from the edge of his area. Richards and Tommy Smith jumped together on the half-way line but missed it. Smith was first to react but inexplicably headed towards his own goal past the covering Emlyn Hughes. Richards was now ahead of both in the centre

The winner against Liverpool from John Richards.

160

of the pitch and, chased by Lloyd, advanced some 50 yards to just inside the box, shielding the ball before firing across Clemence as Lloyd closed in. The ball speared into the corner to spark wild celebrations. The loudspeakers boomed out Slade's 'Merry Christmas Everybody' to mark a second successive League Cup semi-final appearance and, this time, Bailey was convinced it would lead to glory; "I recall talking to Jim McCalliog, who recalled getting to the 1966 FA Cup final with Sheffield Wednesday. He told me there came a time when they thought their name was on the cup and, after the Liverpoool game, I knew what he meant."

Richards then doubled up on the Saturday to send Chelsea home pointless and send fears of relegation receding. His first was a classic as he trapped the ball on his chest before swivelling to rifle a left-footer into the North Bank net. However, there was widespread concern at Wagstaffe being placed on the transfer list after almost nine years with the club. And, after the game, Munro was admonished by McGarry for "acting like an idiot" in chasing 70 yards to scuffle with Peter Osgood and earn a booking and likely two-match ban. Visits to Leicester and Burnley resulted in four and two goals being evenly shared despite a writer in the Foxes' programme claiming that, "Wolves' confidence is shattered."

Suspension duly kept Munro out of the visit of Southampton on New Year's Day. On an icy pitch, Wagstaffe (with his first League goal for just over two years) and Richards secured a 2-1 win and, although Sunderland missed a penalty, he played a key role in both goals. Almost 27,000 were present on a bitterly cold afternoon and most were baying for blood when a poor Saints challenge with the ball nowhere in sight led to Powell being stretchered off with a knee injury. The turn of the year was synonymous with the austerity of the three-day week and eventual collapse of the Heath Government, although I was oblivious to hardship as I watched Wolves on Saturdays and Midland League Stourbridge on Sundays. Inspired by Chic Bates and Ray Hayward, Stour reached the Welsh Cup final and fell 3-0 on aggregate to Cardiff. Richards shares my biased opinion; "Although it was difficult from a national economic standpoint, they were good times for Wolves."

Battle was rejoined with Leeds on the first Saturday in January in the FA Cup third round. McGarry was philosophical about another pairing with the old adversaries; "We could have had an easier tie but would have to play them sooner or later." Although Powell was passed fit, injury again denied Richards the company of Dougan while Leeds' Allan Clarke made way for Joe Jordan. On 55 minutes, Richards deflected in a Sunderland shot to seemingly exact revenge for the 1973 semi-final. But, just seven minutes from time, the flamboyant Roger Kirkpatrick stunned Molineux when judging Powell to have fouled Bremner in the box. Afterwards, the Wolves no 7 vehemently protested; "I never touched him." Peter Lorimer, who had not scored for his club for four months, netted the penalty in front of over 38,000 to earn a replay on the same day a meaningless (for England) World Cup draw took place in Munich. I could only agree with newspaper headlines like, 'Leeds squirm off the hook' and 'You lucky Leeds', although Alan Williams argued in the Express; "Leeds get by on skill, not luck." Although he wasn't playing, McCalliog landed himself in hot water with the FA when he allegedly abused Kirkpatrick at the end.

Munro returned and Dougan was substitute but Leeds won a replay that kicked off at 1.30 the following Wednesday, Mick Jones heading home on 84 minutes. McGarry's view was that; "the referee robbed us again." Comfort came with Palmer informed he would earn his first under-23 England cap at 19 after only 11 Division One games when called up to face Wales at Bristol City; "Bill came down to watch me and John Richards - and he brought us back. He said, 'The others are in tomorrow, so you come in. John, you can have the day off.' So he had me in next morning and, as I walked through the front door, he's there. He took me in the office and said, 'Now you're back from playing with all the big boys, they've probably told you how much they earn. I'm bringing you back to earth now. You've got a match on Saturday. You earn this and that's how much you're worth at the moment.' With that, he sent me home. He'd brought me in for five minutes to get my feet back on the ground."

At the same time, Powell was at the centre of a tug of war, with Welsh parentage offering him another international option. But, after initially being overlooked, he was called up by England. Partly because of the Kenilworth lad's form, McCalliog joined Waggy on the transfer list, saying; "I want first-team football" as Wolves recovered from their Cup exit to inflict a 1-0 home defeat on Newcastle. Richards, watched again by Ramsey, delivered inside three minutes in gluepot conditions, firing home his 11th goal in 13 outings. A 16-page 'Crisis Edition' served as programme for a game which stretched Wolves' unbeaten home run to three months.

The League Cup semi-final draw pitched Wolves against Norwich, who had overcome Millwall to reach the last four. As is often the case, the teams were due to meet in the League at Carrow Road on January 19, four days before the first leg. Jimmy Kelly was included in the squad of 13 but didn't make his debut and, after Ted MacDougall scored just before half-time, Dougan climbed highest to earn a point against a team who remained bottom of the table. Wolves were now unbeaten in seven League games and returned to Norfolk to play under generator-powered floodlights, with Canaries boss John Bond insisting; "One goal will do." Unfortunately for him, that's what Richards managed on 78 minutes. With his white shirt almost fully in the possession of defender Dave Stringer, JR levelled a strike by Ian Mellor, who was in for the cup-tied MacDougall.

Wisbech-born Bailey relished the challenge; "Going there was like going home for me. Even though they went down that year, they were tough at Carrow Road, with Kevin Keelan in goal and, just in front of him, big Duncan Forbes, a colossus."

Parkes remembers the two-leg affair and an escape attempt by a nervous Waggy; "We drew there on the Wednesday and then played them at home on the Saturday because we were both out of the FA Cup. We stayed on Thursday and Friday in the Raven Hotel in Droitwich, brine baths and everything." This was the popular stop-over where coach driver Sid Kipping famously trapped McGarry's head in the coach door. Parkes continues; "Sam used to get up early and saw Waggy getting into a taxi saying, 'I'm going home, I'm too nervous to play'. Sam talked him round. Waggy was better after that but he was going home if Sammy hadn't caught him."

Bailey describes how Wolves' big day was almost undermined by another attack of nerves for the no 11; "I felt confident we would get through but it was much harder than I thought. We had a real problem in the dressing room beforehand, with Waggy so nervous he did not want to go out. He wanted to go home. He was such a brilliant player, a wide player to equal all the great wingers in Wolves' past, so for him to do this to us was unthinkable. I offered him the ball to go out first but, no, he wanted to go last. We couldn't do that because he would have run out of the ground! In the end, when the bell went, we put him in the middle of the huddle so there was no escape. We bundled him on to the pitch, where his nerves completely disappeared."

For the second leg on Saturday, January 26 (2pm), 32,609 streamed into Molineux and provided a fabulous atmosphere on an afternoon of steady rain and gusty wind. It was probably the most one-sided game I have ever seen but, the longer it went on, the greater the concern that Norwich would nick an undeserved goal to extend our hoodoo. Attacking the South Bank end on a cloying pitch, Wolves forced 15 first-half corners as the expectation and tension increased. On 48 minutes, Parkes launched a long ball and Dougan beat Forbes to land the ball at the feet of Richards. With Stringer alongside him, Richards closed in on goal and, as the defender half slipped in the mud, JR needed

WOLVES v NORWICH CITY

Wembley, Wembley, here we come! A priceless JR winner.

163

no second invitation, rifling a right-foot shot past the advancing keeper. There were other chances and a few heart-stopping moments as Wolves stubbornly refused to do things the easy way but they made it to Wembley to meet Manchester City or Plymouth, fulfilling what Richards described as; "the players' dream." He elaborates further; "The semi-finals were very close but on balance we deserved it. The match at Molineux was undoubtedly one of the most exciting I've ever played in. The build-up was very tense and the match was very close. There was one goal in it, a typical flick from Derek to me. You could feel the relief of the fans when the final whistle went. It was a big relief when we got through as we'd lost two semi-finals in the previous year. I think people thought there was a bit of a jinx as to whether we'd ever get any success." It was in a later interview with the Evening Mail's Dennis Shaw that McGarry's desperation for success was clearly stated; "If I dwelt on my career as a player and manager and thought about how little I had to show in terms of major honours, I would go mad. It would seem as though I had wasted my life."

Hardly had Wembley been reached when Parkes picked up a hairline fracture of his ankle in training. He is incredibly philosophical about the crushing disappointment; "I had played in every round but what's meant to be is meant to be. After the semi, we had a fantastic Saturday night and, on the Monday, went training. Bill said, 'We're going to play five-a-side up in the gym. If you want to go to the racecourse with the young kids and do some goalkeeping, that's all right.' So I did that. We'd only been there about 20 minutes when one of the kids had a shot. I started to go down and my studs stuck in the turf. I couldn't stop myself and went over. I did all my ligaments and broke my right ankle." Gary Pierce deputised in a 1-1 home draw with Stoke that was most notable for the appearance of Alan Hudson, Stoke's £240,000 signing from Chelsea, and the dismissal of Munro on the hour for an indiscretion few apart from referee Hackney saw. John Dee summed up Wolves' nervy countdown to their big day, the headline on his Express & Star report saying, "It's the trembley Wolves." Bailey convinced nobody when he said; "What cup final? We don't want to know!"

Defeats against Sheffield United and Everton saw Wolves drop back to 17th, the latter securing their first League win of 1974. Although Munro headed in Wagstaffe's right-wing corner to score the only goal against Birmingham, Wolves continued to hover too close to the relegation zone for comfort and had still scored more goals away than at home. Only hours after captaining Wolves against Blues, McAlle was at his wife Jill's bedside as she presented him with a daughter. Significantly, though, injury problems were mounting when, in the last game before the final, they contested a 0-0 draw at Old Trafford without Parkes, Richards (pelvis), Powell (knee) and Bailey (another broken toe). Powell recalls the uncertainty over his fitness; "Three to four weeks before the final, I damaged knee ligaments." McCalliog returned against United and Peter Withe was handed the no 12 shirt. Daley deputised for Bailey and knew his Wembley chances were dependent on whether the skipper recovered; "I felt I played really, really well against United but Bill said to me Mick would play at Wembley if he was fit, 'You're a young lad, you'll go back there. Mick's coming to the end of his career and may never play there again.' Mick played and I never got a game there!"

In the battle of the treatment rooms, Denis Law, Francis Lee and Rodney Marsh were reportedly doubtful for City, who had beaten Plymouth in their semi. But, when the teams lined up at Wembley for their 3.30pm date on Saturday, March 2, only Parkes was missing. The big keeper knew he had no chance despite testing his fitness in a midweek reserve game with Blackburn; "That was Bill's idea. The only good thing was that I knew from the start I wasn't going to play. I was in the gym doing some exercises when the physio came up and said, 'How is it?' I replied, 'I can hardly walk, what's the matter?' 'Oh, they've got a reserve game and the gaffer wants you to play'. There's no way I could but I said, 'If he wants me to play, I'll play. It ain't a problem. It ain't gonna make it any worse is it?' So I went to see Bill and said, 'Gaffer, do you want me to play?' So they strapped it up and my ankle was huge when I went out, there was so much strapping. Luckily, Blackburn had only sent a young side, I didn't touch the ball and we won 3-0. Barry Powell also played. He'd been struggling and finished as sub at Wembley." Pierce, February Midland Footballer of the Month, would have to play on his 23rd birthday after just 12 matches for the club. Wolves' first Wembley visit since 1960 would, in Percy Young's words, be the game when; "Gary Pierce chose to make his prize offering to the club."

Powell remembers the same practice game; "Bill organised a behind-closed-doors match for Phil and I. The rest of the players had gone to Worthing on the Sunday to prepare and the game was on the Tuesday. Phil had no chance but I got through. Bill, Alan Williams of the Daily Express and me got on the train straight afterwards. The two of them were into the gin and tonics and I was on juice. Bill went to the toilet and I asked Alan, 'Has he said anything?' He said, 'He's told me you're not going down just for the trip.' So I had an idea I was going to be involved. It was between me and Ken who played." Hibbitt realises he was far from certain of his place in the final; "I had a thigh strain and wasn't sure whether I would be playing, nobody told me. I got ready to play, I was fit, but

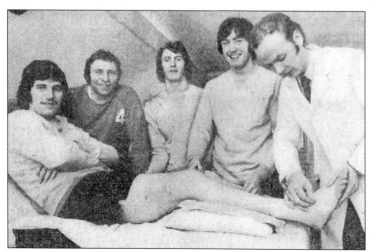

Physio Toby Andersen was kept busy in the build-up to the final.

Barry had filled in for me in the couple of League games leading up to it and had done really well. I didn't know until I walked into the Wembley dressing room and saw my boots under the no 7 shirt. McGarry never said anything, we didn't have a meeting on how we were going to play or what we were going to do, nothing like that."

Richards had been suffering since early January with an abdominal problem at first believed to be a pulled muscle and later diagnosed as a small split in the pubis or pelvic bone. Although he discounts the argument of his then-pregnant wife Pam that he might have been coming out in sympathy with her, the injury strangely disappeared soon after their daughter was born! At the time, treatment had little impact and Wolves' star striker wore a corset for several weeks, even sleeping in it. JR adds: "From January, I was having pains. I had x-rays, all kinds of things but nothing was found. It was assumed it was a muscle and every evening in the build-up to the final, Sammy Chung would come in and strap my legs together so I didn't aggravate it." As both carried injuries, Richards and Bailey recall a leisurely countdown; "Mike and I didn't train that week and, while all the other lads worked hard, we strolled around the pitch." The time spent in the Sussex resort replicated preparation for previous games in the capital, as far as Bailey was concerned; "John and I were injured and did not play for three weeks before the final. We just did some light training. McGarry made perfect preparations by taking us away to a quiet seaside town. I remember the hotel was mainly full of elderly widows. They had their places in the dining room by the radiators, and the lads had a laugh and joke with them and they became quite attached to us. They said we had livened up the place and waved us off as we left on the Friday for a hotel nearer London." Palmer appreciates the effort put into protecting players from the Wembley frenzy; "The whole week just passes you by that quickly. McGarry knew there'd be a lot of problems with tickets, people asking us all the time. He took us away on the Monday so we were away from everything. We trained down there, went out at night, it was good. Then we went up to London."

The squad took a trip to the Strand to watch 'No Sex Please, We're British', where John Richards was pictured with namesake Wendy. Palmer sensed the tension mounting; "You could feel it on the Friday. We were in the hotel and it was something to eat at eight, half nine to bed, watching TV. Next day, it was get up, have breakfast, have the team talk and on the coach." Although he must have felt the burden of expectation, Bailey describes a calmer last few hours; "We stayed at a really nice hotel. I slept well, which was unusual. After breakfast on the Saturday, I had a nice walk in the hotel grounds. The lads were a little quiet at the pre-match meal. They were coping with any nerves in their own way, including Waggy." Concerns over the fitness of the two key men led to the choice of Powell as sub, as he could play in midfield or off a front man, although Waggy reveals he was also doubtful due to a thigh strain picked up in training; "I shouldn't have played. I pulled a muscle on the Wednesday and, if it had been a League match, I would never have played. It caused me a long-term

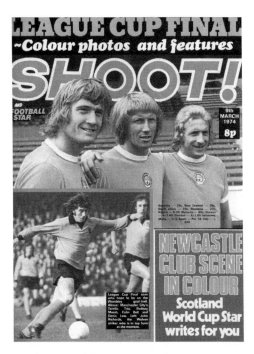

problem the next season but you don't want to miss Wembley. I was only 75 per cent fit and don't think I did the team or myself justice."

The pundits were only too keen to share their views on the likely outcome, with ex-City manager Malcolm Allison highlighting the duel between Wagstaffe, now off the list, and Glyn Pardoe as the key. He argued that, "Wagstaffe's skill will mean torture for City." In the Express & Star, John Dee predicted a 3-1 Wolves win while Arsenal keeper Bob Wilson also felt the Wanderers would prevail. Experts in 'Goal' magazine, however, were convinced City would have the edge. Richards says; "City were expected to walk all over us. As it turned out, it was probably as good a cup final as they had at Wembley in the 70s, really end-to-end." Munro was super-confident; "I didn't think City were favourites. I know people said about their forward line but they were all getting a little past it, even Denis Law, who was a fantastic player. I always thought Frannie Lee was a great player, though, so was Colin Bell, and you had to watch Rod Marsh who could get a penalty by tripping himself! We were 11-8 against, they were 7-4 on but I really fancied us." Parkin also admired the opposition; "To be fair, 1974 will always be the one that stays in my memory when you consider the team City had. Like Leeds, they had really physical players but most of those were forwards, which was unusual. I had some big battles with that bugger Mike Summerbee. He was the new breed of forward and used to kick full-backs! He was a big, strong lad; head down and run and, if you got in the way, he'd run over you. But he was a good player."

Palmer could hardly believe what was happening; "I was lucky my career just took off and I also got picked a couple of times to play for the under-23s. It was as if it was a bit too fast and culminated in a 19-year-old playing at Wembley in front of 100,000. If there was one bloke who was never going to let your feet leave the ground, it was Bill McGarry. With him, you weren't going to get above your station. You're playing Manchester City and you look at their team. Although we had a good side, I thought we were underdogs." Powell recalls how the day passed him by; "I don't remember much. I recall waving to my parents in the crowd but the game and everything just went. I'd never seen a dressing room like it. Afterwards, everyone was strewn about. I was there again in 1988 as Graham Turner's coach for the Sherpa Van final against Burnley. He was doing his team talk, so I walked out to listen to 'Abide With Me'. I stood at the end of the tunnel with tears dripping down my eyes. I then walked out behind the players and remember more about that than 1974."

Bailey recalls the drive to the ground; "The lads looked very smart in their new suits as we boarded the coach. The sun was shining and, as we neared the stadium, a few supporters waved to us. As we drove down Wembley Way, a sea of colour greeted us with both sets of fans cheering us on; a wonderful sight with the twin towers in the background." Munro describes the same scene; "Waggy and I were always card partners but there were so many Wolves fans it was unbelievable. They were banging on the coach windows, incredible. Dave said, 'It's OK for them, I wish the game was at Castlecroft!' Waggy himself adds; "It was a blur. I can tell you now but it goes so quickly. I'm the most nervous person in the world and was absolutely petrified walking out there. I was the same with any game. But, once you walk out, you're comfortable because you're doing your job. I didn't like the build-up but going down the tunnel, all of a sudden it's like walking into a cauldron, absolutely magnificent. There were more of our supporters than City's, I felt completely at home." Richards remembers that the proudest person on the coach was the driver Sid Kipping, who deliberately drove slower to wave to the all the supporters waving to him! Palmer was bowled over by the reception; "I couldn't believe the number of Wolves fans we saw. You think, 'What am I doing here?' We go out on the pitch and we're there, an unbelievable experience. I think I've only seen the match about twice."

The dressing room was in the bowels of the stadium, detached, as Richards explains; "I don't think anyone could prepare you for walking down that tunnel. You'd seen it on TV, you'd heard about it but to experience it was unbelievable. The noise was deafening and two thirds of the stadium was gold and black. Even in the City end, there was some gold and black. I don't know where they'd all come from and it made a massive

difference." Hibbitt agrees; "I had watched the Cup Final on TV from 1957 and been to Wembley in 1968 to watch West Brom beat Everton. I also saw Leeds v Chelsea when they drew (1970) after the horses had been on the pitch. I said I would never go back until I was playing. That day in 1974...no words can explain it. First you want to be a professional footballer, then you want to play at Wembley. The opposition players, Bell, Marsh, all of them had played there 30 times and it was another game for them. Watch the video and look at our line-up, full of youngsters who had never been there before, and we were stood ready to go out with our hands down by our sides or in front of us. You look over to the City players and they're tossing the ball up and flicking it on their shoulders or the back of their heels. They couldn't give a monkey's, they were just going out to whack us. But once we started to walk out, the black and gold that faced us played a massive part. We grew in confidence. I'm not sure what it would have done to us if it had been the other way round seeing the blue. We knew they'd come to watch us win and it lifted us. It was a magnificent atmosphere and I was so nervous, I was shaking like a bloody leaf until we got to the pitch and the ref called us together. I thought 'Go for it, this might not happen again.'"

Parkin remembers McGarry's meticulous attention to detail, his players properly turned out as they filed out alongside a City side managed by Ron Saunders, whose Norwich team had lost the previous year's final. Tracksuits zipped up to the neck, trousers fastened down; "Don't go out like bloody rag-bags, look as if you mean business', that was McGarry. We reached the tunnel from one side, they from the other, tracksuits bottoms with zips half done up. I felt I could do anything that day, anything." Bailey also recalls the last moments; "Our dressing room was positive and relaxed. The players were talkative but not nervously so. Once we were on the pitch, my main worry was the formalities. I was afraid I'd forget a name as I introduced the lads to the Duke of Kent. The City team opposite looked awesome, great players and real characters like Summerbee, Lee, Bell and Marsh. Fantastic players managed by a team-mate of mine at Charton. After the formalities, we broke away and went to the end our supporters were at and gave them a wave. The response was magical. GAME ON!"

Wembley was magical indeed. I had been before for schoolboy internationals, when the atmosphere could not compare with the raw emotion in 1974 among the heaving masses on the west enclosure. Perhaps I had lived a sheltered existence but what I believed to be spilled drinks cascading down the crumbling stone steps was in fact the result of hundreds of grown men relieving themselves almost in unison. As Hibbitt and others describe, I remember the teams coming out at the far end into bright early-spring sunshine, an experience that still sends a chill up Parkin's spine; "It was a tremendous occasion. All we could see at first when we went out was the top of the stand. As we got further and further, the crowd came into view. The hairs on the back of your neck stood up. I thought, this is what I want. Then the day just went 'poof', straight past, all over in a second. So you want to do it all again."

To my then 16-year-old eyes, the match was a classic, with Hibbitt putting Wolves ahead with the outside of his right foot just before half-time. Bailey switched play to Palmer, who fed Sunderland on the right. Back to Palmer, who drifted a ball into the box that Richards just missed but with which Hibbitt connected; "It came off the top of my foot. Geoff can claim an assist with a great cross! John was coming away from goal, banged his leg up and missed it. I had got into position to volley it but lost it for a second and mis-timed it. But it might have been the best thing that happened. Keith McRae in goal went for it and all I saw was him grabbing thin air as it dropped over him. I knew it was in and was on my run before it hit the net. I don't know what I felt, I just ran and celebrated the goal. In fact I can't remember what happened from then until we kicked off in the second half. I was in a dream."

Bailey comments further on the opening stages and the goal; "We settled much quicker than City. Derek Parkin hit Mike Summerbee with a very strong tackle and that seemed to translate itself throughout the team. We looked sharp and our passing was crisp and accurate. After several near misses, Kenny adjusted his feet well to meet Geoff's cross, which came slightly behind him, to volley us ahead." This seemed to spark a City siege that brought the best out of Pierce as he brilliantly tipped over a Marsh free-kick. Bailey said of the half-time team talk; "We discussed how City would come out in the second half like a wounded animal, so we would have to withstand a period of pressure. They hit us with everything and we would have been buried had it not been for some inspired goalkeeping from Gary." Just when it seemed Wolves' goal would remain intact, Bell profited from a lucky deflection off the top of McAlle's head to bring City level. The manager laid some of the blame at Bailey's door; "McGarry felt I was partly responsible as I didn't get close enough to Marsh for the cross." City looked favourites and it was under the greatest pressure that the pugnacious Wanderers captain did exactly what his players still maintain he did best as he took the game by the scruff of the neck. Mike continues; "City did not expect that reaction but we had so much desire to bring a major trophy back to Molineux and our loyal fans. I sensed that we had to get a period of control as we were hitting too many long balls to Doog and John. As we were unable to get up in support, the ball just kept coming back to put us under greater pressure. I encouraged the lads to play shorter balls, keep possession, build more slowly and not get stretched. We gradually got back in the game."

At half-time, Richards had been given pain-killing sprays to ease his growing discomfort but fate took a hand when Wagstaffe broke down on a run down the right and had to go off with a hamstring injury. Powell replaced him but was himself far from fully fit; "In the first tackle, Colin Bell came into the back of me. I felt my knee but it must have had the effect of stretching the ligament out and the knee was fine." It is generally assumed Richards would have come off had Waggy not pulled up. The winger certainly believes so; "John was going to come off, so who knows what might have happened if I had stayed on!" However, Richards maintains the opposite; "I'd always assumed I'd stay on. Although the injury restricted me, I never saw a signal calling me off." McGarry later confirmed Richards had spent the previous two nights with his legs strapped together; "It was not even a calculated risk. He really should not have been playing." JR never played again that season and remembers; "As the game wore on, I became more laboured. The more I did, the worse the pain got. It was really sore." Hibbitt recalls; "I know how hard it was in the second half. John really shouldn't have been on the pitch. If we'd had another substitute, he wouldn't have been. He was in real agony and could have crippled himself but he had to stay on because Waggy had been shot. I still tell him a sniper got him! He was a magnificent player but wasn't the best at preparing for the big occasion. I think the final did him in the end. Of course he wanted to play but I think it got too much for him and that's why he got shot and came off! Our substitute was used and Richie had to carry on. It was a good job as he slid in the winner". He really admires his good friend's determination and bravery; "At the end, John was elated but tender and sore. He could have damaged his pelvis so badly that he might not have been able to play again."

Whatever the truth, Richards somehow found the strength to reward the side's strong finish with the winner. Six minutes left and Hibbitt, socks round his ankles, took a left-wing corner. Wolves had only three players in the box - the Doog at the near post, Munro at the far and Richards lurking on the edge. City had eight men in the area, plus keeper McRae. Hibbitt's flag kick was long and Tommy Booth leapt to beat Munro and head away. But the ball fell to Sunderland on the right edge of the box. He was closed

down quickly by Lee but found Bailey behind him. The skipper threaded a precision pass between Lee and Law to find Sunderland, returned to his original position. Letting the ball run across him and past Willie Donachie, the youngster saw his cross clip Marsh's heel and find Richards on the penalty spot. Mike Doyle couldn't close him down quickly enough and the no 9 drove beyond McRae's right hand. Bailey recalls; "Alan showed great skill in tempting Donachie's tackle by letting it cross his body before delivering the cross." Richards naturally remembers the goal well but is typically modest; "It was a combination of good players. The pass from Mike between two players to Alan Sunderland was beautiful, Alan's cross then deflected off Rodney Marsh's heel. From my point of view, it was laziness. Normally, when somebody got into

Ken Hibbitt comforts an injured John Richards at the end of the final.

171

that position, my run was to the near post, Dougan always went to the back. My job was to get in front of whichever defender was at the near post but, because I wasn't running very well, I didn't. I stayed in the middle of the goal. If I had made a run, it would have missed me anyway because the deflection off Marsh would have taken it behind me. It was just fortunate, not instinct. My shot also went through Doyle's legs. I definitely didn't pick a spot with this one. It was just a case of hitting it hard and low, simple as that. Somehow it threaded its way through and into the corner. I didn't even see it hit the net. It was the reaction of the crowd behind the goal where all the Wolves supporters were, that told me it was in."

We, of course, went barmy and my enduring vision is of my granddad, also at Wembley with Wolves in 1949, hardly able to believe we were back in the big time. It is a continuing sadness that he went to his grave in 1986 more in expectation of Wolves becoming a Conference team than a top-flight one. The game ended with Munro outjumping Law in the Wolves area to head clear, after which Parkin remembers the warmth of the Doog's reaction; "I had suffered this suspected heart problem and Derek was a terrific support. When the final whistle went, he was suddenly there with his arm around me, as if to say, 'See, I told you not to worry'. That was the man I knew." The Wolves bench of Wagstaffe, Parkes, McCalliog and Daley, as well as McGarry, Chung and physio Toby Andersen, poured on. Although McGarry's untypically emotional embrace of Pierce was memorable, it must be the splendid gesture of the unlucky Phil Parkes towards his replacement that lingers longest. Daley agrees; "Phil just shrugged it off, didn't bear people ill will. I would imagine that after that final, he would have been absolutely delighted for Piercy. Annoyed that he couldn't play due to no fault of his own, but the first to say 'Well done kid', absolutely brilliant, Phil's a great guy." Steve is honest enough to admit the difficulty of enjoying the team's success when not in the line-up in comments that might shock some; "If you're not playing, there's a feeling that goes through you, you don't want them to win. People will think, 'What a t**t he is', but if every player's honest I think deep down they'll all think that. You

The Doog - a terrific support to Squeak.

don't want them to break a leg but if they don't win, you've got a chance of getting your place back. If you're not in, you don't want them to win. Others may not want to admit to it but they'd feel that way."

In the commentary, Brian Moore called Pierce; "The man they said would be a weakness but who has turned out to be a strength." Palmer chips in; "He hadn't played many games. You could always tell big Phil was going to be a week short. It was a shame but Gary came in and the rest is history. He was a card he was, all keepers are nutters." Daley agrees; "Piercy was brilliant. He lived in Codsall when I did and couldn't drive. We used to have to report at quarter to two on match-day. Gary would go into The Wheel in Codsall at quarter to one. He'd have two or three bottles of lager and catch the 1.30 bus that dropped him outside the ground at quarter to. He lived on his nerves. That's what made his reactions so good, cat-like."

Hibbitt sums up the joy and relief that swept over both team and supporters at the end; "Gary was man of the match, a star that day. He was just enormous, magnificent. You could see Bill McGarry was elated, not just because of the win but because of the performance Gary had put in. He ran on the pitch in his sheepskin and went straight to Gary, got hold of his hand and shook it. I'll never forget the scene. John was laid out on the middle of the pitch when the final whistle went. You just didn't know who to go to. It was just like a dream, a mist and you were waiting to come through it. We only calmed down when we walked up the steps to get the cup. Mike Bailey must have been a very proud man. He was the best captain I played under." Bailey accepted the cup, wiping the mud from his hands so as not to dirty the gloves of the Duchess of Kent; "As we followed a very sporting City side up to the royal box. I felt enormous pride in holding the trophy up to the Wolves end of the ground."

In the week of a second General Election in two weeks, The Times carried the headline, "Avoiding a recount". McAlle recalls this as the only game that really sapped his energy and needed several days to recover. Hardly surprising as John Dee remarked on; "McAlle the ferocious tackler, who stopped Francis Lee and Rodney Marsh so many times." His captain appreciates this key role; "Gary Pierce's part in our win is deservedly remembered but Munro and John in front of him were magnificent. John never got many accolades but was an outstanding defender, very brave. He was a team player and, the bigger the game, the better he played. He'd be the first man I would want to take to war with me!" Palmer is fulsome in his praise of those around him; "The way Mick Bailey, Derek Parkin, Frank Munro and John McAlle played, and Gary obviously, was amazing. Mike was an inspiration, leading from the front. I've never played under anyone close to being as good a captain as him. He didn't ask people to do anything he couldn't do. If you needed telling off, he'd tell you off. If you needed looking after, he'd look after you. I was the youngest in the team and Squeak, Scouse and Frank looked after me. I had to grow up quickly, especially in the final." Powell agrees; "I didn't realise at the time how well McAlle, Munro and Bailey played, and Pierce of course. City had big-name players but sometimes that doesn't work."

Marsh was heavily criticised by the Daily Mirror's Frank McGhee for a bitter reaction to defeat that was completely out of character for a game played in great spirit. He was accused of; "a sour, rancid attitude and appalling lack of sportsmanship" when he refused a royal handshake and his loser's tankard. Bailey doesn't agree; "The City boys took defeat really well and even Rodney Marsh was not unsporting, as he was accused at the time. He was just so disappointed by his part in the winning goal." The abiding memory for many present is of the Doog and Denis Law, arms around each other with the latter in Munro's shirt, as Dougan remembered; "You walk off the pitch as friends, it's all about rapport." The victory was suitably celebrated at a banquet Munro recalls for more than one reason; "We had a fantastic night at the Hilton Hotel in Park Lane. That's the night I started smoking. I asked a waitress to bring me a packet of Benson and Hedges. McGarry went mad at me, starting at 27, how stupid can you get? I only stopped six weeks ago (November, 2006). Waggy and I went on to a bunny club and a few City players were there as well." Bailey adds; "The club had booked the banquet, win or lose. With our wives, girlfriends and friends, we celebrated putting Wolves back in the limelight. As I was one of the last to go to bed, I saw the cup on the top table. It looked quite lonely, so I took it to bed and brought it down next morning."

Willie Carr reminds us the celebrations were sumptuous compared with those of the 1980 triumph; "We had a 'do' but I don't know whether Barny (John Barnwell) had done a deal with The Mount in Tettenhall. The heater on the wives' coach broke down on the way back, there wasn't room for everyone at the meal and there was a terrible three-piece band." Six years earlier, the winners returned to Wolverhampton to a rapturous reception from thousands of jubilant fans, a true heroes' reception summed up by the headline on the cover of the programme for the Ipswich match; "You made us feel so very proud." The Doog chipped in; "The rousing crescendo of support we had from the stands and terraces in those last 20 pulsating minutes drove us to victory and provided the highlight of my career." Parkin adds; "It was a fantastic day, not just for the players, but for the wives, the chairman, the fans, the club. I think Bill enjoyed the day as well." Supporters had waited for hours in St. Peter's Square and, as the team coach pulled outside the Town Hall for a lunchtime civic reception, the crowd erupted. Mike Bailey picks up the story; "The Sunday was unbelievable. All the dignitaries were there, plus thousands of fans looking up at the 's balcony where we appeared to show them the cup. Quite a few of the lads, me included, then had to drive back to London for the PFA awards dinner! The cup remained in my possession until Tuesday

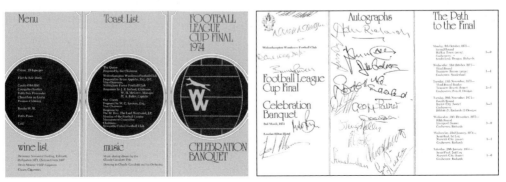

and my son Andrew took it to school. He was very popular as you can imagine. I only took the cup back when people at the club thought it had been stolen!"

As for McGarry, amid the jubilation of his finest hour, he dwelt again on what failure would have meant; "I would have had to go into the Third Division and start again." It seems strange at first that Percy Young should claim that March 2, 1974 was; "the day when the shadows began to lengthen." In Wagstaffe's opinion, Ronnie Allen should have been accorded the lion's share of praise for the success anyway; "Whose players were they? Go back to the League Cup final, McGarry's biggest triumph, and go through the team. No disrespect to Gary Pierce but he wouldn't have been in if Phil had been fit. I feel ever so sorry for Phil. That was the biggest game of his career and Ronnie gave Phil his chance. Palmer, came up through the ranks; left back, £80,000 from Huddersfield, what a buy, Derek Parkin, one of the finest in Wolves history; then you go to Bailey and Munro, Allen's buys at £40,000 and £55,000; McAlle, up through the ranks; outside right, overpriced at £5,000 from Bradford Park Avenue, Kenny Hibbitt - what a buy - unbelievable; Sunderland, up through the ranks; Richards and Powell, came up through the ranks; the Doog, Ronnie's shrewdest buy, taking a chance on Derek when people were saying don't - he loved playing for the Wolves; I was the only one either didn't come through the ranks or was signed by Ronnie!"

As the cup winners got back to bread-and-butter action, the pressing need was to accumulate the points needed to ensure safety. McCalliog was linked with a £70,000 move to Aston Villa while Peter Eastoe was sold to Swindon for £80,000. As it turned out, Jimmy Mac went to Manchester United, the team he would help Southampton beat in the 1976 FA Cup final. With Richards ruled out for the rest of the season and the League Cup paraded before the match, Wolves did well to keep their minds on the job and beat Ipswich 3-1. At 23, Peter Withe, brought back from South Africa by Dougan in the summer, made his full debut and the man who was to score the decider in Villa's 1982 European Cup Final win was on the score-sheet with Sunderland and the Doog. A 0-0 draw at QPR was followed by another single-goal defeat against title-chasing Liverpool. Brian Hall headed the only goal past Parkes, who returned with Pierce

YOUR OWN 8mm HOME MOVIE FILM

'Someone here to tell you how to fight back and win.'

First you see it - then it's gone!

himself hurt in training. The programme for the Reds' visit inadvertently produced the same photograph used in that week's Sporting Star for their Mark the Ball competition - with the ball still in shot! The Corbett family submitted what was clearly a winning entry but the contest was inevitably declared null and void.

Steve Kindon and Powell scored to earn 1-1 draws at Manchester City and at home to Tottenham, stalemates that saw Wolves slip back to 17th. The Maine Road trip was memorable for little else but Hibbitt's decision to write his own name when booked. Any lingering relegation fears were blown away in the rearranged Molineux clash with Derby, though. Managed by Dave Mackay after Brian Clough departure the previous October, the high-flying Rams were soundly thrashed 4-0. Kindon (2), Powell and Sunderland scored and the Evening Mail headline ran; "Pathetic Rams pounded". Kindon's confidence must have been boosted by scoring for the first time at Molineux since joining Wolves 21 months earlier. It was only his eighth full Division One outing in front of the home fans. Physio Toby Andersen left at this time to return to his native Norway to take up a hospital job.

A 0-0 draw at West Ham was followed by a 3-1 home win over Arsenal, Kindon notching his fourth in five games and Sunderland scoring twice. Steve's goal was something special as he picked up the ball in the middle of his own half after a shot by Charlie George had cannoned off Palmer. Setting off on a 70-yard run, 'Tank' shook off Peter Storey, Sammy Nelson and Pat Rice with sheer pace. As Bob Wilson left his line, Kindon let rip from the edge of the box and the ball positively fizzed into the North Bank net. My Auntie June memorably described his fleet of foot; 'When he gooes, he really gooes!' Kindon recalls the goal with affection; "It made me very popular with the crowd and people still write to me about it. I remember picking it up near my own corner flag, running past Peter Simpson and three other defenders and hitting it with my right foot from 20-odd yards. I'm going 'yeh, yeh' but none of my team-mates seemed to be running to me and the crowd were quiet. Have you seen those adverts where you move but everyone else is in slow motion? I thought it was about four seconds, although it was probably 0.4 of a second. I thought it can't be offside, then, all of a sudden, there's a delayed reaction, the North Bank went up and the lads were jumping on top of me." Parkin adds; "That was typical Stevie. Only he could do that. Give him the ball, open the gates and he was off. He was a big lad and, when he hit the ball, he really hit it, although it wasn't always where he wanted to hit it!"

Five points from three matches took Wolves to tenth but a mixed last three games yielded a 0-0 draw with Coventry, a Sunderland-inspired win over Coventry and a 2-0 setback at the Baseball Ground as Derby exacted revenge for their Molineux mauling. In the season that Manchester United were relegated, Wolves were understandably disappointed with a final position of 12th. It was commonly agreed 'Mr. Consistency', McAlle, was player of the year, as John Dee wrote; "He has had a magnificent season at the heart of the defence." Parkin affectionately remembers his partnership with Scouse; "Me and John had the understanding that if he was ever in trouble he'd give the ball to me. If I was in trouble with the winger I'd play him inside and John would kick him. If I'm playing Bestie and he's giving me a roasting, I'd line him up and John would put him into touch. Nine times out of ten it would work!"

Equally, although there was doubt as to whether his best position was midfield or attack, Sunderland was widely acclaimed as discovery of the season. Wolves wound up 1973-74 with a hat-trick of testimonial games in 24 hours, supporting Swindon's John Trollope, Albion's Tony Brown and Watford's Duncan Wellbourne. Left-winger John Farley moved for £50,000 from Hertfordshire and made a rapid return to Vicarage Road. Most significantly Dave Woodfield, by now coach at Watford, was awarded a

testimonial that took place on April 30. It was a fitting end to a wonderful season that a fine Wolves servant was at long last honoured, having left Wolves in September, 1971 after 275 full senior games over 12 seasons. He turned out at no 5 for the Dave Woodfield XI alongside luminaries like Robert Plant, Jimmy Mullen and Elton John in the curtain-raiser against a Don Howe team. Rumours that Rod Stewart would play did not materialise. In the main match, Wolves were humbled 5-2 by an International XI including Frank Worthington, Tommy Hutchison and Geoff Hurst while Gordon Banks stepped out of retirement to keep goal for the Midland Internationals side.

1974-75: Promise Unfulfilled

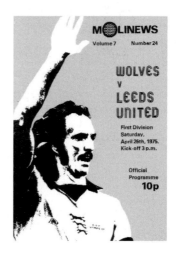

Bob Blackburn of the Sports Argus summed up Wolverhampton's pre-season expectation in summer, 1974 by writing; "Maybe it (the League Cup) will be the springboard to a new era of trophy-hunting at Molineux, when talented cubs turn into fully-fledged Wolves." Derek Parkin reflects; "We should have gone on from there", as it appeared Bill McGarry had unearthed a crop of youngsters to ensure the Wembley success was just the start of a glorious new era. These included the versatile Alan Sunderland, capped by England under-23s at full-back, having switched from midfield to attack after injury had ended John Richards' season; Barry Powell, the Kenilworth midfielder who had been the subject of a battle between England and Wales for his services; Geoff Palmer, another under-age England defender; and Steve Daley, who had enjoyed a relatively quiet few years having burst on to the scene in the final stages of the UEFA Cup campaign in 1972. With a core of experienced professionals like Ken Hibbitt, John McAlle, Steve Kindon and Richards all around 24, and youngsters such as Jimmy Kelly, Nigel Williams, Norman Bell, Mick Bradbury and Don Gardner on the fringes, the future looked bright. According to Richards, there was an extent to which some of the younger players had begun to take success for granted. McAlle, the previous year's Player of the Season, had his boss arguing that the best was yet to come; "He can improve possibly by 25, 30 or 40 per cent." Unsurprisingly perhaps, the only newcomer, Teeside-born winger John Farley, had come in at the end of 1973-74.

Wolves enjoyed an unusually long close season of 11 weeks, partly due to the fact the World Cup in West Germany rendered their Swedish training facilities unavailable. The delay at least gave Richards the best chance of recovery from injury, with the opening friendly not scheduled until July 31. Wolves took on and defeated Swansea at the Vetch Field in an ill-tempered game most notable for the emergence of 18-year-old Dubliner Maurice Daly. But the countdown contained alarms aplenty, when Steve Daley was hospitalised with cuts to his face and glass in the eye when his car hit a

Want-a-move Munro stays, says McGarry

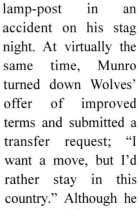

By JOHN DEE

Wolves manager Bill McGarry confirmed today that his former Scottish international Frank Munro had made a written application for a transfer. But, said McGarry, there was no possibility of Munro leaving Molineux.

"I have received Munro's letter asking for a move and it will be put before the board at their next meeting. My recommendation will be to turn it down," he told me today.

lamp-post in an accident on his stag night. At virtually the same time, Munro turned down Wolves' offer of improved terms and submitted a transfer request; "I want a move, but I'd rather stay in this country." Although he had been included in Scotland's original party of 40, Munro was understandably disappointed at being omitted from Scotland's World Cup squad proper but McGarry countered by saying there was no possibility of his star defender leaving.

After 17 years as a professional, Derek Dougan, dubbed 'Methusulah' and 'Old Father Time', confirmed that the new season would be his last. Although it was a decision that had to be made some time, it was still dreaded by his legions of fans. At this juncture, he published 'The Footballer', a novel depicting the story of the life of a soccer superstar. The Doog revealed he had even discussed with the local Liberal party the possibility of a political career. There was then intense newspaper speculation that a bid of £175,000 had been lodged for Albion's talented midfielder, Asa Hartford, with Powell lined up as possible bait. Hartford, on the list for three months, was also interesting Manchester City and Leeds despite a move to the Elland Road having been ruled out in 1971 by a hole in the heart. Neither McGarry nor Don Howe would comment. In his annual report, chairman John Ireland lamented the fact the game had become; "sick about money." It was a view many sympathised with given the brawl at Wembley between Billy Bremner and Kevin Keegan in the Charity Shield; "Football, as we knew it, went out of the window when money came in through the front door. We have to live with it. I don't think anyone knows how to put it right." In a move to tackle the increasing problem of hooliganism and in response to pressure from Minister of Sport Denis Howell, it was also announced that barriers would be extended to form an unbroken line across the bottom of both the North and South Banks. The slightly reduced capacity of 53,500 provided no problem for the last warm-up game. Just over 5,000 saw a Ken Hibbitt penalty earn a draw with Bristol Rovers.

The season dawned with Wolves naming a reasonably familiar line-up for the trip to Burnley on August 17. Eight of the League Cup final team were in action, with only Pierce, Dougan and Wagstaffe missing. Pierce was nursing a foot injury sustained in training at the end of July while Dougan was relegated to the reserves and replaced by Powell. With Kindon on the bench against his former club, Farley stepped up for his Wolves debut at the expense of the unfortunate Waggy, whose hamstring injury meant

All of the hard work seemed worthwhile when John Richards struck at Turf Moor.

he had played only three of the last 11 games in 1973-74. "I just can't get fit," he moaned. But he now recalls the unfair 'injury-prone' tag some labelled him with; "During my time at Wolves, I averaged 35 games a season, that's not bad. Nobody mentions that, they only mention how many you missed."

On only six minutes a revitalised Richards fired past Alan Stevenson from a narrow angle and although Ray Hankin levelled on 39 minutes, Palmer lobbed home right after the restart to secure both points. The following Tuesday, the visit of FA Cup holders and League runners-up Liverpool was a real test of Wolves' ambitions in front of what would be the season's second biggest home crowd of 33,499. Keegan was banned and new signing Ray Kennedy injured while Kindon came in for Farley, who had bruised a foot at Turf Moor. Since only three teams had scored more than once against Liverpool in 1973-74, it was perhaps no surprise defences dominated in a goalless encounter.

The first Saturday home game of the season provided much more entertaining fare as Hibbitt found himself pitched against Newcastle and his brother, Terry. Unchanged Wolves fought back from a John Tudor goal on seven minutes to win in a canter 4-2, the Sporting Star headline running "Canny Kenny Canes Castle". Hibbitt became only the seventh Wolves player since the war to score four in a game, Ted Farmer having done the same when Manchester City were trounced 8-1 in 1962. First Richards set up Hibbitt to run on and hammer home from 15 yards, then on 25 minutes, when Irving Nattrass fouled the Wolves no 9, Hibbitt sent McFaul the wrong way from the spot. On 66 minutes, Hibbitt hit the post and, although Sunderland's follow-up was blocked by Keeley, Kenny forced the second rebound in to make the game safe. With 15 minutes left, Tudor scored, then Terry Hibbitt hit the top of the bar and Malcolm MacDonald missed a sitter. Three minutes from the end, Kenny made the Magpies pay when he smashed home a glorious 20-yarder.

The watching Stan Cullis was full of praise; "Wolves have such a lot of good youngsters who never stop running, and what a shot Hibbitt has!" Willie Carr is equally effusive; "I felt sorry for Hibby. He was like Frank Lampard, always scoring and getting into double figures. He had a good football brain, two great feet and a very good shot. He was unlucky there were a lot of good midfielders at the time, but not

FOUR HE'S A JOLLY GOOD FELLOW ...

many better than him." Daley agrees; "I don't see the game being quicker or harder now. Ken Hibbitt could hit a ball with both feet. He was a great box-to-box player, had great stamina and would really put himself into a tackle."

A week after the Molineux stalemate, unchanged Wolves took on Liverpool at Anfield, where a promising start to the season stalled as Steve Heighway and John Toshack netted second-half goals. On the day McGarry was linked with a move to Tottenham, the Express & Star reported; "the Anfield jinx of 24 years stays with Wolves." The boss himself maintained; "there would have to be something extra special for me to want to leave Wolves", but August ended disappointingly with a 1-1 draw at Birmingham in a match once again marred by disturbances on the terraces. McGarry labelled it a game between "two bloody awful sides" in which Richards negated an opener from Kenny Burns.

The following Saturday brought another Richards equaliser, this time at home to Leicester in gale-force winds, Farley making his home debut by replacing the injured Kindon. The Sun's Hugh Jamieson referred to Match of the Day's coverage of a very poor game as, "an intrusion into private grief". Things had not gone well to date but the wheels well and truly came off when Wolves met Fulham in the League Cup second round. Dougan was handed his first start of the season against a side including ex-England skippers Bobby Moore and Alan Mullery. The visitors looked dead and buried when Richards headed home on half-time and the second half saw countless chances squandered. Misfortune struck on 68 minutes when Les Barrett netted an equaliser that would never be allowed today. A clash of heads in the build-up left

Parkin and McAlle prone in the centre circle as the goal went in. The former took no further part and Viv Busby and Barrett scored in the last four minutes to eliminate the holders and make a mockery of all of their possession.

Shell-shocked Wolves recovered sufficiently to earn a goalless draw at Everton but a lack of punch was further undermined by a hamstring strain to Richards. The only good news was that new England manager Don Revie had called up he, Powell, Sunderland, Palmer and Daley into a squad of 84 for a preliminary international get-together. The loss of Richards left Dougan partnering Sunderland for the opening game of the UEFA Cup campaign when Porto entertained Wolves in the 50,000-capacity Etaeio das Antes. Porto had two World Cup connections; their coach Aimore Moreira had led Brazil to glory in 1962 and Teofilo Cubillas had represented Peru in 1970. A nightmare first half opened with a McAlle own goal on three minutes when, under no real pressure, he headed over Parkes from 30 yards and in off a post. On 35 and 40 minutes, the catastrophe deepened as Cubillas and Flavio extended the lead. Although Bailey shot home on the hour, a retrievable deficit was increased by a Gomes goal ten minutes later. For McGarry, it was Leipzig all over again but he rapidly came to the defence of McAlle, not that 'Scouse' was so kind on himself; "I made three mistakes and was horribly punished for each one. It was my first really bad game in five years. I'll never play that badly again as long as I live."

The return to the League saw Wolves 2-1 up on Spurs with 15 minutes left. Gerry Taylor had come in for Palmer, and Parkin scored his first goal since January, 1972 but Wolves' old tormentor Martin Chivers scored twice late on to pocket the points. The next Tuesday, a woeful 15,187 crowd saw Daley put Wolves ahead, only for Sheffield United to be gifted a point in a match marked by Nigel Williams' debut. A returning Richards gave Wolves their first League win since August 24 - 1-0 at Chelsea - before the first Wednesday in October brought the second leg against Porto.

In front of a meagre 15,294, things soon looked good when, a minute after Dougan had headed against the bar, Bailey deflected in a Richards shot. However, the key moment came on 37 minutes when Cubillas drove across the face of goal. The ball reared off Palmer's arm and Parkes was unable to keep it out. A combination of a 2-5 aggregate deficit and the Portuguese team's blatant time-wasting seemed to have ended the tie but a Daley goal on 46 and a Doog header 11 minutes from time brought it back to life. The huge rescue effort failed to pull the

MY NIGHTMARE

I'll never play as badly again, says shattered McAlle

By HUGH JAMIESON

WOLVES defender John McAlle flew home from Portugal yesterday still stunned by what he described as "my EUFA Cup nightmare."

The 24 - year - old defender put through his own goal inside three minutes.

And he was involved in costly mistakes that led to two other goals as Wolves crashed 4-1 to F.C. Porto in the first round first leg.

Task

"I caught the ball

right after that and lost my way.

"I could have cleared the ball for the second goal but hit a Portuguese player instead, and I got a bad bounce for the third.

"It was unbelievable and something I'll never forget."

Now Wolves are left with a tremendous task in the return leg at Molineux but manager

"He's been one of my most consistent players—especially in Europe—and it's a tragedy this should have happened to such a dedicated boy."

But McGarry admitted: "Blame me—I picked the wrong team.

Hopes

"I reckon I should have played Steve Kindon all the way through instead of bringing him on at

would have made the difference because we had plenty of possession."

Wolves will pin their hopes on the return of England striker John Richards who was ruled out because of a strained hamstring muscle.

And McGarry pledged: "It's not a lost cause. "The Portuguese played well at times but they won't fancy the return, especially if we're aggressive.

It's heroic UEFA Cup failure again, though The Doog sets up a grandstand finish.

game round, though, and Wolves were unable to force extra-time, not helped by an extraordinarily paltry 65 seconds of stoppage-time. Palmer recalls the adventure this provided him with as a youngster; "Playing against different nationalities, Germans and Portuguese, was part of my growing up. But I don't think we had the best of draws. We had some good results at home and seemed to lose ties away." The end of the line in two cup competitions was summed up more bluntly by Percy Young; "Carelessness had caused visions of success in UEFA and League Cup competitions to expire."

The gloom continued at Middlesbrough when transfer-listed Derek Jefferson replaced thigh injury victim Munro. Substitute Derek Dougan scored one of his best goals in a 2-1 defeat, his 95th and last League strike in eight and a bit Molineux years and one gloomily described by Young as nothing more than; "a reminder of a fading time." The visit of Carlisle United brought a welcome win, with Jefferson retained and Pierce preferred to Parkes. The latter complained that his own form suffered from team failings; "The inconsistency and lack of success meant confidence was low through the team and I suffered with everybody else. My confidence went, so did my form." On the morning of the Carlisle game, McGarry saw Wagstaffe face Walsall in the Midland Intermediate League at Castlecroft - and he came through 90 minutes unscathed. At Molineux, Hibbitt had to leave the field concussed after just 15 minutes but the win was assured courtesy of a Withe bicycle kick and another Parkin goal.

Another North East visit seven days later resulted in a 0-0 draw at Newcastle but the real story was Carr's reported £230,000 move from Coventry, a figure well in excess of the transfer ceiling McGarry had called for shortly before. Willie takes up the story; "I'd had both cartilages out in 1973 and was out a long time. It took me a while to get back to full fitness. I got back in the first team in 1974 but just got the feeling Gordon Milne didn't think I was going to be like I was before. McGarry had obviously made an offer for me and Gordon had me in the office and said Wolves wanted to buy me. I came over to speak to Bill, who, like most managers in those days, ruled by fear more than respect. He told you what he was he was going to offer you, not you telling him. He said, 'I'm not paying you more than I pay Bailey' and stuff like that."

As Carr remembers, it was then things then began to go wrong; "I had my talks before going to the Royal for my x-rays and all that. I got back to the ground about three and Bill was in with John Ireland. I was outside with all the reporters. By about five, they hadn't come out so I'd got the idea something was afoot. McGarry came out soon after and said, 'Willie, the X-rays have shown a bit of arthritis in the knee and, with the amount (£240 grand, a lot of money then) obviously we can't risk you breaking down. They probably wouldn't insure you anyway.' I said, 'fair enough' and went back to Coventry. I missed the game on the Saturday but the week after was back in the first team." The official version was that the deal was called off on medical grounds due to 'degeneration of the joint'. Powell believes that he would have been the make-weight had the move gone ahead; "Willie and I should have gone different ways in 1974 but it didn't work out."

Chasing their first win at Leeds since 1946, Wolves lost 2-0 on a day Palmer was stretchered off. Although Wagstaffe returned near the end of October, Hibbitt's penalty could not stop Don Givens inspiring QPR to a second Molineux win in a row. McGarry couldn't understand it when some supporters in the Waterloo Road Stand subjected Bailey to abuse; "I can't believe it. I'm dumbfounded. He gives me 100 per cent every week." Bailey typically took it on the chin; "The boo boys are really doing me a favour." Dougan said this was partly a result of Bailey's failure to develop a closer relationship with the fans; "I tried to tell him, '97-98 per cent of the fans love you, you must have a rapport with them.' But he was cold and didn't communicate with them. I never left the dressing room until I had signed every piece of paper."

However, Waggy remembers a tremendously inspirational leader; "It was just his way and Wolves have never had a captain like him since. Mike had a strong personality and the guts to go with it. He would never shirk a tackle, just the kind of man he still is. A few weeks ago, we had a golf tournament, 75 people, a tough course, Mike went round in 78 (less 10) and won it!" Parkin adds; "Mike had a presence and was well liked among the players, had a strong character and was well respected. If you were a young player, he was always there. If there was trouble, he would sort it out. When you played Leeds, you'd got Bremner, Giles and a few others who liked to put their foot in. Well, nobody liked to put their foot in like Mike." Willie Carr sums it up very

succinctly; "Everyone respected Mike Bailey", although Steve Kindon reckons McGarry expected too

Specialist ko's Carr deal

By John Dee

SHATTERING . . . that was the reaction of Wolves manager, Bill McGarry, after he announced last night the £230,000 transfer of Coventry's Willie Carr was off.

Earlier McGarry firmly believed the transfer, agreed by Coventry and Carr, would go through without a hitch.

Then came the bombshell news. The specialist, who had carried out Carr's medical earlier in the afternoon, advised Wolves not to go ahead with the transfer.

He had diagnosed what was officially stated to be a

the one on which two cartilage operations had been carried out last year and which forced Carr to miss most of last season's First Division games.

Carr, himself, had sensed something was wrong as he waited for Wolves to consider what was in the report.

After arriving in Wolverhampton at around 2.0 pm he first had the medical then went to Molineux for the usual formalities of meeting the Press.

The time then was 3.30 but after McGarry had left him in the Wolves boardroom, the minutes ticked away and it soon became obvious things were not going according to

Waters went into conference in the manager's office and when they re-emerged the expressions on their faces told their own story.

Just before 5.0 pm Carr was called in to see McGarry and was told the news. He was obviously shocked at what he heard and immediately left for his home near Kenilworth.

It was then that McGarry broke the news the deal was off. He said; "I have never been so disappointed in my life. I regarded this as the best signing of my career, but we have to accept our specialist's advice."

Wolves chairman, John Ireland, summed up everyone's feelings at Molineux much of his all-action skipper; "It is not a criticism but Mike wasn't in 1975 what he had been in 1972. He was still an exceptional captain but McGarry was asking him to do the same when he was two yards shorter on pace."

Wolves recovered sufficiently to snatch a bore draw against lowly Arsenal. Waggy was out again while Pierce was hurt colliding with a Highbury goal-post. Redemption came on the first Saturday in November when fourth-placed Ipswich were beaten 2-1 at Molineux. Hibbitt capped a 40-yard run with an unstoppable fifth minute shot and, although Clive Woods replied, Munro nodded in a Farley corner on 67 minutes. Just when things seemed to be coming right, 20-year-old Sunderland broke the tibula and fibula in his right leg in a five-a-side accident with Bailey. Dougan sympathised; "It's cruel when this happens to a youngster moving towards his highest potential."

Wolves' unbeaten London record, going back to August, 1972 was spectacularly lost as goals by Kindon and Richards could not prevent a 5-2 drubbing at West Ham. Wolves were down to 13th and apparently sinking fast as discussion in the local press focused on a lack of goals (only 20 in 18 League games), and stressing; "Richards' need is for a Doog-type partner." Stoke's visit saw Peter Shilton's debut after a £340,000 move from Leicester and he kept Wolves on the wrong end of a 1-0 scoreline until Denis Smith brought down Richards in the last minute. Hibbitt converted but the standing ovation for Wolves and the keeper could not mask the view that it was; "Shilton Daylight Robbery." The traditional Baseball Ground mud put paid to the planned trip to Derby before a Kindon double saw off Coventry at the start of December.

The Coventry game was Bailey's 450th League match and also saw Carr play for Coventry after his aborted move. The popular Scot said; "I promised myself I would prove them wrong." Kindon won the match in a destructive four-minute spell round the hour mark. First, Richards' header was fisted away by Glazier to allow him to bullet home such a powerful header that he joined the ball in the back of the net. Then a second came courtesy of a straightforward tap-in. In the week, Palmer and Powell were named in Revie's under-23 England squad to play Scotland in Aberdeen, then the injured Alan Sunderland was sent a reassuring telegram; "Sorry you can't be with us, all the best for a speedy recovery." This at a time when Kevin Beattie announced he was 'too shattered' to accept an international call-up. McGarry said sarcastically; "I feel sorry for these 21-year-olds earning anything from £150 upwards for doing what hundreds of us love to do, play football."

Alan Sunderland relaxes after his unlucky break.

Good December form continued when Richards and Kindon netted in a 4-2 home win over Burnley, although an injured shin again put Wagstaffe out and Farley in. With many players laid low by a 24-hour flu bug, a creditable 0-0 draw was prised at third-placed Manchester City. Asa Hartford, who had moved to Maine Road rather than Molineux, was most complimentary; "They are one of the best sides we've met so far and didn't just come and sit on their heels in defence." The Boxing Day visit of Everton drew the third highest home crowd of the season (33,120), a Hibbitt penalty and yet another goal by Kindon earning a third win in four as Nigel Williams deputised for the suspended Palmer. Wolves were unbeaten in five games and closing in on the leaders, and Bailey argued; "What a great New Year it will be!" Indeed, as they visited a lowly Luton side who had won only three times all season, they lay just five points behind pacesetters Ipswich with a game in hand. Almost predictably, though, unknown 18-year-old Ron Futcher made his first start and swept the visitors away on a blustery day in the mud. His hat-trick made goals from Munro and Powell irrelevant.

Any promise the New Year may have offered evaporated with a third first-stage cup exit of the season. This time the victors were Ipswich in the FA Cup. Richards put Wolves ahead on 14 minutes but Farley and Kindon were just two to miss chances before a Colin Viljoen free-kick eluded Parkes as half time neared. A disappointing performance was crowned by a Dave Johnson winner with five minutes to go. It was an outcome that had Bobby Robson admitting; "I have never seen Ipswich play so badly and win." On the day Walsall earned a replay by holding Manchester United at Old Trafford, Wolves were eliminated due to an inability to take simple chances. The misery continued a week later when the return of Wagstaffe failed to inspire the team at Coventry, Carr scoring one of the goals in a 2-1 home win. Referee Keith Styles over-zealously awarded Richards a first League caution for failing to ask permission to return to the pitch after an injury. Any remaining Wolves optimism was blown away when Henry Newton steered Derby to success in another match McGarry's men dominated. It was a fourth defeat in succession and the third in a row in the League.

Critics of McGarry began to surface, including 'Disillusioned Wolf' of Dudley; "Every week he makes feeble excuses about the team's performance. He must have one of the worst records in the transfer market. Where would Wolves be without the players Ronnie Allen purchased, Dougan, Hibbitt, Munro and Parkin? I reckon they would be in the Second Division. Unless something is done, we could end up there anyway." J.E. York of Bilston even argued that all true supporters should boycott the club until there was some indication of their intention to seek success.

With no FA Cup interest, Wolves chose as the antidote to their ills a 3,000-mile trip to Kuwait to take on a Kudissa team coached by Peter McParland. Bailey enthused about a land boasting enough oil to supply the world for well over 100 years and where petrol cost 9p a gallon. Although Wolves returned to the good news that Sunderland's plaster had been removed, a visit to second-placed Ipswich on February 1 saw Beattie

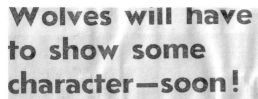

Wolves will have to show some character—soon!

January 1975 was anything but a happy start to the New Year as far as lves were concerned. Three successive defeats following an end of the r set back at Luton made in in fact, the blackest January Wolves have erienced since the 1967-68 season.

en Wolves had just rned to the First Division r a two-year spell in the nd and in January 1968 t failed to win three ue games and an FA Cup at Rotherham. his month league defeats Coventry and home to by came after a quick drawal from the FA Cup n Ipswich won 2—1 at inerix. Wolves ever needed to w their character it is in

JOHN DEE'S MOLINEUX NOTEBOOK

now slipped dangerously in the other direction.

Yet the Derby defeat in many ways could be compared with the game at Highbury last November.

Arsenal had dominated the goalless draw with Wolves riding the luck which came their way and having chances towards the end to take both

bottom of a post and the same player had Gary Pierce moving the wrong way when a shot from him struck the goalkeeper's legs and bounced clear.

What happened against Derby? — John Richards in the first minutes aimed the ball past Colin Boulton. The goalkeeper went the wrong

The Sporting Star reflects on the crisis caused by Wolves' poor January form.

and Viljoen condemn them to a fifth defeat on the trot. In for the injured Munro, Jefferson made his first return to Portman Road since his transfer in 1972 and contrived to concede the free-kicks that led to two soft goals. Plunged to 16th place, just eight points off the bottom, it was hard to see where wins were coming from and even McGarry spoke of; "a cold wind blowing down the corridors of Molineux."

The first win since Boxing Day eventually came in unexpected circumstances in a weekend when injuries, illness and loss of form played havoc with Wolves' line-up for the return match with Arsenal. Parkes again fell victim to the team's decline and was replaced by Pierce. After a Central League run-out against Everton, the keeper was in the first team for the first time since colliding with a post at Highbury in December. Parkin and McAlle, both ever-presents, were kept out by flu and a knee injury respectively and, with six other walking wounded, the 'Express & Star' reported on, 'Rattling Wolves - Emergency Ward 15 at Molineux'.

Richards, himself rushed back after flu, missed from three yards when the ball lodged between his boot and the turf. Typically, though, he fought on undeterred and was brought down by Peter Simpson in the second half, leaving Hibbitt to beat Jimmy Rimmer from the spot. Wolves had collected their first win of 1975 and were probably untroubled by the words of Brian Clifford, himself deputising for flu-stricken John Dee, under the Express & Star heading, 'The day football forsook Molineux'; "Arsenal went down for the first time in 1975 and both teams saved themselves from 19,870 prosecutions under the Trade Description Act." Things appeared to be back on track when a strengthened team stormed into a two-goal lead at Stoke but sadly surrendered a point in the last three minutes.

That same weekend, it was argued in the press that Dougan, unable to return to first-team action, had been earmarked to manage a top club. Although The Doog had previously maintained that management did not appeal to him, Karl Kershaw claimed he had been told by West Bromwich Albion that he had no need to go job-hunting since they felt he could 'do a Jack Charlton' for them. Dougan expressed an interest without being specific; "Knowing it is at last time to retire doesn't mean the game has exhausted me. I hope to continue the relationship in some capacity because football is still my life." The following Saturday, Wolves maintained their improved form with a 3-1 win over West Ham. A blow to Farley's knee in a six-a-side session brought Wagstaffe back to the fray and he contributed to a victory delivered by a goal from Kindon and two from Richards whilst ex-Wolf Bobby Gould scored for the Londoners. Old inconsistencies returned, though, when Paul Hendrie shocked Wolves with a close-range shot on 68 minutes to give Birmingham an away win. With only 30 points banked and 11 games left, relegation was still a distinct possibility, with Sunderland continuing to fight his way back to fitness by cycling and swimming.

The defeat against Blues saw Palmer dropped for the visit to Bramall Lane but his replacement Nigel Williams was dismissed by Clive Thomas, and Eddie Colquhoun won the match for Sheffield United. Palmer remembers; "On the Monday, I came in for training and my kit wasn't there. I asked Sammy where it was. He said, 'The gaffer says you're training with the young lads in the park.' I had to change in the bottom room with the kids. When the first team was training, I'd be with the reserves. I didn't play on the Saturday and my replacement, Nigel, got sent off so I was back the week after. It was the way he went about it. Surely he could have had me in his office and given me a rollicking. Instead he shoved me with the kids. That's how he was. I still wouldn't knock him because I think he put me in good stead for later life."

Unexpectedly, there was a turn for the better in mid-March when Willie Carr, having almost joined Wolves in October, came on board at a cut-price £100,000. It was quite a shock for him to receive a 9am call from Coventry boss Gordon Milne but he had little hesitation in agreeing to the move; "I could have been in danger of getting into a rut but I am sure this will renew my zest for the game," he said then. "I've always liked Wolves, had some great games against them and I am confident I can do well." Hibbitt argues that his good mate was one of McGarry's best coups; "He was a great buy, one of his shrewdest. Wolves were going to pay over £200,000, found a bad knee and got him for half. Then they had him for seven or eight years."

Even the appearance of Slade couldn't inspire a much-needed Wolves victory at home to Birmingham.

Carr recalls; "Around

Christmas, QPR came in. Not going was probably the worst mistake I ever made as far as moving was concerned. Dave Sexton was manager and they had Don Masson, Stan Bowles and Gerry Francis but I just didn't fancy London. By March, I was getting back to something like I was before and, on deadline day, Gordon Milne had me in the office to tell me Wolves had come in again. He said, 'I don't want you to go', but I thought, 'If that's the case, why let me speak to them?' I didn't have a medical that time because they could take a chance at the price." However, he recalls advantages and disadvantages at Molineux; "I wasn't desperate to move in 1975. I'd had ten good years at Coventry but it was just something that happened. And I have no regrets. When I first got here, I thought I'd gone back to the 1950s with the dressing rooms, baths and a weight room that was out of the Ark. I thought bloody hell. The big difference was the fan base, so much bigger at Wolves."

A 21,649 crowd saw Carr's debut against Chelsea, who had already conceded 54 goals in 32 League games and just parted company with Peter Bonetti on a free. Kindon remembers this match for his own good performance; "There's a picture of Willie running out for his first game and, unbeknown to me, I was just in front of him. I had one of my best games and after that always tried to go out just in front of him!" Parkes recalls being required to play despite medical advice to the contrary; "I'd been off Thursday and Friday with flu. I came in on Saturday and saw the doc. He said, 'There's no way you can play, big man. You've got a temperature of 104'. I said, 'That's OK but you're going to tell him cos I ain't'. We went in and the doc said, 'gaffer, the big man can't play today'. McGarry's exact words were, 'Why f***n not?' The doc replied, 'He's got a temperature of 104'. 'So f***n what? You're the doctor, I'm the manager, he's f***in playing. You'll be ok, won't you?' 'If you want me to play, I'll play'. 'Of course I f***in want you to , I've got no-one else."

The match brought Wolves' biggest win in nine years and their best in Division One for 12. Carr began the move that led to Richards putting them ahead on 23 minutes and two minutes later slammed in a great 20-yarder. Although Bill Garner hit back for Chelsea, Hibbitt finished off a Wagstaffe effort to set up a 3-1 interval lead. In the last half-hour, Wolves ran riot against a tiring John Dempsey and Ron 'Chopper' Harris. Bailey sent a magnificent volley past John Phillips for

Molineux goal-fest as Willie Carr celebrates his arrival.

his first League goal since October, 1971 and, with almost 20 minutes left, a powerful left-wing run by Kindon culminated in an unstoppable shot. Two minutes later Kindon turned provider to lay a goal on a plate for Richards, and Waggy smashed home a tremendous effort to make it seven on 83 minutes.

Never satisfied, most of us left asking the inevitable question, 'Why can't they play like this every week?' but McGarry was even more demanding, as Parkes recalls; "We came in after the game and Bill came in. He slammed the door, shouting, 'That was f***in crap, f***in garbage. We should have won 15-1!' With that, he left and slammed the door. Sammy comes round, it's like chalk and cheese. By the time he stopped talking, we'd forgotten what Bill had said and everybody's happy again. If he hadn't had Sammy, I think he would have struggled because he was so intense about winning." Carr looks back on an excellent first outing that still couldn't keep McGarry satisfied; "It was a good debut, it couldn't have gone better. I still got a bollocking off McGarry after the game, though. We were 4-1 up and they had come back into it a little bit. He had a go at me for letting John Hollins make forward runs instead of making him run after me. That was how he was."

Wagstaffe remembers McGarry calling Kindon in after his goal; "He always had it in for Steve and asked, 'Do you know how you did that?' Kindo replied, 'I haven't a clue boss.'" McGarry is often claimed to have coined the description of Kindon that he attributes to Phil Shaw; "Runs like a racehorse, works like a dray-horse and has the brains of a f***in rocking horse." Kindon was amazed to find he had attracted indirect praise from the boss; "Jack Everall, a professional crown green bowler, was a very close friend of McGarry's. I loved my bowls and played a couple of times with Jack. They went way back to when Bill was at Port Vale. Against Chelsea, I can't remember putting a foot wrong, everything I tried worked. I was at home at eight o'clock that night and Jack phoned. He said; 'Now, you've had some game today, haven't you?' 'I have, were you there?' 'He said; 'No, but I've just had my pal on absolutely raving about you.' McGarry hadn't said a word to me, it's the way he worked."

The Chelsea result proved to be a false dawn. Kindon and Richards gave Wolves a 2-1 half-time lead at Filbert Street but a Parkin own goal brought Leicester level and Chris Garland scored almost on time to nick the points. Good Friday brought a 3-0 drubbing at Tottenham, who had not won at home since December 7 and were fighting for their First Division lives. Spurs scored three at home for only the second time that term to notch their first League win in ten. The Molineux men's cause was not helped by the fact they were without Bailey and Richards, the latter replaced by Withe. Even the sight of Dougan on the bench was unable to lift their insipid efforts.

The skipper was again out for the visit of Manchester City the next day, although Dougan returned for his first full game since October. Why he was not able to add to his tally of 532 League games and 219 goals was seen at the time as debatable. Was it back trouble or was there another reason for him making only six full appearances and two as sub? Dougan put the record straight; "I had a back problem and waited until 1979 for an operation I wish I'd had in 1974. I still had the urge and interest but was seriously restricted and lost some of my suppleness. I regret it because I had another year of my contract and had promised John Ireland after the first American tour that I would give him ten years. With my 'dicky' ankle totally recovered, I feel I could have surpassed Sheringham. I miss the camaraderie in the dressing room and the regular training." City, seeking a top-six finish, were rattled when The Doog had the ball in their net inside 12 minutes, only to have the effort ruled out for offside but Hibbitt's seventh penalty conversion of the season ultimately won the game.

Easter Monday provided revenge for earlier in the season when a 5-2 win over rock-bottom Luton made Wolves mathematically safe and even had McGarry looking for a top-ten finish. Carr put them ahead on seven minutes, but John Seaseman and John Ryan had the Hatters ahead by the half-hour before Hibbitt scored twice in ten minutes to wake Wolves up, the first with a penalty. On 58 minutes, Kenny intercepted a Buckley pass and embarked on a 50-yard sprint to fire home the hat-trick goal before Withe made it five with half an hour left. As April dawned, Wolves continued to be rocked by injuries to Bailey, Richards and Palmer, while Kindon soon joined them in the treatment room. The Richards-Kindon partnership had yielded 18 League goals from November 16 to March 22 but it was a patched-up attack who took to a heavily sanded Loftus Road pitch on April 5. Jefferson played at no 4 while Withe, Daley and 19-year-old debutant Don Gardner took on the attacking responsibilities against QPR for a team who meekly succumbed to goals by Don Givens and Dave Thomas.

Powell made his last appearance for the club as substitute for Nigel Williams and explained he had spoken with McGarry about going to the USA; "I'd played about 60 games for Wolves and knocked on his door because I fancied getting experience in the States. McGarry said, 'F*** off from my office, you only want to go because Phil Parkes is going.' I got in the bath in the changing room and Sammy Chung said, 'He thinks you want to go because Phil wants to go.' I went back to see him and he said, 'Leave it with me.' A few days later, I was doing sit-ups in the old pen next to the drying room under the stand. He didn't say anything and just lay down and started doing the same sit-ups; 'I've been thinking about what you said. I think it would be a good idea for you to go. You might finally grow up.' That was all he said and just walked off. There was no changing him."

The end-of-season drift continued when a Bailey error let in Franny Lee for the only goal of the rearranged game at Derby, who so went top and condemned Wolves to an eighth defeat in nine away games. Richards returned to help beat Middlesbrough 2-1 at Molineux but it was top scorer Hibbitt who again netted twice, the winner a special finish on 72 minutes. Hibbitt netted 17 times that season, with Richards scoring 15 and Kindon 10. Unfortunately Wolves' away form continued to be their worst since 1967-68 when ex-Albion man Dennis Martin sealed a 1-0 victory for relegated Carlisle

Wolves defend in depth (above) as their dismal away run continues at relegation-bound Carlisle. Left: Steve Kindon is a lone Wolf among celebrating Cumbrians.

and made it six successive away losses (and nine in ten) and 16 away games without a win. In stark contrast, 12 home wins put Wolves ahead of 16 other Division One sides, with Stoke on the same mark and only Ipswich, Derby, Manchester City and Liverpool ahead of them. Average League gates were down by 2,500 on 1973-74 and fostered more brutal criticism of McGarry from the likes of G.P. Hardwicke of Leamington Spa; "What about a manager who has won just four away games in the last two years? Set up a club post-war record of 16 away games without a win? Scored 14 away goals in 1974-75? Average gates at home reduced by 3,000?"

The visit of European Cup finalists Leeds on the last Saturday in April marked much more than the end of the season. The fact 34,875 packed into Molineux owed more to the fact it was Derek Dougan's last game than to the lure of the Yorkshiremen. In the build-up, the Irishman attracted compliments from across Europe. In Hungary, his extraordinary heading ability earned him the nickname 'The Irish Torres'; "Dougan was a very clever player with a deceptive turn of speed." In France, he was termed; "as elegant on the field as off it, he was the star footballer who demanded attention by sheer presence and personality." A Swiss journalist praised his work as a leader, both on the field and with the PFA; "Dougan is a born winner. He will succeed in any sphere he chooses to work in, whether it's the media or as a football manager."

WAGGY

THE
DAVE
WAGSTAFFE
TESTIMONIAL

Molineux Grounds,
Wolverhampton,
Tuesday, May 6th, 1975.

Official
Programme **10p**

The Doog firmly cemented his relationship with the fans with his pre-match comments in the Express & Star; "In all those years and ramblings, I was looking for a club where I could express myself without feeling inhibited, a club which responded to my particular style and did not try to force me into a mould. I want to let Wolves supporters know how much their encouragement and support have meant to me over the past eight years. Even when I or the side had a bad day, the vocal support has kept us going, especially that uplift from the North Bank." Star editor Mark Kersen presented him with a silver salver before kick-off but it was some 65 minutes before he was allowed to join the action as replacement for Kindon. Honours were even when Frank Gray equalised an early Richards goal with just six minutes left.

Although Waggy was awarded a testimonial on May 6, a disappointing season ended with Derek Parkin being named Player of the Year in a term in which 22 players were used and crowds fell by 5,200 to an average of 23,377.

1975-76: Glories Gone

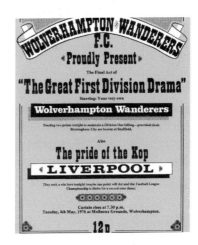

"There is no great enthusiasm for season tickets at the moment. The Wolverhampton people are terribly difficult to sell football to," bemoaned John Ireland as the new season dawned with only 5,506 of a possible 8,500 gone. With a season ticket for the centre of the Molineux Street Stand rising from £12 to £18, perhaps it was no surprise but the price still compared favourably with First Division neighbours Villa and Birmingham. I was most concerned my spot on the terraces would now cost an inflation-busting 70p a time (a 20p increase), although this was the season of my move from South to North Bank and the first of what was to become my regular encounters with the man Tony Eagle refers to as the 'North Bank Nutter'. My friends and I came to know him better as Dougal for some reason but he was definitely the same card-brandishing and note-taking character. The chairman ominously reported a £122,587 loss that placed the club in the red for the first time since 1970-71. Reasons included defeat in the opening stages of all cup competitions, Willie Carr's transfer fee, a nominal payment to Arcadia Shepherds for Peter Withe and an increased wage-bill of £239,592. Ireland could comfort himself only with the receipt of a silver salver marking 21 years as a director.

Although transfer targets reportedly included Coventry's Brian Alderson, Southampton's Mick Channon and Arsenal's Bob McNab, only the 31-year-old full-back signed. Contrary to popular belief, McNab had never played alongside Derek Parkin at Huddersfield; "In 1966-67, Ray Wilson left, so Bobby fitted into his shoes rightaway. I went in alongside Chris Catlin and it was me and him for a season or so. I never played with Bob at Huddersfield." Frank Munro won Wolves' only summer international honours when representing Scotland in a friendly against Sweden and a 1-1 draw in Romania that saw them knocked out of the European Championships. The pre-season nonetheless began promisingly with three wins in Norway, culminating in an 8-2 win over Odds Ballklubb in which John Richards scored a hat-trick. The goal-fest continued in Sweden with opportunities for McNab and young keeper Stuart

Cup failures put Wolves in the red

Wolves trio hit goal trail

Norrkoping 0, Wolves 3
Goals from Ken Hibbitt, John Richards and Steve Kindon helped Wolves to a clear victory at the start of their five match pre-season tour of Sweden.

Watched by a capacity crowd in the tiny stadium of the first division club, Wolves produced a fine performance in perfect conditions.

"We probably have tougher games to come," said manager Bill McGarry, "but this was an encouraging display. If we can maintain this it will do our confidence the world of good."

brought into the game including Alan Sunderland, having his first competitive outing since breaking a leg nine months ago.

Said McGarry: "Sunderland played as if he had not missed anything. He is going to put several players under pressure this season in order to win back his place."

VALUABLE

McGarry also felt new signing Bob McNab — eventually replaced by Jeff Farmer, would be a valuable acquisition to the defence. "He has so much knowledge of the game, I was more than satisfied at his performance."

Wolves, for the first time since 1970-71, are in the red with the balance sheet for last season showing a loss of £122,587.

Main reason for the deficit was the transfer of Molineux of Coventry's Scottish international Willie Carr and the zero amount for receipts from away games in the League Cup.

Carr's transfer and a nominal figure Wolves had to pay Arcadia Shepherds (South Africa) after Peter Withe had made a certain number of first division appearances are listed in the balance sheet at £90,088.

There were no outgoing transfers while the absence of funds from away league cup ties compared with 1973-74, when Wolves won the trophy, accounts for just over £35,000.

Revenue from RUFA and FA cup ties are down, though only marginally, but lack of success in the three major cup competitions — Wolves were eliminated in the first round of all of them

charges but programme and profits were down by over £9,000.

The wage bill rose from £231,227 to £239,393. Travelling and hotels costs dropped by over £16,000.

An extra £7,500 had to be found for the item on rent, rates, lighting, heating and insurance.

The accounts come under the microscope at the annual general meeting of the club at Molineux on August ... when relating directors George Clark seeks re-election.

By John Dee

An explanation of Wolves' restrictive finances.

Garnham, and successes against the likes of Norrkoping, Malmo and Helsingsborg. A few days after Mel Eves had signed professional forms, a Molineux friendly against Bolton and a returning Hughie Curran attracted a mere 5,000. The match saw the returning Alan Sunderland impress as he scored to earn a draw and preserve an unbeaten record in eight friendlies. The gloomy atmosphere pervading the club was summed up by Peter Knowles in an interview under the headline, 'The game I quit is dying'. Knowles, working part-time for a Bilston tile firm, explained; "When I quit, people thought it was some kind of joke but I knew what I was doing." The bad omens for the season seemed to be confirmed by news that, after 13 years, Rev Malcolm McNicoll was moving from St Mark's parish to a posting near Stafford. He was presented with a silver paper knife to mark his link with the club and their staff over more than a decade.

Manchester United, promoted as champions, were the first-day visitors and attracted a disappointing attendance of 31,973 and serious crowd disorder. Twenty five were arrested in Stafford Street for being drunk and disorderly, a gift shop was attacked, a fan was stabbed outside the George Hotel and the United following massed on the South Bank were locked in after the match. On the field, Gary Pierce and Ken Hibbitt were out, the latter due to a knee injury, and even the return of Dave Wagstaffe couldn't save Wolves. The nightmare season to come was heralded by Lou Macari 'stealing' the game with two goals in the last 18 minutes, the second a 25-yard drive. However, the following Wednesday saw things improve with Hibbitt returning at Stoke. Carr gave Wolves a half-time advantage and Richards restored it, only for Terry Conroy to spoil the party by converting a penalty near the end. Despite the loss of a point, Bill McGarry was clearly much happier; "If we could play like this

Hundreds held in Molineux compound
UNITED FANS 'LOCKED IN'

United left their mark in more ways than one.

STEVE THE TANK...

Fashion and injury victim Steve Kindon.

every week there would be no shortage of spectators at Molineux."

The long search for an away League win continued when John Hickton scored the only goal of the game at Ayresome Park. With Gerry Taylor in for an injured Munro, defeat meant Wolves had beaten Middlesbrough only five times in 19 post-war games. Back home, Phil Parkes was in goal for both teams as a Hibbitt penalty earned a 2-2 draw that denied QPR top place. Waggy's deputy, John Farley, was himself injured in the match and replaced by Steve Daley for Arsenal's visit. A 0-0 draw was witnessed by just 18,144 and Wolves were jeered off, much of the anger again directed at McGarry. To compound matters, a back injury put Kindon out for at least a month and, although Pierce once again won back the no 1 jersey, Leeds thrashed Wolves 3-0 at Elland Road to root them firmly in the bottom three with just three points from six games.

During the weekend that Ole Olsen became World speedway champion at Wembley, Barry Powell was somewhat surprisingly released to Coventry for £75,000 after a four-month spell with Portland Timbers; "I'd been to the States and sampled a bit of success. We'd got to the final and lost 2-0 to Tampa Bay. I came back and had two or three offers. One option was to stay in Portland, then there was talk that Birmingham were interested and, all of a sudden, Coventry came in. Obviously, it was coming home. It was a little bit of a shock." McGarry remained defiant on this issue and everything else; "I don't care what anyone else says. I have the players who have proved themselves in the past and there is no reason why they cannot do it again." In retrospect, Wagstaffe disagrees, viewing this attitude as the manager's biggest mistake; "We'd been together for virtually ten years and we were all losing that bit of edge. That was the start of the demise. I was finishing, Mike Bailey was finishing, Derek Dougan had finished. He didn't replace us and we'd been the hard core of the team. He didn't see that three of our major experienced players were virtually going to finish at the same time. You can miss one and get away with it but not three. All of a sudden, the machinery that kept the wheels turning had gone." Richards concurs; "It was the fact we had two separate groups within the team. The older ones were coming to the end of their careers together. Waggy, Mike, Doog, even Phil Parkes to an extent; top-quality players, all going within a two-year span. What the club didn't do was replace them. McGarry tried to get players in to play like-for-like saying, 'This is my style and we're going to play this way regardless of who is in this position'. The fans were to blame as well. They needed to realise that was gone and the players were different." Knowles asserted; "Money is all that is left in football. All the stars, the entertainers, have gone." Whether or not it was his intention, he was certainly highlighting the concern of many fans as to how Wolves would cope without the Doog. Percy Young provides a more stark summary; "In the 1975-76 season, relatively at least, Wolves appeared personality-less both collectively and individually."

Further humiliation almost followed when the second-round League Cup draw sent Wolves to Swindon. Although boosted by Wagstaffe's return, they were two down in 36 minutes, the first from Peter Eastoe. With ex-keeper Jim Barron in the home goal, the margin remained intact until Sunderland and Richards earned a replay with time fast running out. The first League win was just round the corner and the victims were Wolves' potential third-round opponents Birmingham. Munro reveals he played though hardly fit to walk; "I lived at Compton and had a shave before the match. Rushing to watch On the Ball, I fell downstairs. My knee swelled up badly and when I got in, I told McGarry I could hardly walk. My knee was killing me but he said; 'If you can walk, you can play against Bob Latchford!' They got some tape and strapped it up and I had an even bigger bandage on at half-time." Blues also included Peter Withe (signed from Wolves for £40,000) and Terry Hibbitt. When Sunderland was brought down in the area by Ray Martin, it seemed certain Kenny would give Wolves the lead. After all, he had converted all his previous 13 penalties. Although the no 7 this time blasted high and wide, his blushes were spared by a Carr double that at last cheered the Molineux faithful; "Before the game, McGarry had me in the office and said, 'The way you strike the ball, you should be getting more goals.' I played the ball through for Sundy to be brought down and, for my first goal, he nodded back and the ball fell nicely for me to half-volley with my left foot. The other came from a throw-in. I just let it come away from me and whacked it into the top corner."

The League Cup replay with Swindon saw the transfer-listed Derek Jefferson replace Munro for only his 48th Wolves first-team start. He fouled Eastoe on the edge of the box and, with just 18 minutes gone, David Moss gave the visitors a lead that lasted until early in the second half when three goals in 22 minutes from Sunderland, Richards and Hibbitt changed the whole tie, although a simple header from Eastoe a minute later set up an unnecessarily nervy end. Hibbitt's goal was his first in the cup since Wembley, 1974 but JR's record was nine in eight successive ties going back to the visit of Exeter in December, 1973.

SMILING NOW . . . but there'll be no holds barred when brothers Terry Hibbitt (left) and Ken clash today.

BROTHERLY LOVE!

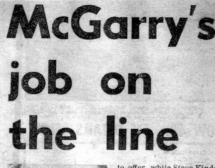

air of sadness hanging
se days as the once
Wanderers pitch from
a crazy helter skelter
m plunging towards

our finger right on it,
hat unless Wolves start
ther very quickly the
ort of one top flight outfit.

Manager Bill McGarry knows the problem well and the loudmouths in the enclosure in front of McGarry's director's box seat le thim hear in no uncertain manner that they want him out.

On Tuesday night in the goalless draw with Aston Villa the crowd baited McGarry for the full 90 minutes. Certain players, too, came in for plenty of stick.

The fans are entitled to their say, although on Tues-

⊛ *Bill McGarry*

to offer, while Steve Kinde is one of the most exciting players in the First Division and John Richard must surely regain h touch soon.

There's been some criticism of McGarry selling Peter Withe for such a low fee to Birmingham. Bi Withe never really did it a Molineux and the Wolve manager says: "I've no regrets about selling him.

"If anything I would sa

Nonetheless, the hard work Wolves had made of lower-league opposition was ominous, given the statistics of 22 shots on target against nine from Swindon, and nine corners against two.

Buoyed by modest cup success, Wolves headed north seeking a first League win at Newcastle since 1959 and a first away victory in 12 months and 19 goes.

Things began promisingly when Daley scored on nine minutes, the youngster having rocked the club with a transfer request when left out of the line-up for the Blues and Swindon games. Two howlers by Pierce blew away any optimism as first he watched a header by Alan Gowling drift into the net and then dropped a ball from John Tudor to gift a second. Strangely turned out in orange shirts and socks and light blue shorts, it wasn't only the kit that was a pale imitation as Wolves tamely succumbed 5-1. The game also saw Richards injured and Bailey booked for only the third time in a long, illustrious career, McGarry claiming the former had been kicked out of it; "He was murdered in the first half. How he played on, I shall never know. His ankle is a terrible sight." However, on September 23, some fans showed little sympathy when mercilessly baiting the manager from the Enclosure below his directors' box seat in a dull midweek 0-0 draw against Villa. Waggy played the last of his 324 League games for the club and Norman Bell went in at no 9 to play the first of 17 matches that term. He was the first of four youngsters to debut in 1975-76.

While some criticised him in particular for selling Withe, McGarry turned both barrels on his players; "We had too many Robin Hoods out there. Too many players were playing hide and seek." Carr remembers being one of those in the boss's sights; "I had a bit of a bad time and fell out with him. Against Villa, somebody played a ball and John Gidman was coming in behind me. I went to dummy but Gidman read it and took the ball away. It must have looked to Bill as if I'd s**t out of the tackle but I knew what I was trying to do. He had me in the office and said, 'You've let me down and let yourself down'. I replied, 'I know what I was trying to do, obviously you think differently.' I hadn't been playing that well and did not play for eight or nine weeks."

The 33,000 crowd almost halved for the visit of West Ham on the eve of my decampment to Liverpool University. On a gusty afternoon, JR returned but Graham

Paddon scored the only goal with a freakish shot from 40 yards. After only one win in ten League games, I could have hardly been in worse spirits as mum and dad settled me into Roscoe and Gladstone Hall. The Sunday newspaper headlines ran, 'Wolves have to bear the fans' taunts', 'We want our money back', 'We want Dougan back', 'McGarry out'. But, with his chairman's backing McGarry was defiant, saying; "It hurts like hell but I won't be broken." As I

HALL DIVES IN TO SINK WOLVES

Liverpool 2, Wolves 0

by Alex Goodman

LINE-UP

Despite the attentions of two Wolves defenders, Jimmy Case fires in a shot.

settled, Wolves prepared for their own Merseyside visit to a far from happy hunting ground. Interest in Liverpool's Ray Kennedy came to nought and the side had enough difficulty getting to Anfield after the coach broke down. Brian Hall, on the hour, and Jimmy Case, four minutes from time, gave Wolves no respite. One win, seven goals and six points from 11 games represented the worst crisis since the 1964-65 relegation season. Perversely, the following Tuesday brought a Hibbitt double and a League Cup win at St Andrew's at a time when the imperative was points.

The following weekend brought my first Student Railcard trip home, rewarded by a 5-1 win over struggling Sheffield United. With Martin Patching as sub, Richards and Hibbitt earned a half-time lead they then doubled. Wolves went nap with a Flynn own goal in a victory that raised them above Leicester, Birmingham and the Blades and out of the relegation zone for the first time. Just seven days later, however, a visit to high-riding Derby saw Wolves three down in double quick time. My good mate Chris Cox informs me Wolves fans started singing 'Those were the days' five minutes before half-time and the lyrics cascaded down the Baseball Ground terraces all through the interval and into the second half. He describes the mood of Wolves' players as they re-emerged as one of collective astonishment but, despite goals by Kindon and Richards, there was to be no reward in terms of points for the tremendous vocal backing.

On Monday, October 20, I made the pilgrimage from Lime Street to High Level Station as one of 25,658 paying their respects to The Doog. His testimonial against a Don Revie XI including Shilton, Kendall, Francis, Bowles and Little was preceded by a Tiswas v All Stars clash. Chris Tarrant captained a Tiswas team containing Gary Newbon, John Dee and Peter Tomkinson and trained by angling expert Terry Thomas. The All Stars boasted Jasper Carrott and Bev Bevan. Although the main game was goalless, Dougan was chaired off and cheered to the echo.

A final farewell to The Doog with a testimonial game and a cuppa in the dressing-room.

During the week loyal servant Gerry Taylor left for Swindon after ten years and 193 appearances, there was more home League disappointment. On 76 minutes, Hibbitt equalised Martin Dobson's opener but Everton grabbed a highly controversial late winner. A shot by Gary Jones struck the underside of the bar and bounced back into play, the linesman appearing to be the only person to see it had crossed the line. A 2-1 defeat at Tottenham soon followed when Pat Jennings, beaten once by substitute Daley, proceeded to defy all-comers, Bailey in particular. It was the day McNab had his last outing in a short, injury-ravaged Wolves stay. Some measure of revenge was exacted when Bailey, Hibbitt and Carr scored to guide Wolves to a 3-1 win over Spurs at Wembley in the final of the Daily Express National Five-A-Side tournament. I watched this Bonfire Night success at Roscoe & Gladstone Hall, with Pierce, McAlle and Sunderland completing the squad. This seemed to spur Wolves to greater things and a third League win, when a second-half Daley strike sent Ipswich home empty-handed in a game in which Maurice Daly debuted as substitute for Farley.

November 12 brought considerable embarrassment with

More cup success at Wembley, albeit in the five-a-sides.

a League Cup exit at Field Mill, where Rod Arnold helped Third Division Mansfield keep Wolves at bay, but there was further League progress three days later at Turf Moor. Richards struck in 18 seconds - believed to be the fastest goal in the club's history - and inspired Wolves to a 5-1 win over struggling Burnley in front of the Match of the Day cameras. Daley and Richards kicked off to find Munro, who played it to Kindon. He was roundly booed by the home crowd but found Farley on the left and he beat Michael Docherty for speed to fire in a cross Alan Stephenson fumbled to allow Richards to slot home right-footed from six yards. In increasingly sodden conditions, Richards scored again, along with Daley (2) and Hibbitt. The no 7, along with Farley and the returning Kindon, had further efforts ruled out but, on a pitch fast becoming unplayable, Richards' second completed the rout courtesy of a surging run by Bailey that found him free just inside the box.

Daley recalls the importance of two points to McGarry; "If we'd got beat, I think that was his job gone. He wouldn't say 'well done' in front of others. He came in the dressing room and said to all the lads, 'Great result, we'll stop for a drink on the way home.' He walked past me, winked and walked off. Brilliant, that meant so much to me." The win was consolidated by a 0-0 home draw with clear leaders Derby but, as November drew to a close, the optimism engendered by three League games unbeaten was blown away by the visit of Manchester City. Weakened by an injury to Parkin that let in Maurice Daly for his full debut, Wolves tamely succumbed 4-0, handing City their first win at Molineux since February, 1970. It was to be the first in a horrific sequence of five straight defeats, with just one goal (a penalty) between then and the last game of the year. I associate the depression with the haunting drama of Queen's 'Bohemian Rhapsody' that dominated the charts up to Christmas. In a move smacking of panic, Bobby Gould, having last played for Wolves in August, 1971, became the first player ever to return to the club for a second spell. Parkin saw sense in the move at a time of low morale; "Bobby was a good lad in the dressing room, a good talker who inspired people. I think that's why he was brought back."

Nevertheless, a 2-0 defeat followed at Leicester, where Parkes replaced Pierce, and even Hibbitt's penalty could not stop Jack Charlton's Middlesbrough completing a double over Wolves. On the last Saturday before Christmas, Richards was dropped to the bench but a brave rearguard action controversially went unrewarded at Old Trafford when Gordon Hill snatched a winner from a Steve Coppell corner so deep into injury-time that the BBC gave the result as 0-0. However, the real talking point was the first sending-off of McAlle's seven-year First Division career. Booked just before half-time for a foul on Stuart Pearson, 'Scouse' maintained he was met in the tunnel at half-time by Docherty saying; "I'm going to get Pearson to provoke you and get you sent off. I'm going to see the ref about you." It was an exchange overheard by Munro and Parkes. Whether or not Docherty carried out his threat, McAlle was sent off by Kevin McNally for a challenge on the same player. In 1985, The Doc returned to haunt

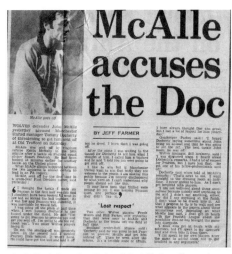

A full airing for John McAlle's allegations - but he enjoys better relations with another famous Manchester resident, Pat Phoenix, alias Coronation Street's Elsie Tanner.

Wolves when fulfilling his pledge to get them out of Division Two - alas through relegation, not promotion.

Coventry's Boxing Day win at Molineux was inspired by Barry Powell and clinched by John Craven and meant Wolves had suffered five straight League defeats in three weeks. Brief respite was gained at Norwich when Bell earned a point with a goal in his second start, the game also marking Carr's return; "Just after Christmas, McGarry came to me and said, 'Little man, I need you to play for me.' I said, 'Bill, I won't play for you. The last time I played for you, you saw what happened. This time it will be for me and nobody else.' By the end of that season, I was playing very well." Bell wore the no 9 shirt again when Arsenal were visitors in a third-round FA Cup tie. With a forward line showing Kindon at 10 and Richards 11, Bell, JR and Hibbitt chipped in to secure a 3-0 victory.

Wagstaffe, meanwhile, kicked off a month's loan stay at Blackburn, only for his potential debut against Southampton - including Jim McCalliog - to be postponed. When Waggy made it a permanent deal, he became Blackburn's player of the season in 1976-77, a time when his

Former Express & Star sports editor George Gillott hands over Dave Wagstaffe's testimonial cheque on behalf of Wolverhampton Sportsmen's Committee.

path and that of his demoted ex-employers would again cross. With Gordon Taylor on the opposite flank, Waggy enjoyed the freedom afforded him by new boss Jim Smith; "I had to play for Bill McGarry was with restrictions. I was getting up and then had to be in a defensive position when they had the ball. Backwards, forwards, backwards, forwards. When I got the ball, I'd be knackered! A year later, it was 'play it as you see it'. 'Just do a job for me', said Jimmy." He argues without bitterness that on monetary grounds he probably stayed too long at Wolves. With a testimonial cheque for £6,477 rewarding 12 years' splendid service and 404 outings, he points to Hughie McIlmoyle, Bob Hatton and Gould who he reckons made more in signing-on fees than he did for over a decade of loyalty. When he made his move permanent, it wasn't in the best circumstances, as Palmer recalls; "He was in Jim Smith's office when the phone went. It was Bill McGarry, reputedly asking if he had signed yet. Smith said no. McGarry retorted; 'Well, tell him if he doesn't sign today, he'll never play football again.' Apparently, the whole conversation was broadcast as Jim had a speaker phone."

League progress came in mid-January when a Carr penalty at St Andrew's earned a win that drew them level with the Blues and above Burnley and Sheffield United in the dogfight. Gould's first Wolves goal since the first day of 1971-72 then cancelled out a McAlle own goal for Leeds to earn a first home point since November 22. A week on and a 0-0 FA Cup draw at Ipswich set up a replay in which Hibbitt filled Bailey's shirt and Gerry O'Hara made his full senior debut at no 7. Gould won the match with a bizarre cross-cum-shot that deceived Paul Cooper and sailed in at the North Bank end. Things still appeared to be looking up in the League when a Carr penalty and a goal by Bell helped Wolves overcome Stoke 2-1. However, within a week, it was back to the doldrums when two headed goals from Gould proved to be no match for QPR's four at Loftus Road.

The fifth-round FA Cup tie at home to Charlton on Valentine's Day saw the unexpected return of Wagstaffe from his loan. He wore his no 11 shirt for the last time to relegate Richards to the bench for the second time that season. However, Richards then came on for the injured Waggy to win the match as the first substitute to score a hat-trick in the competition. The best of the three came when Richards ran towards the area to fire left-footed through the keeper and into the top of the South Bank goal. In injury time, he came out of defence with the ball and swept it to Carr on the left. Closing in on goal, Carr found the no 12

JR shares the match-ball with daughter Kim.

on the penalty spot and he slotted left- footed into the corner to complete the hat trick.

The follow-up at Ipswich brought a reversal in Cup fortunes, a 3-0 setback being best remembered by Parkes for the returning Jefferson standing up bravely to McGarry in what was to be his last game; "I think we were losing 1-0 at half -time and Bill even had a fight with an Ipswich supporter on the way to the dressing room. He came in, stood there and said; 'All you b***ards want to do is get me the sack'. He said nothing about the game, nothing constructive. We were all just looking at the floor. He was walking up and down, up and down. This went on for ten minutes before a voice said; 'Oh, f***in shut up. All you say is we're a load of b***ards, nothing constructive'. Everybody sat there thinking who said that? Everybody was frightened to look up. McGarry said, 'Who f***in said that?' Derek said, 'I did, I f***in did'. McGarry said, 'You're all b***ards' and, as he's walking out, he boots this solid wooden block. He limped out and we found out two days later he'd broken his toe! In the end, we got beat 3-0. We were stuffed out of sight."

Wolves went on to win the vital home game with Burnley, Richards' double and a goal by Bell ensuring a 3-2 victory. Richards made it six in four games when he earned a point at Villa but, as the shortest month slipped by, my first visit to Everton was an unhappy one due to another 3-0 reverse. All the goals were before half-time on the day a certain Dave Jones wore no 12 shirt for the Toffees and Wayne Clarke, reputedly the most wanted schoolboy in Britain, signed pro forms for Wolves.

Cup action took centre stage in early March, Steve Crompton's goal seeing Wolves past QPR and into a Youth Cup semi-final against Birmingham or Newcastle. Then the first team visited Old Trafford for the FA Cup quarter-final. My route took me east from Liverpool with university mates and future best-man Dave Tarsky. We travelled uncomfortably incognito on the bus from Piccadilly to the ground before occupying our places in the paddock opposite the Stretford End. Very much in the minority in a 59,433 gate, we had to tolerate verbal abuse and countless every-day items being hurled in our direction, as wave after wave of United attacks rained down on Wolves' goal. It really was a case of Parkes and the back four against the Reds as they proved equal to everything

THE TEAMS

EVERTON (3) 3		WOLVES (0) 0	
Royal Blue Shirts, White Shorts	TEAM CHANGES	Gold Shirts, Black Shorts	TEAM CHANGES
1 DAVID LAWSON		1 PHIL PARKES	
2 MIKE BERNARD		2 ALAN SUNDERLAND	
3 TERRY DARRACOTT		3 DEREK PARKIN	
4 MIKE LYONS		4 KEN HIBBITT	
5 KEN McNAUGHT		5 JOHN McALLE	
6 MICK BUCKLEY		6 WILLIE CARR	
7 BRYAN HAMILTON		7 GERRY O'HARA	DALEY
8 MARTIN DOBSON		8 FRANK MUNRO	
9 GEORGE TELFER		9 NORMAN BELL	FARLEY
10 JOHN CONNOLLY	GOODLASS	10 BOBBY GOULD	
11 GARY JONES		11 JOHN RICHARDS	
12 D. JONES		12 STEVE KINDON	

Referee: N. J. ASHLEY, Nantwich   Linesmen: K. R. DODD, Rhyl (Red Flag), P. H. WALTERS, Oldham (Orange Flag

Yet more misery for McGarry's men on Merseyside.

thrown at them. Among many close shaves, Pearson hit the bar and Parkes made a fine reaction save to deny Macari. Then, Munro's 55th minute free-kick found Kindon on the edge of the box. He fed it back to Hibbitt, who lofted towards the penalty spot, where Gould headed across the box to Kindon on the left. He drove the ball across left-footed and Richards held off Alex Forsyth to flick home first-time into the Paddock End net. Our unbridled joy, cue more objects and obscenities, lasted just ten minutes until Gerry Daly's shot was deflected in by Carr. Then, in the very last minute, Sammy McIlroy almost won it but Parkes threw up a hand to turn it over.

The replay three days later was preceded by complaints from United fans that admission prices were to be raised by 20-25p, with entrance now costing 90p and £1 respectively behind the goals or in the enclosure. David Smith of the Reds Supporters Club recklessly chose to hold Wolves responsible for any violence that might result; "If there is any trouble, the disgraceful decision to raise the cost will be to blame." John Bird, leader of Wolverhampton Council, joined in the criticism by arguing the match should have been all-ticket. There was much interest on the injury front. Gould shook off an ankle knock suffered late on the Saturday but Munro needed a test on his injured knee, so there was speculation as to whether Bailey would return from his stomach muscle problem and play for the first time since the Ipswich replay on January 27. Munro did eventually make the line-up with Bailey on the bench and the winners taking on Derby at Hillsborough while the other semi would be contested by Southampton and Crystal Palace at Stamford Bridge. Although some fans were locked out and had to wait until half-time to get on to the South Bank, the official gate was only 44,373.

The match was uncannily similar to the Wolves v United Cup matches of 1965 and 1966. Amid ecstatic celebrations, Kindon and Richards put Wolves two up. On 18 minutes, Kindon netted as a Hibbitt throw on the right saw a Gould dummy allow the ball to reach Carr 15 yards outside the box. Carr tapped the ball back to McAlle, who set Parkin free on the Molineux Street side of the pitch. His left-foot cross eluded Richards but Kindon shrugged off Brian Greenhoff to power a header into the top left hand corner, as JR recalls; "It was very rare for him to score with a header!" Just two minutes later, Gould found Kindon drifting to the right side of the box but apparently well covered by Greenhoff. Undeterred, he ran at the defender and cut back, chipping left-footed to the back of the box, where Richards chested past the slipping Forsyth to smash into the same top corner.

Just past the half-hour, Docherty replaced Macari. Although the Scot had a foot injury, McGarry was convinced it was a tactical shift that moved Jimmy Nicholl into defence and Greenhoff into midfield; "Macari had two awful games against us and Carr was simply gobbling him up. I'm sure United sensed this and fetched him off." Whatever the reason, the substitution was a turning point as a right-wing corner on 35 minutes eluded two Wolves defenders to allow Pearson to head in, then Kindon hit the

Newspaper headlines: "Bless 'em ALL in Wolves' finest hour", "Unlucky 13? Gar; does not think so", "Wolves finally fall to Red Army raiders", "United: Out of this world", "Saddlers swoop"

inside of the near post just before the hour. This bad luck proved costly as Hill increasingly tormented Sunderland on the Wolves right. Hibbitt dropped deeper and deeper to help out but, when the decisive moment came, the danger was from the other wing. With 15 minutes left on the clock, Coppell fired the ball into the middle, where Pearson's point-blank deflection bounced out off Parkes to give Greenhoff a tap-in. McGarry sent on Bailey on for Daley, a change that inspired Wolves to pour forward and Carr and Sunderland both narrowly missed. Carr remembers; "We were 2-0 up and I went through and should have scored. I never caught it. I tried to place it past Stepney but put it too close to him. We should have won." Three minutes into extra-time, Parkin clipped the post from 30 yards but this was to be Wolves' last real chance. Almost inevitably, Pearson turned villain again to provide the centre that McIlroy headed in for the 95th minute decider. Although our hurt was obvious when Pat Partridge (who had also officiated in the 1973 FA Cup semi-final) blew for time, we still enjoyed ourselves on Cup Final day, cheering Southampton and Jimmy Mac on to a famous win sealed by Bobby Stokes' goal. Although United forced 33 corners to our four, we did not share Docherty's view of United being, "out of this world."

		P	W	D	L	F	A	PTS.
19	Birmingham	33	10	5	18	44	60	25
20	Wolves	33	8	8	17	38	54	24
21	Burnley	35	7	10	18	38	56	24
22	Sheffield United	34	2	9	23	23	68	13

Vital points were then won at nearly-relegated Sheffield United, Kindon (2), Richards and Palmer scoring in a resounding win. Although the situation was gloomy, the table showed there was much to play for. Four pre-Easter games produced just two draws, though, with defeats at home to Spurs (1-0) and at Manchester City (3-2) courtesy of last-minute goals by John Pratt and Mike Doyle respectively. It was no consolation to be informed City fans viewed Wolves as the best visiting team they had seen all season. And things didn't improve. Richards and Hibbitt seemed to have earned a win at home to Leicester, only for Jon Sammels to equalise with a late penalty and, when Wolves drew 0-0 at West Ham on April 3, they had slid further behind

Birmingham City, having played one more game and collected two fewer points.

A tense clash with Newcastle at Molineux saw Munro return after missing five matches. The centre-half was brought in to curb England striker Malcolm MacDonald, who had faced him eight times in five seasons without scoring. With an ankle problem keeping Kindon out, Gould and Richards (the latter fit after a shoulder injury) led the attack against Gordon Lee's team, who had beaten Birmingham 4-0 in their previous outing. Although Hibbitt quickly struck an upright, the first half was largely uneventful and worryingly goalless. A Richards goal immediately after the interval broke the deadlock, the importance of which was summed up by John Dee; "His perfectly timed goal gave them the confidence that was so badly needed." Hibbitt doubled the lead with 18 minutes left and Richards scored two more either side of a Carr effort to notch a second hat-trick of the season and make it a rout. All the goals were at the North Bank end in a game that marked 250 and 500 career League outings respectively for McAlle and Bailey. Birmingham lost at Burnley, so the side were out of the bottom three, giving credence to the Express & Star heading, "Wolves show all is not lost."

The good work was then wasted with 2-1 and 3-1 losses at Arsenal and Coventry in the following week that allowed Birmingham to stretch their advantage to two points with two games left. An ankle injury kept Bailey out at Highfield Road but Blues lost to Spurs on the same day at St Andrew's. Two days later, Blues were at Stoke, where future Wolf Joe Gallagher crashed the ball past Dave Latchford into the roof of his own net after only nine minutes. It was to be the only goal and Birmingham had lost their match in hand. Survival hopes were kept alive in front of only 16,068 on a sunny Easter Monday afternoon when Richards scored his 25th of the season to overcome Norwich. He headed Patching's right-wing cross over Kevin Keelan and beyond defender Tony Powell, the keeper making fabulous saves to keep Norwich in touch, one especially notable from Hibbitt. At the other end, Pierce surprisingly returned to end an unbroken run of appearances by Parkes stretching back to December 20.

"I'd played for most of the season and, with two games left. Bill McGarry called me in and said, 'I'm gonna leave you out'," Parkes explains. "I said, 'I can't believe that, I've been the best player, I've won Man of the Match for the last four or five games'. 'I know', he said, 'but I can leave you out because I've got Gary Pierce to put in. I can't really leave anybody else out. I'm clutching at straws, I'm looking for anything that might spark something off. I don't have another centre-half, I don't have another full back.'" As it was, Pierce performed wonders to stop Martin Peters from equalising and was spared by an offside flag when Ted MacDougall headed in.

Parkes was so bemused and angered by McGarry's decision that he decided there and then to try his luck in America. He describes how he confronted the manager; "Unknown to Bill, I'd been approached by Les Wilson to ask if I'd be interested in playing for Vancouver Whitecaps in the summer. I told Bill, 'I'm totally p***ed off and want to go to America'. He said, 'You can't, everybody's got their teams sorted'. I said, 'If I get fixed up in the next week, can I go?' He agreed and I made a call that night. I went and told him and he said he'd have to ask the chairman. I said, 'No. I've got your word, your word's always been law at this club, you've never had to ask the chairman anything. You've run this club lock, stock and barrel. You stitched me up, you dropped me'. That's how I came to go to Vancouver." Parkes recalls a comic encounter when he ultimately represented the Whitecaps and Jefferson played for Washington Diplomats; "Derek was a great lad, a 110 per center who played in contact lenses. We went to Washington and I didn't know he was there. He's seen me and hugged me, 'I'll take you out for a drink', he said. I had a couple of young Canadian lads with me and Derek's got this big American car. We're going down this road with cars parked on either side and he hit every one. The kids in the back were hiding behind the seat. I don't think he knew he'd hit them. He didn't see them!"

Daley recalls a potentially more serious outcome when he played in the USA with Lofty in the early 1980s; "I was with Seattle and Phil was on loan from Vancouver to Chicago. After the game, I went with him to a bar owned by one of the directors of Chicago. There were a few people in and we're at the bar as a lady walks by. She says to Phil, 'Excuse me' and he says, 'Sorry mama.' Before we know what's happened, her son's come over, 'What did you say to my mother?' Phil says, 'I didn't say anything.' He said, 'You did, you called her mama.' 'I did yeah. She said excuse me and I said sorry mama.' The guy said, 'Where I come from that's an insult.' I said to Phil, 'What's the matter?' and this lad just hit me and I went over the top of the bar thinking, 'Bloody hell, what's all that about?' Phil pushes this lad away but he's told the barman to tell us to leave because if we didn't, he'd be back in half an hour to shoot us. I said, 'I ain't going anywhere.' The barman said, 'My friends, I'm telling you he will do it, he'll come back and shoot you both.' So I said, 'Come on Phil, let's bugger off.'"

The final League match of 1975-76 was way after the normal end of a season. Indeed, with Liverpool in the UEFA Cup final with Bruges, 15 agonising days passed before things would be decided. I was on The Kop when the Reds came from 2-0 down to defeat the Belgians 3-2. They would not go on to complete that particular job (with a 1-1 away draw) until May 19 and had agreed much earlier with Wolves to change the date of the League clash from April 25 to Tuesday, May 4 because John Toshack and Joey Jones were playing for Wales in Yugoslavia that weekend in the European Championships. The day after Birmingham's loss at Stoke, their manager Willie Bell persuaded a reluctant Sheffield United to do the same. Although Malcolm Page and John Roberts were in the same squad, Wolves felt Bell's real motivation was to buy time to get Howard Kendall and Terry Hibbitt fully fit.

As the big night approached, John Ireland insisted he had complete confidence in his manager; "As far as Bill McGarry's situation is concerned, nothing has changed. It hasn't been discussed and, as far as I am concerned, it won't be. He's as unhappy as

TABLES TELL-TALE | . . . AT BOTH ENDS

	P	W	D	L	F	A	W	D	L	F	A	P
		Home					Away					
1—Q. P. Rangers	42	17	4	0	42	13	7	7	7	25	20	59
2—LIVERPOOL	41	14	5	2	41	8	9	3	22	9	58	
3—Man. United	41	15	4	1	38	13	7	6	8	28	29	54
4—Derby Co.	42	15	3	3	45	30	6	8	7	30	28	53
5—Leeds Un.	42	13	3	5	37	19	8	6	7	28	27	51

	P	W	D	L	F	A	W	D	L	F	A	P
		Home					Away					
18—West Ham	42	10	5	6	26	23	3	5	13	22	48	36
19—Birmingham	41	11	5	5	36	26	2	1	17	20	48	32
20—WOLVES	41	7	6	7	26	22	3	4	14	24	43	30
21—Burnley	42	6	6	9	23	26	3	4	14	20	40	28
22—Sheffield Un.	41	4	6	10	18	31	2	3	16	14	50	21

WHAT WE HAVE TO DO . . .

● To keep our First Division status, WOLVES have to win tonight and BIRMINGHAM CITY must lose their game with SHEFFIELD UNITED at Bramall Lane. If we drop a point, or if Birmingham gain a point, then down we go. At the top of the table, LIVERPOOL have to win here tonight to take the title for a record nine times, or they can draw 0-0, 1-1 or 2-2. If it is 3-3 or higher, then the title will go to Q. P. RANGERS on goal average. Scores from Bramall Lane—and from the Manchester United v Manchester City derby—will be announced over the PA system.

anyone at Molineux about our position, and relegation would be a bitter blow to him. It would have the same effect on me. Going down once in a lifetime is bad enough, going down twice shouldn't happen to anyone." Liverpool needed a win to beat QPR to the title while Wolves had to win and Birmingham lose for their better goal average to save them as they entered the last match with a potentially vital 0.11 in their favour. As Molineux waited to host a championship decider for the second time in five seasons, Wolves' youngsters earned 2-1 home and away wins over Newcastle to reach the Youth Cup final for a then record fifth time, Crompton and Todd scoring in both games. Their opponents were Albion and, after losing 2-0 at Molineux, the Wolf cubs succumbed to a 5-0 aggregate thrashing despite having George Berry and Bob Hazell at centre-half. The final, watched by a total of 27,000-plus, added to the potential ignominy of the recently-promoted senior Throstles replacing Wolves if things did not go to plan on May 4.

Injuries forced McGarry to wait until the last moment to name his side. Bailey was still suffering with an ankle problem, McAlle had damaged knee ligaments towards the end of the Norwich game and was doubtful while the sore knee that kept Munro out of the same match looked likely to require surgery. Both first choice centre-backs would require fitness tests, with McAlle only doing light training on the Monday and Munro struggling to play any part. In Frank's mind, he was never going to be fit; "I was having a cartilage out the next morning and my knee was three times the size it should have been, I could hardly walk. An hour before the game, McGarry asked me to play and I fell out with him. I actually grabbed him but I had great respect for him as well." On match-day, the Express & Star revealed McAlle was out, too.

Bailey remembers a seriously weakened line-up; "I played sweeper, which I was comfortable with, but was asked to go man for man. It would have suited me more if Geoff Palmer had picked up Toshack and Derek Parkin had taken Keegan. I could have plugged the gaps. Both Geoff and Derek were good markers and ball-winners. Instead we were pulled about by a very good Liverpool side." Hibbitt agrees; "Munro and McAlle were the backbone of our defence. They had played together so long they knew each other's game and how to play off each other. Scouse was aggressive and tough, and Frank was a footballer with a real brain. We didn't have them and it didn't help. Keegan and Toshack were part of an amazing side and we did our best."

The makeshift defence ultimately showed Sunderland at right-back but why he was there even in a crisis is beyond Munro; "No-one was more skilful than Alan. McGarry wasted a year of his life playing him at right back. It was a crying shame, he was such a talent. He should have been in midfield or up front. Remember him winning the Cup for Arsenal against Manchester United in 1979?" Palmer slotted in at 3, with Parkin and Bailey at 5 and 6, the latter making his 500th Wolves appearance. Palmer recalls they just had to get on with it; "He didn't ask you to play there, he told you. You were just grateful to pull the shirt on." Kindon and Richards were reunited up front, supported by Jimmy Kelly on the wing. As Liverpool trained at Darlaston, defensive hard-man Tommy Smith warned; "We are coming to win and take the First Division championship in style." They made one change from their UEFA Cup final first leg, with Jimmy Case replacing David Fairclough as substitute. Birmingham had Kendall, Gallagher and Trevor Francis fit and Bell stressed the need for a positive approach; "I will not be looking for the result from Wolves, neither will the lads. We must take the initiative and do it ourselves." The games caused the cancellation of Bailey's testimonial indoor sports duel at Wolves Social Club.

In mid-afternoon, my mates and me arrived with thousands of Liverpudlians by train to learn the team news but Palmer remembers many even earlier arrivals; "There were about 5,000 Scousers watching us train that day on the ground. At 11am, they were already in Wolverhampton and there were so many they let them into the ground. I lived at Fordhouses and me, Lofty and a couple of others had to have a police escort because the Stafford Road was blocked. There were so many people we'd have been late for kick-off. They were up the pylons and everywhere." The gates opened early at 5.30 to accommodate an eventual crowd of 48,918.

Once the action started, Kindon stormed through to put Wolves ahead on 14 minutes and the roar five minutes later told us that Sheffield United had taken the lead against Blues. Our noses were still in front at half time and if only we could have mustered the collective will to persuade referee George Courtney of Spennymoor to blow early.... We truly understood what Percy Young meant when he wrote; "The 1975-76 season was one of intense excitement and dramatic denouement." As John Dee reflected; "In the end, it did not matter but, for almost 50 minutes, Wolves were

A rampaging Steve Kindon gives Wolves early heart by crashing past Ray Clemence in their crucial last-night clash with Liverpool. But the flicker of hope was later snuffed out.

in the First Division and Birmingham the Second." The first blow came on 48 minutes when Terry Hibbitt, only passed fit to play at 5pm, equalised for Blues. The pressure was also mounting at Molineux as Wolves bravely strove to preserve their sandcastle from the crashing Mersey waves. Parkin tirelessly shadowed Toshack and Bailey did the same with Keegan but Young saw that the dam would eventually burst; "Liverpool, the most efficient team in England, bided their time knowing McAlle and Munro were missing from the heart of the Wolves defence."

Thirteen minutes from the end, Keegan ghosted on to a Toshack header to equalise and spark the first invasion from the massed ranks of Scousers on the South Bank. Ian Smith in 'We Are Wolves' recalls being an outnumbered home fan that night. On 85 and 88 minutes respectively, Toshack and Ray Kennedy hammered the final nails into our coffin but Hibbitt explains the personal history behind the evening; "Terry was up at Sheffield and one of us had to go. Our mother sat with a Wolves scarf on one side and a Blues scarf on the other. She was supporting both teams. We went one up but weren't good enough to hold on. Birmingham got a draw anyway so it didn't really matter. It was a depressing evening simply because the champions were in one dressing room and a relegated team in the other. It was the first time I'd experienced both together and it wasn't a good night. I think we'd arranged to go for a meal but we cancelled it and just went home. Even when I was a manager, I couldn't go out anywhere if we lost. My wife Jane knew, another night in, it's the way it was. That was a very sad night, a tremendous atmosphere but we were playing a great side."

Parkin remembers the fear of the invasions; "The crowd came on and I felt really threatened. There were so many supporters about, it was the only time I felt it on a pitch." Palmer recalls the hurt of being unable to hold Liverpool off; "It was heart-breaking. Every time you played them, they had an aura. You'd look at them when they came in and you thought 'bloody hell'! Keegan, Toshack, Jimmy Case, we knew we were up against it." Carr agrees; "Big Kindo scored early doors but they had such a good team, in the end they just overpowered us."

We watched the victorious Liverpool players take their bow in the Waterloo Road

directors' box and, as Young described, their followers painted the town red; "Fans of the ruder kind went about Wolverhampton like the Hunnish despoilers of ancient times." University mates Dave Tarsky and Martin Wiltshire, not to mention Liverpool fan Phil Holman, were with me and we respectively drowned our sorrows or toasted success before crashing out on mum and dad's floor. Twelve hours after relegation, Richards went for a knee operation, his discomfort having been kept a close secret; "I had three operations, all on the right knee. The first was in 1976 when I had some floating bodies which broke off. This was no problem until they grew bigger and stuck in the joints." On the Thursday, Munro also underwent exploratory surgery and the following week a nipped cartilage saw McAlle occupying a hospital bed. 'Operation Knee for Wolves trio' ran the Star headline. Chris Cox fondly remembers that relegation didn't stop Bailey going the next night to the first DDCWWFCSC annual dinner dance in the Dun Cow.

Wolves could have moaned how different it would have been with three points for a win and especially had three up/three down not been introduced in 1974-75. Then, Manchester United and Norwich were the bottom two as Southampton became the first 20th-placed team to be relegated. As the post mortem began, McGarry, his "pride dented" by his first relegation, reflected on the fact Wolves had beaten Blues three times that season; "I think we were too good to go down and, with due respect to Birmingham, we are better than them. But they got more points and stayed up. A few weeks ago, we were leading Manchester City 2-1 with ten minutes left only to go down 3-2. Against Leicester, we led 2-1 but drew when they were short of a keeper throughout the second half. Those three points were the difference between staying up and going down." When inevitably asked about his future, McGarry snapped; "I don't know why you ask. It's nothing to do with me. I am an employee of Wolverhampton Wanderers Football Club and still have two and a half years on my contract."

The Sporting Comment section of the Express & Star reflected bitterly on the fourth relegation in Wolves' 100-year history; "What a way to celebrate a centenary." The writer demanded more modern thinking; "The club will have to accept their outdated outlook must be thrown out of the window. They must wake up to the fact we are in 1976 and act accordingly." Modernisation of the ground was seen as key, transforming Molineux into a stadium fit to stage football in the late 20th century; "Wolves have got what they deserve – Second Division football - because they have tried to reach for honours on a shoestring. Since Christmas, relegation has stared them in the face, yet the only on-field action was to re-sign Bobby Gould. We don't intend to lead any campaign for heads to roll but what we demand of this out-of-touch Wolves board is: POSITIVE ACTION TO GET WOLVES BACK TO THE TOP AND IF YOU CAN'T OR WON'T, STAND ASIDE FOR SOMEONE WHO CAN AND WILL."

Richards remembers the shock of demotion; "It was a big surprise for everyone who saw the team we had. We probably had almost as good a team as when we had a lot of success. It came as a total shock to everybody that we went the whole of the season hovering just above or in the relegation zone, and in the end went down." Carr was equally shocked; "There was just disappointment at going down. I'd got close with Coventry but never been relegated before. I'd just joined Wolves the year before and was supposed to be the final piece in the jigsaw. It's horrible when you're relegated but you have to start again. A lot of people said we were too good to go down but, if you haven't got the points, you're not too good. We had a lot of good players but some were getting a bit old. Like in 1980, we held on to people for too long. Things probably needed changing and we had to replace with as good if not better."

Hibbitt is pragmatic; "We weren't good enough, simple as that. Relegation was no accident. You play 42 games, you have injuries but I can't recollect any long-term ones. We just didn't function. A lot of players had to move on. Changes had to be made but they were not for the better." Daley finds relegation even more difficult to explain; "We used to have meetings about what was going wrong. Looking back, I can't put my finger on it. We didn't play well enough in enough games and didn't create enough chances. Once you're down there, you've got to be strong and hard to beat. Once you're getting beaten week in week out, teams come and fancy their chances."

Parkin agrees there was an insufficient turnover of players; "The club didn't get any money back for any of the players. We got old together and needed new talent. I think I should have gone a bit earlier when the club could have got something back for me. Managers like to hang on too long. For us all to play for that time is quite an achievement. The team more or less picked itself season after season but I always thought we were a couple of players short of really challenging." Munro gives similar reasons for relegation; "We had a team that got old at the same time. Age catches up with everyone and McGarry never really replaced players. I still don't think we should have gone down. It was just one of those things. We proved it the next season when we won Division Two." Daley reflects; "Why did it come to an end? We had a great set of players and when one part of that jigsaw goes and another one, you think, 'This is starting to break up'. They weren't bringing in players of the same quality. It was the same in the late 1970s when Alan Sunderland went to Arsenal. He was determined to go, the wages he would be on there, just married and a little kid. I should have stayed but I got caught up in the hype (in 1979) and went to Manchester City. I played my best football at Wolves, so it wasn't a move for the better."

Kindon has an interesting take on the problems and uses the analogy of Sir Alf Ramsey's fortunes; "He picked his World Cup squad in 1965 for the following year and even had wingers like Terry Paine and John Connolly in the finals. However, he came to realise his best team was wingless and we won the World Cup with a team built around the industry of Peters, Ball and Stiles, and the running of two strikers, Hurst and Hunt. Those players had to work hard for that system to work and four years later he took his team to the heat and altitude of Mexico and we blew up against West

Germany. The Brazilians played two wingers and wingers give you a break. When other players had retired and others were ageing, Ramsey put new players into the magic formula, instead of seeing what players he had and building a formula around them (as he had done four years earlier). In the same way I think McGarry hung on too long to the likes of Waggy, Bailey and Dougan. I'm not criticising players but at 32-33 they weren't what they had been at 28-29, and that's why we got relegated. Don Revie made the same mistake with Leeds. He had fabulous players but they grew old together. McGarry kept the same system without the players to play it. I could never head like the Doog but I was faster and stronger. He also tried to turn Farley into a crossing winger when he was darting. You aren't going to get another Waggy."

Bailey's reaction three decades on shows the depth of the hurt; "After so many successful seasons, it was a very low time in my career. I had injuries and lacked that sharpness you need to compete at the top. I still thought we were very unlucky. At times we were all over the opposition but could not score. We hit the woodwork, had balls cleared off the line, it was very frustrating. Our opponents would have one shot at goal and win or draw. Our fans were very understanding but a small group started barracking - me in particular. I was disappointed but I knew I was doing my best."

No-one could have any real complaints in a season in which Wolves won just two of their first 15 League games and lost 22 of 42 overall, with their lowest points return (30) since 1965. Parkin agrees; "Just like today, get a good start and it gives you confidence, but a start like that and it's hard work." The skipper agrees but is more sanguine; "Why did we go down? Because in the end we were not good enough over 42 games. Some of us were nearing the end. The team talks we had all heard before didn't have the impact required. We had an exceptional squad for eight years, with European experience, and replacements of the same ability were hard to find." Relegation was indeed not a case of bad luck as shown by the fact McGarry used 25 players in a desperate search for the winning formula. Under the circumstances, the fans were tolerant, with an average attendance of 23,000 only 450 down on 1974-75.

Just like Stan Cullis 12 years earlier, McGarry paid the ultimate price. John Richards doesn't feel there was any particular loss of respect for him, believing things to be more complex; "It was as much our problem. We weren't playing as well as we should have. It was just circumstances and McGarry was too stubborn with the way he tried to keep the same style instead of moving away, looking at the players we'd got and starting afresh." Hibbbitt is more positive on McGarry's achievements and feels he should have been retained; "He put together a decent, hard-working side and was never scared of introducing youngsters. He brought us all on and knew that was the future. He had quite a successful time with us and I think the club got rid of him too soon. He had been there nearly ten years, won the League Cup and got us into Europe. It was a great period, probably the best other than the 1950s. We did have a bad time that year but I thought the players were good enough and think the club should have been more patient with him. Unfortunately, I don't think McGarry was well liked by Marshall and one or two others. He deserved an opportunity to get us back and, with no changes, we came back as champions." Daley agrees; "Wasn't he one of the most successful Wolves managers? It was a shock to the younger side of the team and I think he should have stayed. Bill was the hard disciplinarian, the exact opposite to Sammy, who was a great coach and a great guy to get on with. The two combined well. It was the same with John Barnwell and Richie Barker, John was the soothing one and Richie the hard guy. If McGarry had been kept on, I think he would have turned it round. We proved it the way we came back the next season."

Others disagree with this view, for example Carr argues; "It was probably not a surprise when Bill went. He had been there a few years and people can get stale. I couldn't say he lost the plot or anything like that. He could be strange. If you did alright for him, he was ok but, if you went against him, he was a hard man. A lot of managers ruled by fear then." Parkin certainly feels changes were needed; "Teams run their course and managers run their course. I think it was probably right. Bill had done as much as he could, although that's not to say he was finished in the game. Players sometimes need a change. We got tired, we needed new faces and it didn't happen. We weren't a bad side and proved that when we came straight back but we had to regroup and freshen up, make things happen." In retrospect, Squeak's full-back partner, Palmer, is even more critical; "I don't think it was a surprise to see McGarry go because results had gone against us. It was funny. Clearly you're one of the worst teams but you never think you are. Things start going wrong, there's unrest, then you are at the bottom and stuck there, you just can't get out. He was always on at the young kids. Whether you think he was doing it for your own good, you thought he didn't like to shout at the older blokes. Although he gave me my chance, the way he dealt with people wasn't the best in my eyes. His man-management was, 'you either do it my way or you don't do it at all', there was no, 'we can work at it'. He was always having a go and shouting at me. Sometimes he was doing it to make you play or play better but you could only stand so much until something snapped and you're at loggerheads." Wagstaffe is especially damning, laying the blame squarely at McGarry's door; "He didn't let us express ourselves. It wasn't as much fun as it should have been. Nobody at Man United said, 'George, Denis, Bobby, you've got to chase back, do this, do that'. They played their own games. We didn't do as well as we should, though we were as good individually as other sides. There wasn't anything flamboyant, it was like England under Eriksson. Maybe McGarry was afraid to lose and too busy thinking about keeping his job."

Chung's appointment was a move Richards welcomed, believing the foundations for a quick return were there; "We still had good players and it was a bit of a travesty we got relegated. But we bounced straight back when us five or six players were joined by younger ones like Sunderland, Daley and Patching." Palmer agrees; "Six to 12 months after the League Cup win, it was time for some players to go. The Doog retired,

Waggy went to Blackburn, Mick Bailey left, it was a progression. There was also a time after the 1980 final when it was time for me to go and others to come in." He also sees the long-term difficulties Chung would face; "The hardest thing was not to call him Sammy. He wanted us to call him boss but that lasted about ten minutes. Every manager I've called gaffer but he was always Sammy."

Hibbitt admired Chung but could not view him as the no 1; "He was a great coach and it was fantastic working with him but he was never going to be a great manager. A manager has to be different to a coach and I don't think Sammy was a manager." Richards adds; "Sammy Chung was a very good coach, probably the best I've worked with. He had the respect of the players but didn't have the support from his coaching staff he'd given McGarry." Powell adds; "Sammy was so close to the players. I've seen him on a Friday afternoon massage 20 players and give them a cold dip to prepare them. If you're that close, it's difficult then to become a manager and be aloof from them. Sammy was a lovely fellow and a good coach. His forte was with the younger players but could he handle the older players? I think he found that hard, to be fair."

Parkin agrees; "Sammy was a great trainer but too familiar with the players and not really treated as a manager. He just let us play." Waggy also recalls Chung's role in the McGarry era; "He was the go-between, sometimes he would turn a blind eye in training or on the field and say, 'You shouldn't have done that' and, if he reported to McGarry, oh my God!" Parkes adds; "Sammy was a good man", and Palmer concurs; "You went from one extreme to the other with the change but Sammy was a very good coach." Carr admired Chung as a coach but highlights the same problem; "Sammy's training was always really interesting. Whether he'd been too close to the players, I don't know but I felt he was just too nice to us lot. If it had been somewhere else, it might have worked as manager but nobody would take him seriously. He'd been there for such a long time." Daley emphasises this; "Purely and simply, Sammy was too nice a guy. If he gave you a b****cking, you really didn't take any notice because it didn't sound like it was coming from Sammy. If McGarry had given it, it would register in your head and and you'd think, 'I won't do that again.' By the same token, Sam sent us out just to play because, in his first season, I don't think we needed coaching. We just needed a fitness level, a couple of good sessions a week, then go and play. We just took teams to the cleaners." Kindon recalls what he felt to be a fatal mistake made by Chung on his first day; "Sammy called us all in and said; 'Right lads, as you know the directors have asked me to be manager and I'm very very pleased. I've worked with you all for many years and I still want you call me Sammy.' I turned to John and said; 'Wrong! He shouldn't have done that.'"

It was at this time John Ireland became life president, making way as chairman for Harry Marshall. Parkes feels the change was a negative one; "I think that when he stepped down, the club started going down as well. I left right after the Liverpool game and went to Vancouver." Marshall had succeeded his father Jim as a director in 1964 but Palmer also sees Ireland's switch as a step in the wrong direction; "Mr Marshall was totally different. He'd say well done but otherwise would not speak to you. Unlike Mr Ireland, who always spent the journey chatting with the players, he rarely came up the coach." Carr agrees; "Harry Marshall was different altogether, a bit aloof whereas Mr Ireland would talk with you. Marshall was a shy sort of bloke who kept people away from him. He was not as sociable as Mr Chairman, who loved the players and you were his boys. It surprised me about the fans not liking him (Ireland). I don't know why because he was a lovely man who was great with the players. He smoked these Villager cigars and came with his pack on to the coach, and the lads would take about three or four, not one. On tour, he liked to join in with us. He was like an American with his hat and camera." Daley chips in; "He was a great bloke and used to call us his lads, 'my boys'. One Christmas party at the Castlecroft, he wasn't due to come but turned up and everyone was round him. On a trip to Norway, about ten of us went fishing on a boat and he came along. As we're coming back into harbour, he thinks he's Captain Pugwash, foot on the bow looking out. He couldn't see we were going to hit the quayside. He takes off and lands flat on his face. We all rushed to check he was ok. He said, 'I'm fine but I've squashed my tobacco tin!' Unbelievable, a great guy."

In addition to the loss of Wagstaffe and Taylor, the lesser lights of Jefferson, Williams and McNab all moved on before the new season was in view. There was premature speculation that Wolves were preparing to strengthen for Division Two with the £100,000 acquisition of former Manchester United striker Brian Kidd but it never materialised. As the bulk of the squad flew to Gibraltar for games against English opposition, Parkes, Jefferson and Jimmy Kelly headed off to play in North America. Sammy Chung and his men began to plan for an immediate return to the big time in Wolves' centenary year.

1976-77: Paradise Regained

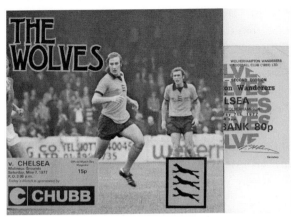

At the start of their centenary season, Wolves were to all intents and circumstances back where they had been almost a decade earlier. With Sunderland, Bristol City and Albion having escaped, they returned to a second tier that contained only eight of the teams they had left behind in April, 1967. New boss Sammy Chung had to deal with the expectation that they were firm favourites to win the Second Division; "Although I don't normally concern myself with such things, I cannot ignore that we are highly fancied." However, he was quick to make his priorities clear; "The number 1 aim must be to try and regain our place in the First Division as soon as possible." John Richards agrees; "With the squad we had, we were expected to be near the top and we fulfilled those expectations." Willie Carr is a little more straightforward; "I wasn't surprised when Sammy got the job. The team were good enough to go up anyway and didn't need much messing about. More or less from the start, we knew we were going back up. Sammy came in and we p***ed it really!"

Pre-season preparations went well, starting with a tour of Sweden that was highly successful in terms of PR and on the field. Bobby Gould scored four as Leksand were demolished 9-1, then 3-0, 1-0 and 4-0 wins were secured over Domsjoo, Hudiksvall and Ope. Back in England, there were wins at Oxford and Wrexham, Richards, one of three players recovering from cartilage operations, netting twice at the Racecourse Ground. The final friendly brought top-flight Coventry to Molineux. Richards again and Ken Hibbitt (penalty) gave Wolves a clear half-time lead that was disappointingly pegged back. Chung's reaction was measured; "I thought the first half was superb. The team played magnificent possession football and their confidence was sky-high. But the second half was a complete contrast. The team were as disappointed as I was." The squad focused on remedying what the boss called; "a rather inexplicable fade-out", but took comfort from the fact they had emerged unbeaten from seven warm-up games.

Although new chairman Harry Marshall assured fans the finances were reasonably healthy, he appealed to fans to support the Development Association and Social Club;

"It costs a considerable amount in these inflationary times to run a League club and ensure success as a viable financial concern." Before a season in which goal difference and not goal average would count for the first time when points were level, there were no additions to the squad. Indeed, in the year of Mike Bailey's testimonial, Wolves were at least temporarily shorn of key figures. Norman Bell was sidelined by a calf muscle injury sustained in training while Richards was still far from fully fit. Phil Parkes, Derek Jefferson and Jimmy Kelly had not returned from their summer in the US and, although Kelly's arrival from Portland was imminent, Parkes and Jefferson (in Vancouver and Washington respectively), would not be back until September due to play-off duties. Although Marshall was well aware of the imperative of promotion, he realised it was not guaranteed; "Wolverhampton Wanderers do not, of course, have a divine right to be with the elite of the Football League any more than the other member clubs. It will obviously take a lot of hard work and effort."

A home clash with another relegated club, Burnley, set the campaign in motion. Almost 20,000 witnessed a goalless draw against an outfit who had Mike Summerbee at no 11 against his 1974 League Cup final adversary Derek Parkin, who was making his 300th League appearance for Wolves. The line-up was familiar; Pierce, Palmer, Parkin, Daley, Bailey, McAlle, Hibbitt, Carr, Sunderland, Kindon, O'Hara. With the temperature in the 80s, the Clarets were given the run-around, their boss Joe Brown revealing his side had lost a collective 70lbs while gaining a point. Alan Sunderland's frustration at not scoring was interpreted as dissent by some supporters, many of whom were mystified by the fact Richards was on the bench and did not make an appearance. Chung explained his fitness position and that Kelly's re-registration with the League had proved impossible as his Oregon club had failed to cancel his registration. Richards was very soon to undergo a second cartilage operation.

The following Tuesday, Kelly replaced O'Hara for the trip to face a third relegated club, Jimmy Sirrel's Sheffield United, who had lost 2-0 at Luton on the opening day.

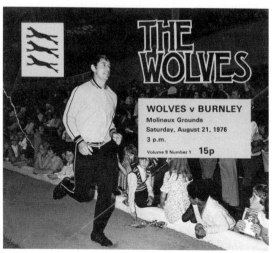

WOLVES v BURNLEY
Molineux Grounds
Saturday, August 21, 1976
3 p.m.
Volume 9 Number 1   15p

A good first-half performance brought Wolves a lead through Carr but goals by Keith Edwards and Ian Hamilton for the Blades and a fine right-foot volley by Sunderland saw honours finish even. Sunderland was to flourish in the season, as Carr recalls; "He was a bit of a lad but could play anywhere. He had a lot of skill and was a very good player." Barry Powell met up with his old team-mate later in their careers; "I managed Aberystwyth and we got into the Inter Toto Cup against Floriana in Malta. Alan was living there and acted as interpreter. We had a great time and I asked him to do a bit of scouting but I think he watched the wrong team!" The last League game in August seemed the most challenging, taking Wolves to the City Ground to face Nottingham Forest under the charge of Brian Clough and Peter Taylor. However, with Gould scoring twice and Daley turning in an action-man display that saw him score for both sides, Wolves left with a hugely satisfactory 3-1 win via a display Chung described as; "not far short of perfect."

Steve Daley in dominant form against Brian Clough's Nottingham Forest at the City Ground.

Interest in the League Cup ended in the second round for the second time in three years when Third Division Sheffield Wednesday snatched a 2-1 Molineux victory. Trailing at the interval, Wolves appeared back on track when Parkin equalised in the 68th minute. However, Len Ashurst's team produced a resolute rearguard action and a fine display by keeper Chris Turner, and snatched a win four minutes from time with an offside-looking goal by Roger Wylde. Supporters had a home win to cheer, though, when Charlton were beaten 3-0 on the first Saturday in September. They still had to be patient, the breaking down of the Londoners' mass defence by Gould (2) and Sunderland not materialising until the last 20 minutes, the last a tap in before the North Bank. An otherwise good afternoon was marred by the poor behaviour of a small section of fans, described as "a lunatic fringe" by the manager, who was concerned at; "The antics of a few spoiling the entertainment of the vast majority. It's as distasteful as it is unnecessary." This was a worrying trend and would return to haunt the club at other times in 1976-77.

Next day, Kindon represented Wolves in the 75m dash at Meadowbank Stadium in Edinburgh. As he recalls, the man known as 'Tank' won handsomely to earn the tag of Britain's fastest footballer; "Ladbrokes had started the fastest footballer in Scotland competition but Kenny Thompson from Dunfermline had won it three years running, so they opened it up to all of Britain. I won, Kenny was third and Malcolm MacDonald fourth." Although the visit to Fulham resulted in a disappointing performance and 0-0 draw, the day is memorable for George Best playing his second game for the

Steve Kindon - the fastest footballer in Britain.

Londoners. Almost 28,000 turned up after Best had scored after 71 seconds on his debut a week earlier against Bristol Rovers. Fulham's team were packed with personalities such as Bobby Moore and Rodney Marsh but benefited from Wolves' failure to turn their supremacy into goals.

In mid-September came the good news that Richards had left hospital after another cartilage operation on his knee. He was making good progress and hoped to be playing before Christmas. Bell had high hopes of putting his calf muscle injury behind him in order to play soon in the reserves. The first team returned to Molineux and blasted Oldham away in a splendid first-half burst that saw them storm into a 4-0 lead. Man of the match Kindon netted two and was given ten out of ten by one Sunday paper. Daley, Hibbitt and Sunderland all chipped in to complete the five-goal display as unbeaten Wolves occupied top spot on goal difference from Chelsea. Chung argued; "I doubt whether any side could have lived with us in the first 45 minutes."

But his warnings about complacency and the need to learn from the League Cup exit went unheeded with three defeats in the next four games. Seventeenth-placed Luton came to Molineux and won as Jimmy Husband and Dixie Deans outscored Hibbitt, with Wolves falling short in many areas. As October dawned, though, it seemed things had been put right as Hereford were thrashed at Edgar Street. John Sillett's team had just come up as Third Division champions but were swept away 6-1 by goals from Carr, Daley, Sunderland, Kindon and Gould (2).

In early October, Farley and Jefferson were loaned to Blackpool and Sheffield Wednesday and, in his next programme notes, Chung explained the benefits of temporary

Party-time as Oldham are swept away at Molineux.

moves. Promotion hopes then suffered a big setback through back-to-back defeats against Southampton and Hull. Lawrie McMenemy's FA Cup winners arrived at Molineux lingering close to the foot of the table but boasting talents like Jim McCalliog, Mike Channon, Peter Osgood and Ted MacDougall. In what was Bailey's last competitive start at Molineux, the Saints stunned the home fans by going in three up before a Hibbitt penalty and an effort from Daley flew past Colin Boulton in the Saints goal. The visitors scored three more, though, to inflict Wolves' worst home defeat since Liverpool's 6-0 romp in 1968. Although John Dee argued; "Southampton made everyone aware of the realities of Second Division football", Hibbitt couldn't believe it; "We won by six at Hereford, then got beat six at home. They had seven shots and scored six goals. We'd dominated the game but every time they went down the wing and crossed, bang! It was one of the strangest games of my career." Carr agrees; "After half an hour, we had about four decent chances. If we'd scored a couple, it would have been our game."

There were rumblings that Chung's leadership may be lacking but Palmer did not think so; "We knew his coaching was second to none and, with the ball-work, it was enjoyable, a fun season. The Southampton game was a rude awakening that brought us back to earth. From there, we stuck together and knew what we had to do. John was still there, so was Hibby and we had some good young lads." Although admiring Chung, Hibbitt feels a successful season was assured irrespective of who had been in charge; "We were so good, we took ourselves up. No disrespect but my grandma could have done it. We had power and goals, five players in double figures, and you're going to be a successful side with that." There were to be no immediate cures, though, as four days later, Wolves lost their undefeated away record in a BBC-televised match at Boothferry Park, where Munro had his first outing of the season. He replaced the injured Bailey while Gould gave way to Gerry O'Hara. The changes made little difference as John Kaye's Hull were inspired to a 2-0 win by new skipper Billy Bremner. It was no comfort that both McMenemy and Kaye told Chung they would have settled for a draw against a Wolves side now dropping back into the pack.

Richards reflects on this serious dent to the early optimism; "Three defeats in four games and the critics and sceptics were out in force. Aren't they always? But it was six months before we regained that top spot." In midweek, Bailey's astounding loyalty to the club was rewarded with a testimonial match against Albion. He eagerly anticipated the event; "I am very grateful to Johnny Giles for agreeing to the game. The Albion manager never takes any game lightly and it should be a cracker. It will be the chance for us to prove we are still a First Division outfit despite our relegation." Player-boss Giles brought a full-strength team to Molineux for a game preceded by a TV XI/Rock Star XI encounter. While Mike was also planning a dinner in November and a celebrity pro-am golf event in the new year, he was delighted to mark his ten Molineux years; "I'd like to thank everyone concerned for making the night so successful."

Relatively normal service was resumed with Bailey on the bench for a 4-0 home win over a lowly Carlisle side containing Billy Rafferty. Sunderland hit a hat-trick and Carr chipped in. Physio Kevin Walters was closely monitoring Richards' progress and resisted the clamour for an early return; "The manager has set no date. That would place unnecessary pressure on the player. We are just going along quietly, day to day." On the same last Saturday in October that the team visited Blackpool, Richards made his comeback in a third-team friendly against Colton Hill School. Just eight weeks after a cartilage operation, he scored a hat-trick and came through so successfully he then played in a midweek Central League match at Newcastle.

Against the second-placed Seasiders, Wolves emerged with a creditable point after swiftly going two down. The first was unluckily deflected in off Kindon, the second was the result of poor marking. Just before half-time, Hibbitt fired a low shot into George Wood's bottom left hand corner to halve the deficit but disgraceful throwing of missiles by visiting fans forced the referee to lead the teams off for eight minutes after the interval. Having been caught in heavy traffic on our trip up the A57 from Liverpool, I and a group of friends got there just in time to witness the chaos. Chung spoke for all associated with the club when he condemned those damaging their image; "If these incidents are repeated, it could do untold harm to the club and disgrace to the supporters. Everyone in the club wishes to be disassociated from the hooligans who caused the trouble at Bloomfield Road. These people are in a minority and they are in a minority who we would rather not have along to our matches. The only thing I have to say to them is 'If you want to cause trouble – STAY AWAY. We don't want you." Fortunately, in Bailey's last match for Wolves (25 goals in 436 matches), the visitors came back strongly to grab a draw courtesy of a powerful Munro header.

On the following Wednesday, Wolves won the Daily Express Five-A-Side competition at Wembley's Empire Pool for the second successive year. The successful team of Pierce, Sunderland, Carr, Hibbitt, Daley and substitute Patching overcame Stoke 2-1 in the final. Although it was claimed Hibbitt had fired the winner straight into the

Sammy Chung leads the players off at Bloomfield Road.

net from an indirect free-kick, the triumph was the culmination of excellent form that saw off Bristol City, Ipswich and Rangers. Wolves drew admiration from many for their one-touch football, vision and running into open spaces, and Gould was not surprised by the success of his colleagues; "I doubt whether any other side plays as much five-a-side as us. Whenever the weather is inclement, you can always find us playing five-a-side in the gym."

DOUBLE KINGS . . .

What the Daily Express said:

By David Emery

WOLVES last night became the first team to carry off the Daily Express five-a-side championship for a second time.

But they needed a goal of such dubious merit to beat Stoke 2—1 in the final that it almost sparked a mini-rebellion at the Empire Pool, Wembley.

If anyone needed proof that footballers treat this prestigious tournament with deadly seriousness it was there on the anguished faces in the Stoke dressing room after the game.

With the score at 1—1 and only the superb referee of Peter Shilton keeping Stoke in the battle, referee Ray Lewis awarded Wolves an indirect free kick on the edge of the penalty area. Ken Hibbitt toe-punted the ball into the net and Lewis awarded a goal, believing it had clipped the foot of Stoke's Garth Crooks.

Stoke went wild, with Crooks protesting long and hard even after the presentation ceremony had been performed by Sir Max Aitken, chairman of Beaverbrook Newspapers.

"It never touched me," Crooks said. "To have worked this hard and have it thrown away . . . it's tragic."

Even Hibbitt admitted "I feel desperately sorry for Stoke. I tried to play the ball against a defender but as far as I could see it went straight into the net."

That final conclusion did not disguise the fact from the capacity 8,000 crowd that Wolves richly deserved their success.

Their 3—0 annihilation of First Division strugglers Bristol City in the opening round gave evidence of their intent.

They needed a penalty miss by Mick Mills to edge past a powerful Ipswich side in the second round and a fine left-foot drive by Steve Daley to send Scotland's lone representatives, Rangers, back to their shuttle service after the semi-final.

Results

Winning line-up. Front: Martin Patching, Willie Carr (capt.) Alan Sunderland, Kenny Hibbitt. Back: Sir Max Aitken (Chairman Beaverbrook Newspapers), Steve Daley, Gary Pierce, Brian Owen (coach).

Picture: Daily Express

The day before the Bonfire night visit of Millwall, Farley and Jefferson returned from their loans, although the latter almost immediately joined Hereford for a month. Wolves had climbed back to third behind Blackburn and Chelsea with a game in hand as Kenny Todd replaced sciatica victim Carr. The problem had surfaced at Bloomfield Road and left Carr mystified and somewhat despondent; "I felt a slight hamstring strain and it gave me problems during the five-a-side championships. It then spread to my back and I have not been able to do anything about it." Looking back now, Willie adds more detail; "Brian Owen had seen an American video about using heavy weights and he'd had us doing these for two or three weeks. I managed to get through games but my hamstring felt tight all the time. We went to play at Wembley on the wooden floor and afterwards I couldn't sit still, I was in agony. I came home and next morning could hardly move and had shooting pains down my leg. I went to see Kevin and he said he thought I probably had sciatica. It upset the apple cart because I'd been playing well. I just lay on the floor at home for six weeks. As soon as I got back to training, I jogged and my calf went. It was another four weeks after that before I was right."

With all goals scored in the first half, two from Sunderland and one from Daley sent Millwall home on the back of a 3-1 reverse. A week later and a fine performance from Pierce kept Wolves in contention in a difficult game at Meadow Lane. Gould went on 12 minutes from the end for Todd and snatched a very late equaliser against Notts County, making him second top scorer with seven. The November 20 visit of Blackburn failed to be a celebration of Sunderland's 100th appearance for the club and his tenth League goal of the term. Jimmy Smith's newly-promoted team featured Dave Wagstaffe on the left and Paul Bradshaw in goal and stole a 2-1 win. The setback raised more question marks for some as to whether Chung could succeed with the players he had. One of the positives on a dismal day was the return to first-team duty of Richards, who wore no 8 alongside Sunderland. It was to be Wolves' last League defeat until

March and highlighted a period when Daley blossomed in the absence of Bailey as a true leader and goal-scoring revelation.

Richards comments on the marked change that came over the team in a 16-game undefeated run that lifted them hard on the heels of Chelsea; "This was the spell that virtually clinched promotion and most of the credit must go to our midfield quartet of Daley, Hibbitt, Patching and Carr. Time and again, they showed just why they were described as the best in the division." Richards particularly appreciated Chung's tactics that saw Hibbitt slotting in just behind the front two; "Against strong opposition, he was given the manager's job, at which many were expecting, hoping, for him to fail, and he developed a style that suited the players. Sammy's style came to be appreciated by the crowd." Richards bounced back the following week with a hat-trick in a 4-2 win at Orient, then doubled up in a 4-0 win at home to Plymouth in which Sunderland and Hibbitt also scored. Victory over an Argyle team featuring ex-Liverpool player Brian Hall was secured on a frost-bound surface that Wolves found to their liking. The programme introduced fans to the Daventry Dun Cow Wolverhampton Wanderers Football Club Supporters Club and their chairman Chris Cox. The DDCWWFCSC had been founded a few months earlier and their honorary member Mike Bailey kindly refereed a first anniversary match against London Wolves when Bert Skelton scored a hat-trick in a 5-3 win. Hibbitt was to be their first Player of the Year in 1977.

By Christmas, it seemed Chelsea would not be caught and that the only battle was between the likes of Blackpool, Bolton and Wolves for second place. The crunch came at Stamford Bridge on December when Wolves sought to close the five-point gap between them and the leaders. In front of a 36,137 crowd that included outgoing American Secretary of State Henry Kissinger, the visitors raced into an early lead. Early on, Munro found McAlle just inside the centre circle and the big no 6 passed low and hard towards the heavily sanded and icy penalty area. Gould dummied to allow Richards to turn away from two defenders and fire right-footed under the keeper and into the centre of the goal. A Gould header gave Wolves a 2-1 interval lead and, when Richards headed a third, a win seemed on. A throw from Palmer found Sunderland on the right edge of the box with his back to goal. He knocked in a first-time ball that eluded David Hay but found Hibbitt, whose header across goal was nodded into the corner by Richards. Unfortunately, two defensive errors in the last five minutes cost Wolves a point and Chung revealed that several players' ears were burning after the game; "It was an absolute tragedy to see a 3-1 lead destroyed in five careless minutes. The pity was that the side, the midfield and attack in particular, had played so well to almost run Chelsea off the park. Then we made two bad errors to squander a point."

A week later, Chung was pleased to report that both Carr and Bailey were close to returning to contention. The club captain had successfully overcome Achilles tendon problems in a reserve game with Bolton in a week when he had been presented with a £10,621.82 cheque from the proceeds of his testimonial. At the same time, Sunderland

A deserving Mike Bailey is in the money.

and Patching won England recognition, Alan for the under-21s against Wales at Molineux and Martin for the youth side against Albion under-19s at The Hawthorns. In his Christmas message in the programme for the Bolton game, chairman Harry Marshall marked the forthcoming Centenary Year with an appreciation of the fans' support and the promise of an exciting forthcoming announcement about the club's future. Jefferson made his move to Hereford permanent for £12,000 before Ian Greaves arrived with a Bolton team containing a young Sam Allardyce, Willie Morgan and Peter Reid. But Gould snatched a vital second-half winner in a game played in a veritable blizzard. This took Gould to double figures in just 11 pre-Christmas outings but he made only four substitute appearances in the rest of the season before joining Bristol Rovers in the summer, leaving him with an overall Wolves record of 39 goals in 93 games. Outplayed in the first half on a pitch that was icy at one end and muddy at the other, Wolves earned three vital points with a battling performance John Dee enjoyed; "It stands out as perhaps the best so far despite only one goal being scored."

The winning run continued in style the day after Boxing Day when Sunderland (2), Hibbitt, Kindon and Daley saw Bristol Rovers off at Eastville 5-1, a result that saw the goal tally to 50. It also brought frenzied speculation as to whether Wolves could hit 100 League goals for the first time since 1960-1961 - a target dependent on them scoring an average 2.38 goals a game from now on. Frost and snow forced the home games Cardiff and Blackpool to be postponed and New Year's Day was marked by a fighting draw at Millwall, secured by a Hibbitt goal. Carr's return on the same day was delayed when the Central League match against his old club was wiped out by the icy conditions. Wolves may have lost some impetus but Richards recalls them gaining an edge over their rivals at this time; "While we were not playing, Chelsea began to drop points. This gave us the inspiration we needed. Though we still had to win the games in hand, the chance was there for us to overhaul them."

Wolves returned to action a week later with Third Division Rotherham visiting in the FA Cup third round. Although Chung warned that the Yorkshiremen should not be underestimated, they were beaten 3-2 as a result of a Richards double and a goal by Daley, having pushed the Wanderers hard. The weather then caused a third Molineux

Centenary celebration under-way

postponement and saw to it that there would be no home League match until February 1. Indeed, Wolves would not play again until a 0-0 draw at Burnley on January 22. A bombshell came in the meantime; 34-year-old Mike Bailey would shortly be leaving, possibly to become a player-manager. The impending end of an association of nearly 11 years was truly the end of an era for the talented squad of the period.

Appropriately, the hiatus in playing action was filled by a banquet at the Park Hall Hotel to mark the club's centenary. In addition to great names from past and present Wolves history, dignitaries like FA chairman Professor Sir Harold Thompson, League vice-president Bob Lord and former FIFA president Sir Stanley Rous were also present to see Thompson hand Marshall an illuminated address.

Wolves were back on the road in late January with a Cup trip to Portman Road, where they were fortunate to draw 2-2. Bobby Robson's First Division high-fliers were almost overcome as Richards twice put the visitors ahead and had a perfectly good first-half goal disallowed. The second, that seemed to clinch the tie, came when two Ipswich defenders failed to deal with a big punt from Pierce. Hibbitt found substitute Kindon on the right and he drew two defenders, Richards being left unmarked in the centre. In a single movement, the striker controlled and slid under the advancing Paul Cooper. It was a full three minutes into injury-time when George Burley netted Ipswich's second equaliser but it proved not to matter as JR headed home at the South Bank end to win the replay. He had now scored at least once in six successive FA Cup ties - the last three of the previous season and the first three in 1976-77.

Bailey's departure became reality when he moved for £15,000 to Minnesota Kicks in the North American League after being unable to secure a position in England. Although sorry to be going, he saw it as an exciting challenge; "Naturally, I am sad to be leaving Wolves. They are a great club and I trust they will achieve their aim of winning promotion. I am really looking forward to playing and coaching in the States. It is a developing soccer country and I hope I can make a valuable contribution." Looking back, however, he is less positive; "When Wolves disposed of Bill McGarry and replaced him with Sammy, John Ireland also resigned and a new regime took over. I was also surplus to requirements and, after 11 fantastic years, I took up a position as player-coach to Minnesota. I left Wolves sad in the knowledge that had Mr Ireland remained chairman, he wanted me to be the Wolves manager."

Putting a successful Cup run to one side, Wolves kept their minds on the main prize in a tricky match against a third-placed Nottingham Forest who were one point better off and two positions higher than them. Over 30,000 fans saw the Molineux men win 2-1 courtesy of a Larry Lloyd own goal (although Richards claimed the ball went in off his head first) and a Carr strike. This clinched the January Manager of the Month award and a gallon bottle of Bell's whisky for Chung who described it as; "the best week of my career as manager." The momentum was maintained in midweek with another 2-1 win, this one over Sheffield United inspired by Richards and Sunderland. A hugely successful month was completed with a hard-earned point on a very heavy pitch at Charlton and a 5-1 home thrashing of Fulham that saw Wolves breathing heavily down the neck of top two Chelsea and Bolton. At The Valley, Kindon made his 100th League appearance for Wolves while England youth international Patching flung himself forward late to level. Then, braces from Hibbitt and Daley and one by Richards destroyed Fulham in George Best's last competitive game at Molineux. Free-scoring Wolves had notched 61 League goals and, as they turned up the heat, Luton, Bolton and Forest slipped.

Wolves were coming strong on heavy pitches and Chung claimed; "It proved, if nothing else, that the players' fitness can't be faulted." February closed with the Cup visit of Third Division Chester, the home team preparing in Southport for a change of scenery including golf and squash. It didn't work perfectly because Alan Oakes' side were composed on a trying afternoon for most of the 37,803 crowd. Patience was the key as I took my girlfriend (and future wife) for her first visit to the ground. Our nerves were frayed on the open terrace on the Molineux Street side of the South Bank until Hibbitt fired home with nine minutes left.

Fifteen games without losing became 16 as another rearranged home game, this time against Blackpool, brought another 2-1 win. Hibbitt netted again and was joined on the score sheet by Daley. On the following Wednesday, Patching won another England youth cap against Wales at Albion, with

Kenny Hibbitt sees off plucky Chester in the FA Cup.

Bob Hazell topping his dream debut with the equaliser. The bubble of optimism was punctured when a visit to Kenilworth Road resulted in a 2-0 setback that earned Luton the double over Wolves. Chung offered no excuses as the visitors fell to two first-half goals and a first defeat since November 20; "We didn't play well. Luton did and they stuck away two goals to deservedly take both points." A 2-1 home win over Hereford, in which 'old timer' Hibbitt was joined in the scoring stakes by Kenny Todd, playing only his third senior game in a career that saw only four full appearances and one as sub. This tricky encounter was typical of how teams dispatched at ease on their grounds made life much more difficult at Molineux but it nonetheless set Wolves off on another unbeaten League run that this time totalled seven games. The returning Jefferson was unable to upset his former employers and, after Bailey had flown to Minnesota to join up with former Birmingham boss Freddie Goodwin, Sunderland and Daley scored to earn two vital points at Oldham and send Wolves top for the first time since the 5-0 win over the same team in mid-September. Chung gave Pierce much credit for the victory but denied making what some papers claimed was a comment that nothing could now knock Wolves out of the promotion places.

After four successive League wins, the Cup run was unluckily ended when Jimmy Armfield brought mid-table Division One outfit Leeds to Molineux. Wolves' hearts were broken in front of 49,770 when Eddie Gray netted a second-half goal that rendered meaningless the home team's valiant pressure. The disappointment was soon forgotten when a home clash with Billy Bremner's Hull was negotiated via yet another 2-1 win. Ex-Wolves youngster Jeff Wealands played a blinder but was beaten as Richards met a near-post cross from Daley at the North Bank end, Hibbitt scoring the other in an encounter covered on Match of the Day. There was more frustration when the scheduled April 2 trip to Carlisle was postponed but, on the following Tuesday against Bristol Rovers, Player of the Season elect Daley sent Wolves top again when, on 28 minutes, he fired spectacularly into Jim Eadie's net. It proved an unnecessarily nervous night as Wolves failed to capitalise on numerous chances but Chung thanked fans for their patience after a labouring victory against defensive opponents fighting for their Second Division lives. The manager knew Easter would be vital and nerves appeared to be taking hold as points were squandered in 2-2 draws at Cardiff and at home to Notts County. Daley scored in both and Hibbitt, a 43rd minute substitute for Kindon, netted at Ninian Park. Richards squeezed a powerful shot past two County defenders and Eric McManus at Molineux but a 2-1 lead was spurned.

Hibbitt and Richards scored again the following Saturday to take both points off a Blackburn team now languishing in the bottom half. JR's strike was described as the best at Ewood Park for many years but the pendulum swung back Chelsea's way when Hibbitt's goal could not prevent a 2-1 reverse at bottom-but-one Carlisle, the home team's winner coming four minutes from time. Wolves were a point behind the table-topping Londoners with six games left and two in hand. A 1-0 home win over Orient was not sealed until the second half when Richards scored his fourth goal in two games against them that season. Orient often packed their defence with nine men but Wolves were again a point clear, with Chelsea losing. Richards recalls the cut and thrust at this time; "We were having great results and a very close rivalry developed with Chelsea towards the end of the season." The advantage was reinforced by a 4-1 demolition of Cardiff, with the less prolific Palmer and Carr joining Hibbitt and Sunderland as scorers. Chung overcame the Manager of the Month hoodoo when he received his second Bell's award and decided to divide his spoils among his backroom team.

Although promotion was still not certain, ELO drummer Bev Bevan was not deterred from presenting John Richards and Steve Kindon with gold records to mark the return to Division One - a gesture that was captured in a photograph in the Cardiff programme. Kindon said long-term fan Bev was confident Wolves would secure their place back in the elite; "John and I were promised a gold record if we bounced back into Division One. He was so sure we will make it, he has decided to make the awards before he flies off to Spain for a holiday." The star's optimism was well-founded as the win over Cardiff left one point needed, something that became a reality with a 0-0 draw at Plymouth on Saturday, April 30. Joyous visiting fans accounted for some 4,000 of the 16,794 crowd at a match that was to see the last Munro-McAlle pairing. 'Scouse' limped off to be replaced by Todd and did not play again that season, although he would play many more times for Wolves. Munro, though, moved on loan that summer to Celtic and then permanently for £20,000 in the December after 371 Wanderers games. He recalls the move with some regret; "What really annoys me with Wolves was that four weeks short of ten years, I went to a club I really didn't want to join. Wolves promised me a testimonial and I had a letter from the chairman Harry Marshall which I lost over the years. Billy McNeill, then manager of Aberdeen, phoned and I was tempted. The only reason I didn't go was because I'd given Jock Stein my word."

Maybe over-zealous celebrations were responsible for the follow-up 1-0 defeat

Bev's confidence is well placed - before promotion is joyously celebrated at Home Park.

at Southampton in a game that saw Colin Brazier replace McAlle and start for the first time. A less auspicious triumph came when I was part of the Roscoe and Gladstone seven-a-side team who won a Liverpool University inter-departmental competition along with Phil Lakeland, Kev Bird, Mark Anderson, Rob Davidson, Dave Tarsky and Steve Bottoms. Although the Saints completed the double over Wolves, all was forgotten when second-placed Chelsea arrived for a match that would decide the title and the visitors' promotion fate. The eagerly-awaited showdown was marked by an Express & Star promotion special in which John Dee wrote; "Wolves are poised to regain their place among the top clubs in English football as champions of the Second Division. One point against Chelsea will be enough to bring to Molineux a trophy Wolves have won just once before, 45 years ago." He also spoke out in favour of the manager; "The choice raised quite a few eyebrows. Supporters wanted a big name but the board went for a man with an intimate knowledge of Molineux." In the same publication Richards asserted; "We will be aiming to add the icing to the cake by cinching the championship. So we are now left with the perfect finale, the top two meeting for the championship. The only thing that could better it is the perfect result. And you all know what that is!"

Before the game, Harry Marshall handed Daley the Player of the Year award, Dee summing up the midfielder's importance; "He took over from Mike Bailey to mature into an exciting prospect." Daley has less positive memories of the occasion; "The golden boot? Everybody thought I kept that but they took it back immediately and I never saw it again. The club kept it and gave me a cup worth about £20!" George Berry was unexpectedly given his debut and was given reassurance by a Wolves great; "I remember John Richards saying when we were coming out; 'Don't worry son, I've never seen a bad debut yet. If you're in trouble, just look for me'. It was an important game but I didn't know I was playing until 2pm. I thought I was in the squad just to make the numbers up but I was told I was playing."

Tommy Langley put Chelsea ahead in the first half and it seemed the trophy might be snatched from Wolves at the very last, as Berry recalls; "When we went one down, it was a case of, 'Oh my God, we've blown it'." Ray Wilkins played a lovely ball to

John Richards fires the title-clincher against Chelsea - cue yet more celebrations at Molineux.

Langley on the left edge of the six-yard box and the striker beat Pierce inside his post. Berry need not have worried, though. Richards kept the promise made on his return in November that he would score 20 in the season. Attacking the North Bank end, Wolves won a corner on the right from which Carr tapped to Hibbitt, whose left-foot cross found Richards. Though thumped in the back by Ron Harris, he was strong enough to flick to Munro, whose shot was saved by Peter Bonetti's foot. The ball flew out to Richards, who reacted first to smash home a right-foot shot. Berry remembers it fondly; "John Richards being John Richards, his reflexes and reactions were so good, he just stuck it in the net. I was so happy it was untrue.".

At the end of a highly-charged affair for a 35,603 crowd, both teams settled for a point that gave Wolves the title for the second time and promoted Eddie McCreadie's Chelsea. Hibbitt recalls the eventual stalemate; "When we equalised, they thought 'We'll take the draw'. We were in each other's halves playing round with it. We won the championship and they were second, an amazing season." There were ecstatic celebrations at the end and Richards remembers slowly having to force his way through the crowd surging on to the pitch. He was accosted by a fan who pulled him to the ground and removed his shirt and some fifteen years later the very same Vic made himself known to JR. Chung clearly felt entirely vindicated in sticking with the majority of the players relegated a year earlier; "The players have responded to my faith and that of the board of directors by giving 100 per cent effort and dedication throughout the season." Richards agrees; "We'd got quality, First Division standard players. Playing against a lesser standard, we were always going to do well. Only Chelsea were anywhere near us because we'd still got virtually all the players we'd gone down with."

In what had proved a glorious Centenary season, all that was left was a final trip to Burnden Park, where Bolton needed to win to join Wolves and Chelsea in Division One and pip Brian Clough's Forest. Sid Kipping, Wolves' bus driver for 20 years, made his last journey with the club before his retirement. Hibbitt feels that Sid summed up the family feel of the club at the time; "He must have had 50 of my ties. He would ask in a real posh accent, 'Have you got me a tie today?' I got on really well with him. He was wonderful, God rest his soul." John Holsgrove managed to catch up with him after leaving Wolves for Sheffield Wednesday; "It was about six months later, I was driving up the motorway and passed the empty Wolves coach coming back from the airport. I got Sid to pull over at the services and have a cup of tea with me and my wife. He was a lovely man." Palmer also describes the team's travels with fondness; "After a match, there would be two crates of beer, bottles of M & B Springfield. But, until McGarry said you could have a beer, it stayed where it was. You got on the coach and we would be waiting for him. We could have been driving an hour, then he'd say to Sammy, 'Tell them they can have a beer'. Sammy would come up the back; 'The gaffer says you can have a beer'. Mr Ireland also used to come up with a big box of cigars and there would be Frank and Waggy. A bottle of beer and a cigar, they thought the world of that." He appreciates now it probably wasn't as elegant as it appeared then; "They were always on the back, so if you were on there before Frank and Waggy, you got your arse kicked! We'd got some tables you could play cards on and like a bed on the back, we thought it was the bees' knees. It was probably the rickiest old coach you've ever seen but it had 'Wolverhampton Wanderers' on the front."

Wolves were unchanged in the Lancashire sunshine except Colin Brazier returned at no 6 for Berry. There was little at stake for them but they were stirred by a wild challenge by Sam Allardyce on Hibbitt. This raised the tempo and Carr played Hibbitt in to smash home and break Bolton's hearts, from what Daley calls; "The cocked-up free-kick!" Hibbitt adds; "Ian Greaves managed Wolves for a short time and I thought he was brilliant. He nearly kept us up. A few weeks after he joined, me and Willie were walking towards his office. He went, 'Oi!' 'Yes, gaffer', 'It was you two b******s who scored at Burnden and stopped us going up. I forgot about that, you b******s!' We ran out on the pitch and waved to him. It had taken him ages to remember. The goal was a free-kick that went wrong but right. I ran over the ball but caught it with my foot so it ran away from Willie. He was fantastic because the hardest skill is to chip a ball running away from you. I saw it coming over the wall and whacked it full on the volley. The keeper got a hand on it but it trickled inside the post. It was a great feeling." Carr says of the free-kick and the Bolton manager; "We'd set the kick up for me to play it into Richie for him to lay it back for Hibby. But when he touched it, I had to check and chip it. It was like the Alamo after that. They had some six-footers like Sam, Jones and a big lad in the middle of the park, not to mention little Reidy. When Ian Greaves came to Wolves, I thought he was great, a man's man and a great coach. He had you tackling a ball against the wall and if you could burst it he'd give you a tenner."

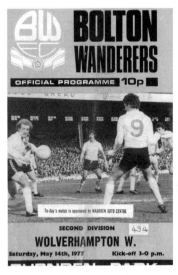

SID'S LAST TRIP

BOLTON 0 WOLVES 1

SID TIPPING, the Wolves' coachdriver, who has driven them back to the First Division, made his last trip with the club for the vital game at Bolton on May 14. Sid, who has driven the Wolves for 20 years, is retiring this summer from the National Bus Company. Before leaving Molineux Steve Daley, Gary Pierce,

Martin Patching, Kenny Hibbitt, Colin Brazier, Frank Munro and John Richards gave him an "armchair ride" to his coach. Kenny Hibbitt (Below) made it an even happier farewell for Sid by scoring his spectacular goal to take Wolves to their 1-0 victory over Bolton. Happy retirement, Sid.

Palmer adds; "There wasn't anything in it for us as we were already up. Something started us off, I think it was Allardyce on Hibby, and we beat them 1-0." Hibbitt elaborates; "It was the two big centre backs, Allardyce and Jones, they kicked lumps off us. Until then, we couldn't give a monkey's who went up. After the way they had kicked, whacked and pushed us, we said at half-time, 'The b******s, they're going to have to work twice as hard if they want a win'. We went out with a determination not to get beat." Carr later played with Allardyce for Peter Anderson's Millwall in 1982; "I could never see him as a manager. He was like a big daft schoolboy."

Some 8,000 away fans swelled the gate to 35,600 and watched their side survive a frantic finish with Gould in goal for Pierce, helped off late on by Brian Owen with an injured left knee. As Hibbitt again recalls, this reduced them to ten men as Gould had already replaced the injured Munro; "We tried to protect Bobby but, every time they got a set-piece, they banged it up there, quite right. But we survived." Defeat for Bolton was something Chung sympathised with; "It must have been a bitter blow for them, particularly as they were also pipped for promotion the previous year. I can appreciate how Ian Greaves and his players must have felt." Daley chips in; "Roy Greaves, big Sam and Reidy in the middle were putting it about. We woke up quickly and put it about. It became a bit of a kicking match. At the end, in their dug-out, Ian Greaves couldn't believe it. His eyes were glazed. For a split second, I felt sorry for him." Palmer also felt for the opponents; "In the players' lounge, some of their wives in tears." It was a sympathy shared by Hibbitt; "Big Sam from Dudley, who watched us a boy, obviously had a feeling for Wolves, but we kept Bolton down."

Although Pierce played all 48 League and Cup games that season, as did Palmer, Parkin and Daley, he did not figure at all in 1977-78, initially because of Phil Parkes' return from the US. Indeed, Pierce played only three more times for the club (in October, 1978). Failure for Bolton secured promotion for Forest, who won the First

Division and European Cup in the next two seasons. Sammy Chung and his Golden Wanderers had scored 84 League goals and fallen seven short of the ton in all competitions. They had suffered only seven League defeats, five players had notched double-figure Division Two goal tallies; Hibbitt 17, Sunderland 16, Richards 15, Daley 13, Gould 10. Carr revelled in the success; "Ability-wise, that was the best Wolves team I played in. It was very enjoyable because there was me, Hibby and Stevie in the middle and we scored nearly 40 between us. It was a great balance because Hibby always scored and Stevie got forward as well. Whoever went forward, the other man sat back." Daley agrees; "We stormed it, the best season I had at Wolves, playing with Kenny and Willie. There was a telepathy, we knew what each other was doing. It was incredible. That was the best midfield I ever played in. There was a different belief and great determination. It was a great season and we just hammered teams."

Daley is particularly appreciative of the role played by his good mate, Sunderland; "When we were younger, we used to travel on the train back to Sheffield straight after a game. In the bar, have a few beers, get on, have a few more and still be asleep when we pulled in. Alan was a great player and great lad, up front, on the wing, full-back or the middle of the park; a lot of strings to his bow. Quick and good in the air, you don't need to be the best lip-reader in the world to see what he said when he scored the winner at Wembley in the 1979 FA Cup final! He's out in Malta now." Kindon emphasises the closeness of that squad; "We were tightly bonded. It was: cut him, you cut me." But he returned to Burnley within months when disenchanted with his perceived worth to the club; "I had played for four years but was increasingly seen as a substitute. At the start of the following season, John got injured, missed a week's training and went back in the team, no argument. If he was fit, he was in. Soon after, Kenny got a knock, was out a few weeks, got fit and was back in. I rode a racing bike three and a half miles to work each day, keen as mustard, to keep fit. A car knocked me off my bike, broke a little bone in my heel and I missed five days' training. Sammy says, 'I want you to have a run in the reserves.' 'Why?' 'To prove your fitness.' 'You didn't ask John or Kenny to prove their fitness, why ask me? Sammy, I'm 26, I've f***in had enough of this. When I was 21, I was told there were two better strikers at the club than me. By the time I was 23 and they were 33, I was better than them but McGarry didn't believe me. I'm asking for a transfer.' Two directors came to my house that night asking me to retract my request if Sammy put me in the team. I said; 'No. He doesn't see me as a first-team player in the same bracket as Kenny or John.'"

Nine days after the Bolton match, Wolves welcomed Manchester City for the Centenary match and the parading of the trophy. It was Second Division champions against First Division runners-up. Richards and Sunderland were both missing due to their participation in England's under-21 tour of Scandinavia while City skipper Mike Doyle was out injured. With Pierce absent, Parkes made an unexpected return and, in front of a disappointing 14,729 crowd, City won 2-1 with Todd replying to goals by

Denis Tueart and Paul Power. Hibbitt admired Daley as a player and dressing-room joker; "Everyone had different ways of dealing with the tension before a game. Steve told jokes and was happy. He never stopped rabbitting while I used to sit in the corner and read the programme. I wasn't actually reading, I was looking at it, looking into it but actually thinking about the game. Steve was the opposite and you just wanted to say, 'Just shut up, Steve', but that was how he was. Willie used to be sick in the toilet, you could hear him. It was just the tension but, when you got over the line, it went." Barry Powell concurs; "Coming through in the game, I found them a good set of lads to be around. Willie would be physically sick before a game. Frank and The Doog would have a cup of tea, not worrying about anything."

Chung had always felt confident of securing the ultimate prize; "We knew we were good enough to go straight back up, so we didn't chase new signings. I remember telling the directors I thought we had enough." John Dee praised Chung's role in the promotion effort; "He was so well respected by the players. He was also, as time was to show, a Wolverhampton manager and not just Wolves boss. The public mattered to him. To get Wolves back and at the same time vastly improve their PR was a daunting task. But Chung has succeeded without having to win anyone over by using the cheque book." Looking forward to a brighter future Dee added; "Chung has learned a great deal and, with First Division football only three months away, who's to say Wolves are not on the threshold of even bigger things?"

Of course it was not to be. As Daley reveals this was partly due to an attitude . that would lead directly to the drastic decline of the mid-1980s; "Things changed with Harry Marshall. When we got back up, he wouldn't see the lads as a group. When you went in to see him and talk about a pay rise, he'd have the financial yearbooks of Stockport, Torquay and other teams, and say, 'We don't want to end up like this you know!' Ironically, he let lots of young players leave and Wolves went that way. With the white elephant stand it was exactly what they did, end in the Fourth Division."

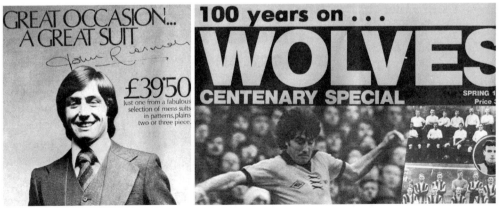

A role model off and on the pitch - and all smiles at the end of Wolves' historic season.

1977-2007: Back To The Future

In the 30 years up to their Centenary in 1977, Wolves had only six managers; Ted Vizard, Stan Cullis, Andy Beattie, Ronnie Allen, Bill McGarry and Sammy Chung. In this time, the club won three League titles, two FA Cups and one League Cup, reached a UEFA Cup final and were twice promoted from Division Two, once as champions. In only three years (1965-66, 1966-67 and 1976-77) were they out of the top flight. In 30 years up to 2007, Wolves have had a staggering 15 full-time, and many caretaker, bosses; Chung, John Barnwell, Ian Greaves, Graham Hawkins, Tommy Docherty, Sammy Chapman (x2), McGarry (again), Brian Little, Graham Turner, Graham Taylor, Mark McGhee, Colin Lee, Dave Jones, Glenn Hoddle and Mick McCarthy. These years have yielded just one League Cup, the Division Three and Four titles, the Sherpa Van Trophy and two promotions from Division Two, one through the play-offs. Only seven seasons (1977 to 1982, 1983-84 and 2003-04) were spent in the top division.

The propensity to chop and change in pursuit of success has, of course, become increasingly common but the progress of the likes of Arsenal and Manchester United shows it won't work. Near the end of Wolves' 2003-04 Premiership stay, Ken Hibbitt sensed something lacking; "I took my wife to the last game and she said; 'Something's not quite right about this club. There's no soul.' There were pictures in the place of players who had only played 30 times. With expectation not as high now, there is more of a feel, given what Mick McCarthy has done. But give him time. They must rebuild." Steve Daley wonders whether a change back is ever possible in the money-driven, modern game; "The money players make now wasn't about when we played. We were incentivised to play; so much if you were in the first-team squad, so much if you got on, so much to win, so much to draw, nothing for losing. Basic wages are so high now, irrespective of incentives. A few months ago, I was having a beer with a Wolves player from the 1970s and asked him what the most he ever earned as a player was. He told me it was £80 a week at Wolves (£4,000 a year). It took him 20 years to earn what Frank Lampard does in a week. And Lampard couldn't lace his boots."

My abiding impression from meeting many of the players who made possible the wonderful adventures of the late sixties and early seventies is one of mutual self-respect and great fellow feeling. Hibbitt reflects on the terrific spirit; "Apart from Alan Sunderland (to Arsenal), no-one else wanted to move and that shows the camaraderie we had. Five or six of us spent ten years there. You'll never see that again. Most of them still live in the Wolverhampton area, although a lot of them aren't from there. I only moved to the West Country because of my job at Bristol Rovers. There was a great spirit and they were great times, it's great to still see them all. Willie Carr was my best mate. We shared rooms for seven years and had good fun but worked our socks off in games and our preparation was first-class." Daley remembers Willie; "He sings, 'The wee little lassie from the Inverary Inn', not when he's sober, only when he's had a few whiskies."

This affinity with fans is something Kenny recalls as very special; "We all had bad games but the one thing I learned early on was that if you worked hard, they'd accept your bad and indifferent games. They knew the harder you worked, the quicker you got out of a rut." Daley agrees; "I never had the fans on my back, they were absolutely brilliant. I must have showed a lot of potential first off and they took to me. I couldn't wait to play in front of them. They were great to me, though it was different altogether at City!" Derek Dougan offered a view that both complements this and summed up his approach to the game; "Whether the crowd was 10,000 or 50,000, home or away, if one person left thinking 'I enjoyed watching Dougan today', all my efforts were worth it. The trouble now is that clubs take fans as mugs. But fans know exactly what they want because the game is an entertainment. It's all about taking people out of their daily life and putting them into a scenario where they're thinking, 'It could be me running up and down that pitch'." Derek Parkin agrees; "The crowd will forgive anything but lack of effort. They'll forgive the bad games as long as you don't hang your head. You must give 100 per cent. We didn't have the money kids are on today. I'm not having a go at that and wish I was still playing. But remember that those lads on the terraces have mundane jobs and use any spare cash to support you." Daley adds; "Down here, if the players are giving 100 per cent, the fans are happy. They always have been. If they see a fancy dan tiptoeing about, they'll crucify him, but if you go out and show you're giving your best, even if it's not going for you, they'll say, 'I tell you what, he didn't have a good game but he bloody grafted.' They want value for money."

Most of the players of that time share a love for the area, as Geoff Palmer says; "Frank, John McAlle, John Richards, Lofty, Squeak, Waggy, Stevie and me still live round here. Apart from me and Phil, they're not local lads." And their much-respected skipper Mike Bailey sums up; "I had 11 eleven years at a club which is very dear to my heart. My children Andrew and Victoria were born at Cosford. We lived in Brewood and Barbara and I have good friends we still see today. Many of the lads live in and around Wolverhampton and the gold blood runs freely through our veins." Dougan agreed; "I found the area to my liking. It struck me as warm-hearted and generous, a friendly place to live." Daley adds; "I have the greatest affection for the Wolves. So many of us still live here. It's just something about Wolverhampton but I don't think it will happen again." Carr adds; "I've been in this house for 32 years and Scouse used to live here. I can't envisage leaving. My kids have grown up here. It's a lovely environment and I've always found the people very friendly. We're a close-knit bunch. It's a nice place and the people are lovely." Hibbitt agrees; "I had a fantastic time at Wolves and that was why I didn't move on. My wife was from Wednesbury and my children were born in Cosford at the RAF where all the players' wives had their babies. I just loved the Midlands and the fans were fantastic with me."

Palmer outlines the spirit; "The banter with the lads on a Saturday and in training is something you miss. Some of the things we did, Danny Hegan was a joker, and so was Stevie Daley." Parkin chuckled to himself when recalling the players' humour but found it safer to keep to himself; "So many laughs, I could write a book but I'd be up in court! That's the one thing you miss when you come out of it. The banter and some of the things that happen are hilarious." Daley agrees; "If the lads all sat down and got together, they could write a fabulous book." Steve Kindon adds; "A great bunch of lads and superb footballers. Steve Daley and Alan were so close they were like brothers, like Kenny and Willie, like Squeak and Scouse, like me and John." Hibbitt would like to see more credit extended to the team who got closest to the achievements of the great 1950s sides; "It would be nice to be thanked by the club for all we did. and helped give it the name it had." As the years pass Frank Munro asks his team-mates to make a promise; "The only time we meet is when somebody dies, sad to say. But if we don't keep in touch, this is what will happen". All Frank wants is that they see each other more often. Derek Dougan's recent death serves only to emphasise this view and a telegram sent by the Doog to McAlle at the time of his testimonial, underlines this.

Carr regrets the way clubs have lost touch with their roots; "I appreciated it more when I went into the Southern League at places like Stourbridge and Willenhall. You were drinking with the fans and it was like the big old Wolves Social Club. I'll go in the Great Western now before games." Wolves need players and a manager who live locally and are genuinely in touch with fans, sharing the highs and lows. We need players who are talented but fully committed, not overpaid mercenaries. It can be argued, albeit partly out of necessity, that Wolves are nearer this state of affairs than for years, certainly since the late 1980s Bully-led recovery. But this time we must not lose sight of this if or when success comes. The emphasis must be on a sustainable and secure future. Barry Powell stresses what made the club so special; "It has lost its family feel now and become a business. Clubs have to do that to succeed but everyone then wanted to make it a homely club. It was of the reasons I joined."

It is my belief this issue has to be urgently addressed if the club are to establish a sustainable, long-term future in the community. Wishful thinking maybe but Wolves will only survive if they again become a club in touch, top to bottom, with their supporters. Perhaps football has changed forever but, if one lesson can be learned from the last 30 years, it is that there is no such thing as a quick fix. The perils of short-termism are well worth remembering as Wolverhampton Wanderers continue their struggle to recapture the lost glory days.

336791 PO WV G
BHAM TGMS

E 34 1246 WOLVERHAMPTON BM 22

MR JOHN MCALLE WOLVERHAMPTON WANDERERS FOOTBALL CLUB
WOLVERHAMPTON

I HOPE YOU GET THE BUMPER GATE YOUR LOYALTY AND DEDICATION
DESERVES
    DEREK DOUGAN

336081 PO BM G
336791 PO WV G

239

Bibliography

The Wolves, an encyclopaedia of Wolverhampton Wanderers Football Club, 1877 to 1989. Tony Matthews. Paper Plane Publishing Ltd. 1989.

Stan Cullis, the iron manager. Jim Holden. Breedon Books. 2000.

Talking with Wolves. Steve Gordos. Breedon Books. 1998.

Forever Wolves. David Instone. Thomas Publications. 2002.

Memories Of Molineux. Express & Star. Breedon Books. 1996.

Wolves Against The World, European nights 1953-1980. John Shipley. Tempus Publishing Ltd. 2003.

Match Of My Life, Wolves. Simon Lowe. Know The Score Books. 2005.

Centenary Wolves. Percy M Young. Wolverhampton Wanderers (1923) Ltd. 1976.

We Are Wolves, Wolverhampton Wanderers - the fans' story. Edited by Charles Ross. A Load of Bull. 1997.

Running With Wolves. Peter Lansley. Thomas Publications. 2004.

Videos/DVDs:

Wolverhampton Wanderers vs Manchester City, 1974 League Cup Final.

John Richards, A Life In Football.

Wolves Match Of The Seventies.

Wolverhampton Wanderers, The Official History DVD. 2006.